NO COP CITY, NO COP WORLD

LESSONS FROM THE MOVEMENT

EDITED BY
Micah Herskind, Mariah Parker,
and Kamau Franklin

Haymarket Books
Chicago, Illinois

© 2025 Micah Herskind, Mariah Parker, and Kamau Franklin

Published in 2025 by
Haymarket Books
P.O. Box 180165
Chicago, IL 60618
www.haymarketbooks.org

ISBN: 979-8-88890-374-2

Distributed to the trade in the US through Consortium Book Sales
and Distribution (www.cbsd.com) and internationally through
Ingram Publisher Services International (www.ingramcontent.com).

This book was published with the generous support of Lannan Foundation, Wallace Action Fund, and Marguerite Casey Foundation.

Special discounts are available for bulk purchases by organizations
and institutions. Please email info@haymarketbooks.org for more
information.

Cover artwork and design by Dio Cramer.

Printed in Canada by union labor.

Library of Congress Cataloging-in-Publication data is available.

10 9 8 7 6 5 4 3 2 1

Praise for *No Cop City, No Cop World*

"In this time of unbridled police domination, when, as Antonio Gramsci put it, the old is dying and the new struggles to be born, *No Cop City, No Cop World* provides us with a methodology of struggle, a praxis of revolutionary optimism, and a blueprint for what is to be done. The diverse and powerful voices represented in this volume warn us about the real-time dangers of police and policing—and guide us on the necessity of organizing against these and other forms of state and imperialist violence. This is a book for those who not only demand freedom, liberation, sovereignty, and self-determination but who are also willing, against all odds, to fight for it."
—**Dr. Charisse Burden-Stelly**, associate professor of African American Studies at Wayne State University and author of *Black Scare/Red Scare: Theorizing Capitalist Racism in the United States*

"In the Weelaunee forest as in the Atlanta City Hall, the future is being made. Across the petitions, protests, direct actions, and encampments to stop Cop City, the future is already here. The fight to Stop Cop City is among the most urgent, most riveting movements of our time. *No Cop City, No Cop World* brings together some of the sharpest insights from the frontlines of the abolitionist movement, be they forest defenders or community organizers, lawyers or media workers. Like the movement it chronicles, this book shows abolition to be a proliferation of strategies in pursuit of something called freedom. It takes all of us, dear reader, including you."
—**Dan Berger**, author of *Stayed on Freedom: The Long History of Black Power Through One Family's Journey*

"*No Cop City, No Cop World* encapsulates precisely what is historic and crucial about the Stop Cop City movement and its place at the radical intersection of abolitionist, antiracist, anticapitalist, Black liberation, Indigenous, territorial, and climate struggle. The text, like the movement, refuses to treat these fights—and the oppression they face—in isolation. The essays collected here, from scholars and frontline organizers, reflect Stop Cop City's insistence on tactical and strategic diversity. These are lessons we must take forward if we are to forge a No Cop World."

—**Natasha Lennard**, author of *Being Numerous: Essays on Non-Fascist Life*

"Over the past few years, the Stop Cop City movement has shaped how people across the country think about policing and power. *No Cop City, No Cop World* traces the story of this fight from principles to practice, and dares to ask what true justice and safety look like. This book is not just about one movement—it's about all movements that center the people over punishment. It's a fascinating book about hope, about the fight for justice, and about a better future—not just for Atlanta, but for the world. I loved every second of it."

—**Josie Duffy Rice**, writer, journalist, and host of the *Unreformed* podcast

"Our world is a world of police, and every city is a cop city. But this reality is neither inevitable nor eternal, and the turn to cop cities is a testament to the desperate fragility of police power. They expect resistance, and we will give them that and more. This book provides an essential map of the terrain and a strategy for the battles on the horizon."

—**Geo Maher**, author of *A World Without Police and coordinator*, W. E. B. Du Bois Movement School for Abolition & Reconstruction

"*No Cop City, No Cop World* is a story about organizers in motion who battled and continue to fight for their community against politicians, police, and organized capital. You will leave with more questions than when you began. This is the mark of an excellent book. The lessons from Stop Cop City should inform our current organizing efforts everywhere. The book underscores that criminalization is the indispensable fuel of fascism. It's timely, necessary, and required reading."

—**Mariame Kaba**, organizer and coauthor of *Let This Radicalize You*

"*No Cop City, No Cop World* is no David versus Goliath story. Rather, it is about waking a sleeping giant—a united coalition of grassroots social movements—to challenge a corporate-backed, ecocidal police state. Together, these powerful essays on the struggle in Atlanta offer vital lessons for how to resist the many cop cities on the horizon. The lesson is clear: only a people united, moved by visions of abolition and militant action, can stop a Cop World."

—**Robin D. G. Kelley**, author of *Freedom Dreams: The Black Radical Imagination*

"*No Cop City, No Cop World* is a bold and uncompromising call to action. Blending powerful storytelling with incisive strategy, the authors bring Angela Y. Davis's chilling warning to life: 'If they come for me in the morning, they will come for you in the night.' Through the lens of Atlanta, they offer a glimpse into the global rise of policing as a response to the anxieties and unrest of late-stage capitalism. This book is a rare and exquisite fusion of unflinching diagnosis and visionary prescription, a sharp tool for cutting through the noise as we resist and reimagine the carceral status quo."

—**Ruha Benjamin**, author of *Viral Justice: How We Grow the World We Want and Imagination: A Manifesto*

"Few books will give you a better sense of our times. Or of the love, kindness, joy, music, dancing, intellectual expertise, and irrepressible determination that form the backbone of the social movements resisting authoritarian repression. Share this book with someone in your life, discuss its profound lessons, absorb its spirit together, and take its teachings out into the world."

—**Alec Karakatsanis**, founder of Civil Rights Corps and author of *Usual Cruelty and Copaganda*

"A master class in mapping power and movement building delivered by a chorus of community organizers on the front lines of the fight to Stop Cop City. This inspiring collection points toward what is possible through principled struggle and a collective commitment to a multiracial, multigenerational, multi-tendency, multi-tactic, united front to fight for and practice a world beyond policing, extraction, displacement and organized abandonment of Black and Indigenous communities and the lands they call home. The experiments, lessons, reflections, and strategies for navigating solidarity, struggle, conflict, repair, realignment, and resistance to repression reflected in these insightful and beautifully written essays are essential for everyone committed to fighting the violence of policing, authoritarianism, and fascism in the US in the current moment and those to come. Next step: Stop Cop Nation!"

—**Andrea J. Ritchie**, cofounder of Interrupting Criminalization, author of *Practicing New Worlds: Abolition and Emergent Strategies,* and coauthor of *No More Police: A Case for Abolition*

Contents

Introduction   1

PART 1: HOW DID WE GET HERE?

1. Why Cop City? Why Here? Why Now?   13
   Micah Herskind

2. Boss Terror: How the Capital of the South Funded Cop City   29
   Mariah Parker

3. A Brief History of the Atlanta Prison Farm   39
   Atlanta Community Press Collective

4. Becoming External Enemies: From Occupy Atlanta to Stop Cop City   49
   Kayla Edgett

5. How the Black Misleadership Class Provides Cover to Cop City   63
   Eva Dickerson

   Timeline of the Movement   73

PART 2: NO COP CITY

6. Mvskoke Migrations   79
   Mekko Chebon Kernell

7. Eviction Notice from the Mvskoke People to Mayor Dickens and Cop City   87

8. The Saboteurs   89
   Paul Torino

9. Base Building to Stop Cop City: Successes, Failures, Reflections, and Lessons for Future Organizers   101
   Ashley Dixon

10. Is This Enough Black Folks for You, Andre Dickens?   117
Curtis Duncan and Kamau Franklin

11. Protecting the South River Forest   129
Jacqueline Echols, interviewed by Matt Scott and Mariah Parker

12. A New World in the Forest   137
Anonymous

13. Students vs. Cop City   145
Narek Boyajian, Dr. Andrew Douglas, Oren Panovka, Daxton Pettus, and Jaanaki Radhakrishnan, interviewed by Kamau Franklin and Mariah Parker

14. There Is No Cop City in the Beloved Community:
An Open Letter from Members of the Morehouse
College Faculty   157

15. The Roots of Resistance: Building Narrative Power   161
Hannah Riley

16. Let the People Decide   173
Mary Hooks and Kate Shapiro

17. Children Have Always Been at the Center   187
Rukia Rogers, interviewed by Nolan Huber-Rhoades

18. Dear Andre Dickens, Save Weelaunee   195

PART 3: VIVA, VIVA TORTUGUITA!

19. Little Turtle's War   203
David Peisner

20. Statements by Tortuguita's Parents   209

21. In Their Own Words   213

PART 4: REPRESSION

22. How Georgia Indicted a Movement   225
Zohra Ahmed and Elizabeth Taxel

23. Thirty-One Days in DeKalb County Hell   233
Priscilla Grim

24. Defending the Movement: Lessons in Anti-repression   241
Marlon Kautz

PART 5: NO COP WORLD

25. You Can't Reform a War Away: On Creative Aggression   253
    Craig Gilmore and Ruth Wilson Gilmore

26. From No Cop Academy to Stop Cop City   283
    Benji Hart

27. Cop Cities in a Militarized World   289
    Azadeh Shahshahani

28. Atlanta's Attack on Protesters Should Be
    a Warning to Us All   299
    Angela Y. Davis and Barbara Ransby

29. Please Keep Playing: A Letter to My Son, Remix   303
    Ariana Brazier

Conclusion: No Cop City, No Cop World   307

Acknowledgments   315

Notes   317

*For the forest defenders in Atlanta and across the world,
for everyone opposing cop cities and building abolitionist futures
in their place, and for Tortuguita*

Introduction

A suspension bridge built across a stream in the forest. Cop cars on fire. A clipboard painted green with the words "Let the People Decide." A friendly but unexpected knock at the door, inviting you to a town hall on Thursday. An open mic night at a local church. An excavator destroyed. A line of people, hundreds long, winding down the marble staircase in the atrium of City Hall. A fleet of police motorcycles going up in flames. A potted fern you can have for free, if you'd like. A child at a rally, turning shyly to her mother for the go-ahead to speak as she raises a megaphone. Surveillance cameras smashed. One of the largest urban forests in North America, at stake in a battle between a broad coalition of everyday people and the big money and guns that run the city of Atlanta.

These are scenes from the Stop Cop City movement, a decentralized effort to stop the construction of a $120 million police militarization facility and the devastation of the Weelaunee Forest. In this book, you'll find many scenes like these, as well as lessons for future battles against conjoined threats of police militarism, environmental collapse, and rule of the rich.

In March 2021, then mayor Keisha Lance Bottoms—backed by a powerful coalition of private sector corporations, nonprofits, and Atlanta political elites—announced plans for a sprawling police complex that would be branded as the "Atlanta Public Safety Training Center." Organizers quickly labeled the facility "Cop City," highlighting the plans to include a mock city block on-site for police to train in various urban counterinsurgency and control tactics. Though the plans for Cop City have been shrouded in secrecy from the start, at various points the designs for the pretend city block have included a convenience store, hotel, night club, houses, park and splash pad, gas station, school, and bank. Cop City would also include a K-9 unit kennel and training center, a burn tower, an emergency vehicle training course, horse stables, a shooting range, and classrooms and administrative buildings. Initially, the plans also included a Black Hawk helicopter landing pad.[1]

The proposed site for Cop City is a 381-acre plot of forest land owned by the city of Atlanta but located outside city limits—a detail that allowed the city to sidestep traditional procedural safeguards required for projects within city limits.[2] Located in a majority-Black working-class and deeply disinvested area of unincorporated DeKalb County, the land was known as the South River Forest until the Mvskoke descendants of its original Indigenous stewards returned to Atlanta in 2021 and reclaimed the South River as Weelaunee—meaning "brown (*lane*) water (*ue*)"—and the forest as the Weelaunee Forest.[3]

More than 175 wildlife species make their home in Weelaunee.[4] Hardwoods and Bradford pear trees sway alongside sugar hackberries, with their tough, pimpled bark, and the native loblolly pines that carpet the earth in their needles. Dirt paths are fringed with irises and daffodils, fungi and ferns. White-flowered dewberry brambles feed the white-tailed deer and the Carolina wrens.[5] In 2017, Atlanta's City Council had formally committed to permanently preserving the forest.[6] But just four years later, the Atlanta City Council reversed course, voting to lease the city-owned forest land to the Atlanta Police Foundation (APF) to build and operate Cop City.

APF is a private nonprofit organization that raises corporate donations for Atlanta's police department, operates a massive city-wide surveillance network, and uses its extensive corporate ties and deep pockets to wield massive influence over city politics.[7] Its board of directors is a snapshot of Atlanta's ruling class, containing the interests of finance, real estate, media, and sales titans like KPMG, Wells Fargo, Invesco, Loudermilk Companies, Amazon, Cox Enterprises, and more.[8] Many of these same corporations also organize themselves through "public-private partnerships" like the Atlanta Committee for Progress (ACP), a blue-ribbon committee whose membership includes the mayor of Atlanta, university presidents from across the Atlanta metro area, owners of major sports teams, and a host of multinational and locally headquartered corporations. ACP was one of Cop City's earliest backers, releasing a statement of support in April 2021 noting that its board chair, Alex Taylor, would be spearheading the fundraising campaign for the facility.[9]

Alex Taylor is also the CEO of Cox Enterprises, another APF board member and a massive media conglomerate that owns the *Atlanta Journal-Constitution* (*AJC*, the city's main media outlet) and an array of other Atlanta-based news sources. Unsurprisingly, the *AJC* has consistently published slanted coverage in favor of Cop City and its backers, continuously stirring up fear over crime and offering Cop City as a solution.[10]

In addition to the plan's private backers, a broad array of public officials have shepherded the proposal through the necessary government hurdles. Mayor Bottoms first announced the plans in early 2021, and her successor, Mayor Andre Dickens, took up the reins upon his election. A supermajority of Atlanta's Democrat-dominated City Council has consistently voted in favor of building and funding the facility, while Republican governor Brian Kemp and other state officials have vocally supported the project and the repression of its grassroots opponents. Local, state, and federal police and prosecutorial agencies have been the project's muscle, regularly responding to protests and dissent with extreme charges and police violence.

In short, Atlanta's ruling class—composed of local and state elected officials, private corporations, university leaders, a handful of nonprofits, corporate media outlets, and police forces—has coalesced around Cop City.

The Movement

Since the spring of 2021, everyday people in Atlanta and across the country have organized and agitated under the loose banners of Stop Cop City and Defend the Atlanta Forest to save the forest and prevent the construction of Cop City. The decentralized movement has no single unifying political framework. It includes abolitionists, anarchists, communists, liberals, libertarians, environmentalists, Black radicals, neighborhood associations, faith congregations, voting and civil rights activists, Indigenous and anti–settler colonialism organizers, disability justice advocates, and many more. Opponents of Cop City do not collectively identify with one particular political philosophy, but they all choose trees over cops, transparency over backroom deals, and community resources over a burgeoning police state.

No Cop City, No Cop World is a book about this movement: its context, strategies, tactics, formations, goals, setbacks, victories, and lessons learned.

Creating a book about an ongoing movement is challenging. There are no tidy narratives about what the movement accomplished, or how it ended or won or lost. Our goal in *No Cop City, No Cop World* is not to provide a final or comprehensive narrative or analysis of a movement that is still unfolding. Indeed, most of this book's contributions were written near the end of 2023 and the beginning of 2024—there is no way to know exactly what will have happened from the time that we sent this book to press to its publication date.

Instead, this is a book of writings mostly from organizers that offer strategies, reflections, and insights from the Stop Cop City movement and its connections to struggles across the globe. By providing snapshots from and of the movement, we hope to both document what exists of this movement thus far, draw out initial lessons and reflections, and provide tools for those who may be fighting a Cop City in their neighborhood in the coming years.

Across this book's pages, you will see many themes emerge. Perhaps most centrally, the Stop Cop City movement demonstrates the power of a decentralized movement that works on many fronts and against many targets. The movement's decentralization and diversity of tactics have been among its greatest strengths, building an astonishing breadth and depth of local, national, and international support. Through decentralization, the creativity of small groups of movement actors has flourished, inspiring a broad range of actions against not only politicians and obvious villains like APF, but also APF's board members, funders, contractors, and media propagandists. Rather than acting according to one group's strategic direction, those in the movement have taken many forms of action, often under an overarching ethos: Overwhelm the enemy on all fronts and with all tactics to make Cop City as untenable, toxic, and challenging as possible for those working to build it.

At the same time, decentralization does not necessarily mean disorganization (though sometimes it does!). Different corners of the movement feature different degrees of organization, often depending on the tactics pursued. This book provides windows into some of these tactics and how they fit within the picture of the broader movement: While some activists pressured Cop City contractors, others hosted town halls and block parties for residents surrounding the forest. While some engaged in sabotage of destructive machinery, others worked through the courts to challenge construction permits.[11] While movement journalists filed open records requests to expose the city's backroom dealings with APF, attorneys and jail support organizers fortified infrastructure to support criminalized protesters.[12] While forest defenders fended off attacks by putting their bodies on the line, independent formations across the country targeted Cop City financiers and contractors at their various nationwide locations by vandalizing storefronts, gluing ATMs shut, and burning machinery. While student organizers protested on and off campus, electoral and civil rights nonprofits that had once stayed on the sidelines brought new resources and support to the fight.[13] While faith congregations offered their houses of worship as organizing spaces and imbued the struggle with righteous outrage, activists in other cities formed local Weelaunee Defense Society chapters and completed two nationwide tours to share about the struggle in Atlanta and its connections to other cities.[14] Ultimately, the decentralized action seen across this book's pages has allowed the movement to take root not only in Atlanta, but across the country.

While pursuing decentralized action, the many who make up the Stop Cop City movement have nonetheless maintained a commitment to principled unity across the struggle. The state has continuously tried to divide the movement along the lines of race, respectability, and legality through rhetoric denouncing 'violent' protest and 'outside agitators,' attempting to peel off "respectable" formations from underground ones. But in general, the movement has resisted these designations, recognizing that such divisions only serve the enemy. For example, despite repeated prompting from journalists to denounce acts of sabotage and arson, the ballot initiative campaign to put Cop City to a vote by Atlanta residents—led primarily by visible, established nonprofits—regularly affirmed its support for a diversity of tactics, rejecting the division between violence and nonviolence and offering full-throated support for the movement's more radical elements. Likewise, while many in the movement were split on the value of the referendum effort, activists have generally kept tensions internal, working out differences through conversation and relationships. Importantly, principled unity is not the same thing as total agreement. In this book, you will see recurring tensions—not all our contributors agree on the utility of various tactics, and some may say that certain tactics undermine parts of the movement. As the editors of this book, we certainly do not agree with each other on everything. But what unites people across the movement is a commitment to struggle, and a recognition that we need people in as many lanes as possible to win the fight.

Even as the movement has drawn together people with varied political orientations and motivations, struggling together has nonetheless had a unifying effect. While many, or even most, who oppose Cop City may not identify as abolitionists, a common thread running through the movement is that for all who want to stop Cop City and preserve the forest, police are standing in the way. The movement's many political education and mobilization efforts have cultivated a growing abolitionist consciousness in Atlanta, even for those who might not identify it as such. For example, when many hundreds of people showed up to City Hall in June 2023 to oppose $67 million in public funds for Cop City, they revealed the extent to which abolitionist frameworks have taken root in Atlanta. Hundreds who spoke articulated not just what they don't want—Cop City and the destruction of the forest—but also what they *do* want to see in their communities. Atlantans spoke to a vision of safety that included well-funded schools, mental and physical health care, affordable housing, streetlights and paved streets, bike lanes, parks and green space, public transportation, arts and culture, childcare, and an array of other public services—not more police.[15] These moments were made possible through the varied base-building, media, and other political education efforts you will read about in this book, each of which has made connections across struggles and clarified that environmental justice requires abolition, which requires the abolition of capitalism and militarism.

Finally, a recurring theme you will see in this book is that it is worth it to fight, even when we do not know the outcome of our struggle. We do not wish to paint an overly rosy picture of the movement. Repression takes a heavy toll. Organizing is difficult. The state has thrown everything it has at the forest defenders, neighbors, educators, students, organizers, children, advocates, and others who oppose Cop City. As of this writing, much of the forest has been clear-cut, and the construction, though significantly delayed, is moving forward, displacing wildlife and shattering the forest ecosystem. As a result, the surrounding Black neighborhoods have already experienced increased flooding, and the river that runs through the forest has been further polluted with sediment from construction.[16]

But as we write these words, the fight goes on. The movement continues to find new forms of creative aggression. An ethos of care continues to pervade the movement, through direct support for community members and expanded defense infrastructure for Cop City's political prisoners. Over the years of this struggle, many moments that felt like the end of the movement—a massive legislative setback, particularly severe repression—instead gave rise to new tactics. For example, when the Atlanta City Council first approved the Cop City plans in September 2021, the movement was given new life when forest defenders took to the Weelaunee Forest and began camping out, building tree huts, erecting campsites, and challenging initial deforestation efforts.[17] Forest defenders created a rush of new energy in some of the darkest moments of the struggle, issuing an uncompromising call to defend the forest by any means necessary—in the process, deepening analysis of and resistance around the connections between police militarization, climate disaster, environmental racism, Indigenous displacement, genocide, and more. By putting their bodies on the line, forest defenders clarified the stakes of the struggle and made clear that nothing about Cop City would end on the terms of the powerful. City Council could approve the project, APF could secure contractors, and the funds could be raised—but none of that meant Cop City will be built. Instead, the movement continues to fight.

The book is organized in five parts. The first part, How Did We Get Here?, lays out the history and context of the Stop Cop City struggle, asking how we should understand Cop City within the context of Atlanta's complicated political landscape as a city with a majority-Black Democratic leadership and overwhelmingly white economic power structure. How have the forces of capital and policing consolidated to produce Cop City, and how has Atlanta's history of radical struggle produced the movement against it?

Part 2, No Cop City, offers lessons and reflections from organizers in the movement: stories of Mvskoke comrades returning to the Weelaunee Forest to fight against Cop City, base-building efforts around the forest, environmental racism and climate justice organizing, resistance to corporate media, student and faculty organizing, child and neighbor mobilization, people of faith rising up, sabotage against the architects of destruction, ballot campaigns, and more. In a truly decentralized movement, there is no central leadership committee—just many groups and formations of people pursuing a variety of tactics with varying degrees of coordination.

Part 3, *Viva, Viva, Tortuguita*, is a tribute to Tortuguita, the queer eco-anarchist Indigenous Venezuelan forest defender murdered in cold blood by Georgia State Police in concert with local and federal police agencies. As many in the movement chant, *Tortuguita vive, la lucha sigue!* Tortuguita lives, and the fight goes on.

Part 4, Repression, details the devastating repression of the Stop Cop City movement—including domestic terrorism and criminal conspiracy charges that carry the potential of decades in prison—as well as accounts from political prisoners in the movement and those engaged in anti-repression work to sustain our movements and protect them from the state.

The final part, No Cop World, focuses on connections between movements against policing, racial capitalism, and imperialism at home and abroad—from the No Cop Academy struggle in Chicago to the connections between police expansion and the murder of land defenders in the US and Latin America, to struggles over austerity, land, and criminalization from Atlanta and Los Angeles to South Africa, France, Indonesia, the UK, and Brazil. From the local to the global, our struggles are connected.

Essentially every moment of working on this book was interrupted by our own participation in the movement. We are all organizers involved in various ways with the fight to stop Cop City, as are most of this book's contributors. And for each contributor, there are many more unnamed organizers, activists, and everyday people who made the tactics and strategies described possible. Some of the most critical actors in the movement cannot show their faces or names, given security concerns, while others are facing serious criminal charges. Here, we have sought to uplift the work of those who have stood unswayed against the police state's violence and criminalization of the movement.

Finally, the book is an invitation to fight back against police repression and elite domination. The stakes could not be higher. Whether practicing civil disobedience, knocking on your neighbor's door, engaging in strategic sabotage, working in or out of the electoral process, organizing your workplace, or engaging in political education with your community, we need you. We need a true diversity of tactics, including the tactics we have not yet discovered. We invite you to join us in saying, "No Cop City, No Cop World!"

PART 1

HOW DID WE GET HERE?

ONE

Why Cop City?
Why Here? Why Now?

Micah Herskind

As the Stop Cop City movement has garnered national and international attention, it has also left many wondering: Given such widespread opposition, why is the city of Atlanta so intent on building Cop City? And if city leadership insists on building Cop City, why build it on such precious forest land? And why now, when the plans were first proposed as early as 2017 and the city had previously committed to protecting and preserving the land in question?

Making sense of Cop City requires understanding the shifting dynamics of class and racial oppression in Atlanta, marked by organized abandonment: the state's retreat from the provision of social welfare and the interrelated buildup of policing and imprisonment to manage inequality's outcomes. Or, as abolitionists Ruth Wilson Gilmore and Craig Gilmore put it: "profound austerity and the iron fist necessary to impose it."[1]

Put simply, Cop City is the Atlanta ruling class's solution to a set of crises produced by decades of organized abandonment in the city. These crises included the threat and reality of mass uprisings against police violence, extreme and racialized income inequality and gentrification, corporate media narratives in the wake of the 2020 uprisings that threatened Atlanta's image as a safe place for capital investment, and a municipal secession movement that threatened to rob the city of nearly half of its tax revenue following the uprisings.

Confronted with these crises, Atlanta's leadership opted to seek a "solution" in the form of Cop City. Designed and propelled by a mix of state, corporate, and nonprofit actors, Cop City would address Atlanta's crises in three ways: First, it would provide a material investment in police capacity on the heels of the uprisings, as a project to prepare for and prevent future rebellion. Second, it would represent an ideological investment in the image of Atlanta, signaling to corporations and those attracted by the influx of tech and other high-paying jobs that Atlanta is a stable, securitized city that will protect their interests. Finally, Cop City would be a geographical investment—one that would repurpose publicly owned land in a disinvested area while opening up new opportunities for development. But while Cop City may have been an imagined solution to the crises facing Atlanta, the city's drive to destroy the Weelaunee Forest opened up a new crisis in the form of the militant Stop Cop City movement—one that has the potential to upend Atlanta's status quo altogether.

Organized Abandonment and the Atlanta Way

When thousands of Atlantans took to the streets during the nationwide uprisings of 2020, they were responding to more than the recent police murders of George Floyd, Breonna Taylor, and Rayshard Brooks.[2] They were responding to decades of organized abandonment, including social disinvestment, displacement and gentrification, and police expansion—and calling for a reversal of these dynamics.

Twenty-first-century Atlanta has featured rapid, publicly subsidized development and gentrification, the disintegration of the social safety net, the expansion of surveillance and policing, and rising inequality. Since 1990, the share of the city's Black population has decreased from 67 percent to 48 percent, while the median family income and the share of adults with a college degree in the city doubled.[3] Investment firms have gobbled up housing stock, with bulk buyers accumulating over sixty-five thousand single-family homes throughout the Atlanta metro area in the past decade.[4] As the city has attracted major tech companies like Microsoft, Apple, and Google—and along with them, more middle- and upper-class white people—the city has pushed its Black and working-class residents further out of the city. Choices by policymakers have made Atlanta a lucrative place for big business, but a difficult place to live for the rest of residents. In 2022, for example, Atlanta was named by *Money* as the best place to live and was identified by *Realtor Magazine* as the top real estate market in the country.[5] The same year, Atlanta was proclaimed the most unequal city in the country. At the same time, Atlanta is the most surveilled city in the US.[6]

How did we get here? Atlanta has long been home to what is known as "the Atlanta Way"—the strategic partnership between Black political leadership and white economic elites that work in service of corporations and upper-class white communities and to the detriment of lower-income Black and working-class communities. Though the Atlanta Way emerged in the 1900s, we can begin with the lead-up to the 1996 Olympics in Atlanta as a key accelerant of the Atlanta Way. As historian Dan Immergluck explains, the decisions made in preparation for the Games "effectively set the stage for long-term gentrification and exclusion in the city, focusing primarily on making the city more attractive to a more affluent set of prospective citizens."[7]

Atlanta underwent a fundamental transformation in its effort to attract the 1996 Olympics. As historian Maurice Hobson has documented, city and corporate leaders worked together to fashion an image of the city that "had it all: the citizens, the dynamism, and the charm along with an economic and social robustness that made it one of the world's most vibrant new cities."[8] This meant infrastructural upgrades and new Olympic stadiums, but it also meant redefining the city's image as a "prosperous, authentically global city"—an image that required erasing the city's disproportionately Black poor and homeless population.[9]

Driven by a coalition of state and corporate actors, Atlanta's Olympification was a process of organized abandonment that included the displacement of roughly thirty thousand people from 1990 to 1996; the discriminatory arrests of over nine thousand homeless people from 1995 to 1996, in part through the Atlanta Police Department's (APD's) use of pre-printed tickets with categories filled out for "African American," "Male," and "Homeless"; a city partnership with a nonprofit that purchased one-way tickets out of town for homeless people, who were required to sign pledges not to return; the demolition of public housing, including the US's oldest federally subsidized public housing project; the passage of new city laws hyper-criminalizing homelessness; and the construction of a 1,300-bed jail downtown to clear homeless people from the streets.[10] As housing activist Anita Beaty explains, the Olympics were "a dry run, a dress rehearsal for the developers and the elites to take over the city, to take over the planning, housing construction—to eliminate public housing."[11]

In the following decades, developers and elites did indeed take over the city, seen perhaps most clearly in the city's posture toward major development projects and the gentrification that accompanies them. For example, the Beltline, a publicly subsidized and privately constructed 22-mile path around the city, has drastically raised property values in the surrounding neighborhoods since construction began in the early 2000s.[12] And as Immergluck has documented, while city officials promised to earmark funding to keep people in their homes as property values rose around the Beltline, in practice they instead focused on building amenities that raised property values and accelerated gentrification.[13]

Public-to-private transfers of wealth in the service of major development continued apace in the following years. There's the $1.6 billion Mercedes Benz Stadium for the Atlanta Falcons in downtown

Atlanta, opened in 2017, which received an estimated $700–900 million in public funds through a socialize-the-costs, privatize-the-profits financing scheme.[14] There was the $142.5 million from the city in 2016 for a renovated State Farm Arena, home to the Atlanta Hawks.[15] There was the 2017 sale of the Turner Field stadium to Georgia State University—a deal that received roughly $5 million in tax breaks, and was fought by community members who established a tent city and demanded a community benefits agreement to offset the impending gentrification.[16] And there was the fiercely resisted $1.9 billion subsidy for "The Gulch," a plan approved in 2018 that transferred significant public dollars and forty acres of publicly owned land in downtown Atlanta to a private developer for the creation of office, retail, and hotel space and mostly unaffordable housing.[17]

As Atlanta has poured money into major development projects, city leadership has refused to capture the increased tax revenue associated with its investments. Sometimes this happens through financing mechanisms that divert new tax revenues from the area surrounding the development back into the corporations behind the projects, siphoning money away from schools and other public goods. Other times, it is done by failing to adequately assess the value of major commercial properties (meaning they are taxed at far less than they are worth).[18] One estimate suggests Atlanta and Fulton County are leaving approximately $500 million in annual property tax revenue on the table—leading to significant corporate underpayment of taxes and fewer funds for public goods.[19]

At the same time, money for affordable housing has been scarce, as funding promises have been made and broken.[20] In 2017, as the housing crisis persisted, the city officially closed Peachtree-Pine, the largest homeless shelter in the US Southeast, deepening the decimation of options for unhoused people.[21] Meanwhile, APD's budget has continued to grow, today accounting for a third of Atlanta's annual budget.[22] The Atlanta Police Foundation (APF), founded in 2003 and now the largest police foundation in the country, helped establish Operation Shield—an ever-growing network of over 3,300 surveillance cameras throughout the city. APD has continued to kill and maim while filling up Atlanta-area jails, like the Fulton County Jail, where 90 percent of people detained are Black.[23]

Despite the Atlanta Way's hostility toward low-income and working-class Black people, the 2010s saw some promising reforms, won through a combination of sustained struggle and mass mobilizations.[24] From 2013 to 2019, organizers notched a series of wins, defeating a sex worker banishment ordinance, creating the city's first alternative-to-police program, passing local bail reform, cutting the city's ties with Immigration and Customs Enforcement, and winning a city resolution to transform the city jail built in preparation for the 1996 Olympics into a community resource center. Amid severe inequality there was, it seemed, an encouraging trend.[25]

A Breaking Point

Then came 2020. The COVID-19 pandemic. Nationwide uprisings. In May of 2020, protesters took to the streets, smashing windows and burning police cars in righteous anger. The demand to defund and abolish the police, and to invest in community safety, went mainstream. Protests in Atlanta and across the country intensified again just a couple weeks later following the police murder of Rayshard Brooks.

On June 20, 2020, roughly a week after Brooks was murdered, the Atlanta City Council considered a budget amendment that would later be known as the Rayshard Brooks bill, framed widely as a bill to defund APD. While the bill itself was not a true "defund" bill—it would have merely withheld 50 percent of APD's budget until the mayor's office and City Council formulated a plan to "reimagine public safety"—it was nonetheless symbolically hefty, a test of whether Atlanta electeds would heed community calls or not. The council ultimately rejected it by the slimmest of margins in an 8–7 vote.[26]

The narrow vote against the Rayshard Brooks bill marked a turning point—not in the fundamental nature of the ruling-class consensus or the "Atlanta Way," but in the way that consensus manifested in Atlanta politicians' outward posture toward policing and incarceration. In the months that followed the uprisings, there was a palpable sense of backlash against the city's recent criminal legal reforms, with many Atlanta politicians sharply changing their tune on reforms that they had previously championed.

Police revolted, with 170 officers calling out sick in the days after Atlanta police were charged for the death of Rayshard Brooks.[27] They were quickly rewarded with $500 bonuses, funded by APF and authorized by then mayor Keisha Lance Bottoms. "Crime wave" narratives took off as corporate media outlets in Atlanta and across the country promoted the idea that crime was out of control, that police were demoralized, and that the defund movement was responsible. (These narratives, of course, turned out to be almost entirely false.)[28]

Corporations, organized through "public-private partnerships" like the Atlanta Committee for Progress, sounded the alarm on crime, pledging to work with city leadership to fight gang violence, car break-ins, and nuisance properties while manufacturing panic around street racing and "water boys," or Black children selling water bottles at street intersections.[29] Seizing on and amplifying crime fears, the disproportionately white and wealthy area of northeast Atlanta known as Buckhead launched a secession movement in July 2020, falsely touting the supposedly rampant crime in the area.[30] Buckhead accounts for roughly 40 percent of the city's tax base, and its attempt to separate from the city immediately caused panic among Atlanta liberals who feared the corresponding loss of tax revenue.[31]

It was in this climate that, just one year later, in September 2021, the Atlanta City Council voted to approve Cop City despite mass community opposition.[32] Long-standing patterns of organized abandonment had come to a head: the people had been in the streets, inequality was on the rise, long-standing patterns of gentrification and uneven development had taken their toll, the city's wealthiest area was threatening to secede over a crime panic, and Atlanta's corporate class was demanding stability in response to uprisings.

Capitalizing on the Crisis

It was a web of corporate, state, police, media, university, and nonprofit actors that came together at this moment of crisis to push forward the Cop City proposal.[33] APF had been working on the plans for Cop City as early as 2017, even approaching councilmembers, long before they went public.[34] But the plans didn't appear to be considered in earnest until years later, and were not publicly announced until spring of 2021, when Mayor Bottoms created an advisory committee to rubber-stamp APF's recommendations for Cop City.[35]

The announcement came on the heels of rollbacks to reforms and promises Atlanta leadership had made just years earlier. In November 2020, the Atlanta City Council rolled back its 2018 bail reform after racist fearmongering about street racing, an effort led by the Buckhead Council of Neighborhoods.[36] In December 2020, three councilmembers—one of whom, Matt Westmoreland, had voted for the "defund" bill—announced that they were donating $125,000 from their office budgets to the "Buckhead Security Plan," investing further in surveillance and policing in the Buckhead area.[37] Despite her promise to close the Olympic jail, Mayor Bottoms dragged her feet for years until August 2022, when the new mayor and City Council voted to *increase* the jail's population by leasing jail beds to Fulton County.[38] More broadly, crime and its relationship to the Buckhead secession movement was central to the 2022 mayoral election cycle, with each of the candidates pledging to crack down on crime, hire more police officers, and keep the city intact.[39]

Announcing the Cop City plans, Bottoms argued that the facility would "improve officer morale and retention" following the supposed dip in morale and increased vacancies after the 2020 uprisings.[40] Likewise, APF touted the proposed facility's size and state-of-the-art nature, giving it a "tremendous amount of appeal" to other Georgia law enforcement agencies.[41] An FAQ document released by APF argued that nowhere else could accommodate the department's needs, and that Cop City would be a "beacon for what we call 21st Century policing."[42] Dave Wilkinson, APF's CEO, echoed these talking points at a September 2021 press conference, saying that APF is "building this training center as a tribute to the community," and that it is "the most important security measure that this city could introduce in our generation."[43] The plan's proponents frequently tied building Cop City to social justice, arguing that it would provide the "most up-to-date methods of community policing, including de-escalation tactics and cultural awareness."[44] In fact, Cop City's original proposed name was the "Atlanta Institute for Social Justice and Public Safety Training"—a name that was quickly scratched, perhaps because even the project's proponents realized this was a bridge too far.[45]

Many of the city's most powerful corporate, university, and nonprofit institutions quickly announced their support for the project, while the city's main media outlet, the *Atlanta Journal-Constitution* (*AJC*), repeatedly published pieces in favor of Cop City while failing to disclose that its parent company had donated $10 million to APF.[46] For example, after the Cop City legislation temporarily stalled in City Council in August 2021, the *AJC* published an editorial arguing that supposedly improved training at Cop City "may well save lives during routine encounters with the public."[47] Of course, the editorial board didn't cite any evidence to justify this claim, and certainly did not acknowledge, for example, that the Atlanta police officer who killed Rayshard Brooks underwent over two thousand hours of training.[48]

As the plan met community resistance, APF and the corporations backing it leveraged the threat of Buckhead secession and narratives about rising crime to demand the plan be pushed through. As emails obtained through an open record request show, during the summer of 2021, APF heavily pressured the mayor's office to push for the approval of the legislation.[49] For example, in the lead-up to a June 2021 committee vote, CEO Wilkinson sent emails to the mayor's right-hand man demanding that the mayor push forward on Cop City, citing frustration from major CEOs over the "crime surge and lack of support for public safety over the past year." Wilkinson also forwarded an email from an unidentified "prominent CEO" in Buckhead who had written to Wilkinson objecting to the "shootings over the past few weeks, parties in the streets this weekend and the water boys running around on scooters"—all the products of organized abandonment in a city that has pumped money into policing at the expense of youth programming and other community investments.

At the same time, APF heavily circulated suggested scripts to its email list encouraging residents to call the City Council, identify as Buckhead residents, and demand the building of Cop City: "Hi, my name is _____ and I live in Buckhead, and I am concerned with the uptick in crime, and something must be done! Please vote yes on the building of the Public Safety Training Center."[50]

It all made for a perfect storm, and in September 2021, City Council sided with APF against Atlanta residents and voted 10–4 to approve the plan.[51]

Resolving the Crisis

Though the public justifications for Cop City revolved around policing and the need to combat rising crime, even those who voted for the plan knew that the facility would not be built for at least two years after its approval.[52] In that sense, Cop City would by no means be an immediate response to crime concerns. And in the following years, despite APD's reported crime rates continuing to drop, the city continues to charge forward.[53] But Cop City was never about stopping crime—instead, it is a solution to Atlanta's multiple crises of organized abandonment that would 1) materially invest in police capacity, 2) ideologically invest in the city's image, and 3) geographically invest in future development.

This is not the first time that police expansion has followed rebellion. As detailed in the 2022 documentary *Riotsville, U.S.A.*, the parallels between the response to the uprisings and rebellions of the 1960s and those of today are eerie. In the 1960s, after uprisings in communities like Newark, Watts, and Detroit, the US military constructed mock cities on military bases. These bases were referred to as "Riotsvilles," where, much like the plans for Cop City, police could role-play responses to uprisings and protests.[54] More recently, in 2019, Chicago's City Council and mayor approved a plan proposed in 2017 for what organizers branded "Cop Academy"—a $128 million police training center that, like Atlanta's proposed Cop City, would include a "tactical scenario village" with a full fake city block.[55] While Chicago's political leadership made many of the same claims in pushing for Cop Academy that Atlantans have witnessed with Cop City—better trained, reformed police—#NoCopAcademy organizers made the connections between the slashing of social services and massive investment in police infrastructure in a majority-Black part of the city that had faced significant disinvestment.[56]

Just as Cop City followed Cop Academy, new proposals for similar facilities have continued to emerge across the country in recent years. One estimate puts the number of proposed facilities nationwide at sixty-nine, as local leaders across the country work to lock down their cities and lean further into austerity.[57] While libraries shrink their hours, hospitals are shuttered, and pools close during the summer heat, police budgets continue to grow.

Expanding police infrastructure to control the masses is certainly not limited to the United States.[58] Israel, for example, is home to the Urban Warfare Training Center, known by the soldiers who train there as "Mini Gaza"—a $45 million, 60-acre facility that is "meant to simulate the urban environments in which Israel's soldiers often operate."[59] Beyond urban warfare training to combat so-called terrorism (note that both Palestinian freedom fighters and Stop Cop City protesters have been called terrorists), the link between Israel and Georgia is even deeper, as the Georgia International Law Enforcement Exchange program has operated since the 1990s as an exchange between Israeli and Georgia police forces.[60]

Cop City is thus part of a historical and ongoing pattern of governments, at home and abroad, expanding police and jail infrastructure and honing urban repression tactics in response to, and in preparation for, uprisings and threats categorized as terrorism. And, importantly, Cop City is but one piece of a broader lockdown strategy. While Atlanta's leadership works to build Cop City, it has also threatened to withhold funding for policing alternatives, expanded the city's network of surveillance cameras, and opened new police precincts.[61] And as Atlanta leadership reversed its promise to close and repurpose the city jail, Atlanta's Fulton County is considering a proposal for a new $2 billion jail that would double the county's jail capacity.[62]

Just as Cop City offers a material investment in Atlanta's police capacity, it is also an investment in a particular image of Atlanta that is friendly and welcoming to major events, tech and real estate capital, and middle and upper-class white newcomers. Think back to the 1996 Olympics and the moves city leadership made to rebrand Atlanta as a world-class city by demolishing public housing, displacing poor and Black residents, building a jail and using it to lock up homeless people, lining the pockets of developers, and investing in events-based infrastructure. Think of the projects since then: the Beltline, major mixed-use commercial properties, stadiums, The Gulch—all projects that have enhanced the aesthetic appeal of the city for the corporations and individuals who flood in, as Black and working-class residents are criminalized, evicted, and priced out of the city.

Atlanta prides itself on being a world-class city, focusing on its ability to attract major events and tourism. In recent years, Atlanta has hosted the 2019 Super Bowl, the 2021 NBA All-Star Game, and the 2021 World Series, and is preparing to serve as one of the host cities for the 2026 FIFA World Cup (which the city is preparing for, in part, by recruiting at least four hundred additional police officers).[63] Mayor Andre Dickens and other Atlanta boosters also poured significant time and resources into an unsuccessful bid for the 2024 Democratic National Convention and the supposed revenues and prestige it would generate for the city—a process through which leadership emphasized the city's hotel capacity, its scheduled improvements to its event infrastructure, and its ability to collaborate with at least twenty-seven other police and fire departments in the metro Atlanta area.[64]

Attracting big business and big events requires investing in policing and surveillance as a promise of stability and safety for those who would come here. As historian Destin Jenkins has demonstrated, even a city's ability to borrow money to finance projects is tied to its investments in policing and the bond market's perception of a city's stability—perceptions that are deeply threatened by mass uprisings.[65] In that sense, Cop City is meant to play a stabilizing role for Atlanta's image in the wake of the uprisings; it is as much about the reality of Atlanta's police capacity as it is the story *told* about Atlanta's police capacity. Cop City is meant to communicate that Atlanta is a place that takes "public safety" and the protection of property seriously—a place where people with money can come and safely turn that money into more money.

Identifying Cop City as an investment in Atlanta's police capacity and image doesn't explain why the forest that was officially slated by the city in 2017 for incorporation into a broader stretch of park land was chosen as the site for the project.[66] Why, as climate catastrophe worsens, destroy more of Atlanta's already diminishing tree canopy?[67]

There are various elements of the land that make it appealing to the city and APF. Perhaps most importantly, the Cop City site is city-owned land—it is "free" for the city to destroy, convert, and develop as it so chooses. Additionally, the land is located within a majority-Black and deeply disinvested area of DeKalb County; it is surrounded by a number of carceral facilities and industrial waste-producing sites, has been used as a shooting range by the Atlanta Police Department, and is home to one of the ten most endangered rivers in the US.[68] Further, because the land falls outside city limits, it is not subject to the more demanding input processes required within the city, and its residents do not have any formal political representation on the Atlanta City Council.[69]

But the Weelaunee Forest is not just a seemingly convenient location for Cop City. It also represents an opportunity for the city to repurpose publicly owned land in a way that materially and ideologically invests in policing while serving the area up for future development.

Consider what's happening in the surrounding area: Directly adjacent to the site, and part of the same stretch of forest land, is public park land owned by DeKalb County, known as Intrenchment Creek Park (ICP). In 2020, the DeKalb County Commission approved a highly controversial deal to "swap" forty acres of ICP land with developer Ryan Millsap and his company, Blackhall Studios, in exchange for far less valuable land—a deal that is still being challenged in court.[70] And while Millsap's original stated plan was to take the ICP land and convert it into an expanded Hollywood soundstage, he has since sold Blackhall Studios and now claims to independently own the land.[71] It is unclear exactly how he plans to use it—but it is clear that he plans to destroy the parkland, as he has already (illegally) started to do.[72] As one reporter concluded, "In the end, Blackhall Studios was really just a real estate play."[73]

While the Cop City proposal itself might seem like less of an obvious real estate play—the city will technically retain ownership of the land, even as control of the land shifts to APF—the city has consistently put forward the site's supposed green space, parklands, and trails, framing the project as offering enhancements to the surrounding area. Reflecting Atlanta's pattern of "green gentrification" as seen in projects like the Beltline, any parks and green space built by the city will not be for the benefit of those who currently live in the area, but rather those who will be attracted by new development.[74]

Given the centrality of real estate development to the twenty-first-century Atlanta Way and the web of corporate interests behind Cop City and APF, it's not hard to see how the destruction and development of the Weelaunee Forest, whether by Millsap or APF, begins to create new markets for real estate development and displacement in what is currently a majority-Black working-class area of the metro Atlanta area.

While the pledged $60 million of private funding for Cop City has been framed as a boon for Atlanta—the city gets a state-of-the-art police and fire training facility for a fraction of the price!—here's another way of looking at it: Cop City is a project that allows the already-powerful APF to dole out over $67 million worth of public money and $60 million worth of tax-sheltered private donations into non-competitive contracts for the destruction and redevelopment of forest land, while tilling the soil for future development in the area. At the same time, the city can cash in on new revenue streams generated by renting the facilities to other police departments and even film studios looking to use the space.

When you take the fact of city-owned land being transformed into Cop City, with flashy renderings of supposedly significant park and community space, and county-owned park land being transferred to a private developer to use as he will, a different image of the space comes together: Through transfer from public to private or privately controlled land, an entire stretch of forest land has instead been slated for various forms of destruction and development. And if the plans for Cop City and the land swap go through, both the land and its surrounding neighborhoods will be fundamentally transformed, as current residents are pushed out and new, wealthier white residents move in.

⚖

So, why Cop City, why here, and why now? Because, after the 2020 uprisings, Atlanta's leadership chose to repurpose city-owned land in a way that fortified police legitimacy, signaled to corporate elites and wealthy white communities that Atlanta is safe for their interests, opened up new real estate markets for hungry developers, defanged crime narratives and the threat of Buckhead secession, doled out over $120 million in tax-shielded or public dollars to many of the companies that make up Atlanta's ruling class, and promised protection and stability for capital in an increasingly unstable world.

Ultimately, Cop City represents the Atlanta Way: a status quo that benefits a few at the top while sacrificing the many at the bottom. But the Stop Cop City movement is fighting for a new status quo, one that upends the city's ruling-class structure and creates an abolitionist future in its place. As the Defend the Atlanta Forest Twitter account wrote: "The Weelaunee Forest will be the graveyard of the Atlanta Way."

A version of this piece was originally published in Scalawag Magazine *in May 2023.*

TWO

Boss Terror

How the Capital of the South Funded Cop City

Mariah Parker

In times of mass uprising, the powerful band together. And not just politically, but financially. This was certainly true for passive investors who, amid mass protest following Trayvon Martin's 2012 killing, poured hundreds of millions into publicly traded firms that contract heavily with the police.[1] They did so again when Martin's vigilante murderer, George Zimmerman, was acquitted, and again when police killed Michael Brown in 2014. While unrest simmered, firms that deal in carceral tech saw their stock value shoot seven percentage points higher than those of non-policing firms in similar industries. In the three weeks after Minneapolis killed George Floyd, firms with tight financial ties to policing gained $474 million in value.[2]

After mass shootings, another prominent genre of American terror, investors don't splurge on carceral tech in the same way. A white gunman commits unspeakable violence against nine Black churchgoers in Charleston, South Carolina, or murders twenty-three Walmart shoppers in El Paso, Texas, and the line on the graph stays normal, because white supremacist killings *themselves* are not the problem. Mass uprisings, their attendant economic disruption, and the specter of a widespread redistribution of power—that's what shakes the elite most deeply and what fuels lavish investment in militarization.

Police foundations have also enjoyed skyrocketing revenue

29

since Black Lives Matter became a household phrase. The Atlanta Police Foundation (APF), the primary entity behind Cop City and the most well-endowed police foundation in the country, has seen a fifteen-fold increase in revenue since Trayvon was killed in 2012 and a 45 percent increase in revenue between 2018 and 2019, from $7.5 million to $10.8 million.[3] Most of this funding comes from the philanthropic suites of high-profile corporations, whose economic might is built on exploited labor. Foundations then use their stockpile of private capital to coerce militarized public investment with next to no public accountability, raining free money for policing onto local governments with couch-cushion change to spare for much else. Police foundations and their elite boards can leverage the threat of austerity and the loyalty of the city's paramilitary forces to ensure their will is done, their cop cities built, and future working-class uprisings neutralized on their donors' behalf. In this way, police foundations consolidate corporate and militarized police power in a proto-fascist arrangement that gravely threatens democracy.

In the words of George Jackson, fascism is, at its core, an economic arrangement. When workers refuse exploitation en masse and threaten the corporate bottom line, fascism attempts to renew the legitimacy of the economic elite by bearing down upon and diffusing unrest. If we are to clear the path to liberation of cop cities and other snares, movements must build on Atlanta's current experiments in undermining the economic arrangement of the police foundation as an institution. What we're seeing today isn't new; the kinship of capital and policing in the American South has a long history. And Atlanta, the capital of the South, sits squarely at the center of that history. APF is one of the most novel and dangerous versions of this arrangement, but it is by no means the first.

Capitalism in Crisis at the Turn of the Century

When American capitalism entered a period of crisis with the fall of slavery, the southern economic elite made use of (para)military violence and dehumanizing propaganda to diffuse conscious organization of the newly freed, constrict democracy, and ultimately re-entrench their own power—a repertoire that European fascists observed and expanded on in the decades following Reconstruction.[4]

Fascists famously hurl accusations of corruption to undermine the legitimacy of their political opponents. When newly enfranchised Black voters swept the first thirty-three African American members of the Georgia General Assembly into office in 1868, they were barraged with claims of corruption that, in the mind of the public, green-lit violently coerced resignations.[5] This political representation did not last long, however; in short time, a quarter of the Black electeds were imprisoned, assaulted, murdered, or intimidated into resigning.[6]

All the while, white business tycoons elected to public office nakedly wielded their posts in their self-interest to their enormous economic benefit. Three years after founding the Chattahoochee Brick Company in 1878, James English was elected the mayor of Atlanta in 1880 and wielded the city's newly professionalized police department to supply his enterprises with a steady stream of exploitable labor. The police rounded up free Blacks, often for petty or invented crimes, who were then leased to the Chattahoochee Brick Company, which English had founded and part-owned. The depraved working conditions at the brickworks later earned the site the nickname "the Black Auschwitz of Georgia": Captives toiled under the constant lash of overseers' whips and the searing heat of the kilns, fabricating millions of bricks a year that to this day line the streets of many iconic Atlanta neighborhoods and the walls of many historic municipal buildings.[7]

English was not a wholly selfish man; indeed, he managed control of the city's police and political apparatus to the benefit of the city's elite broadly. In July 1881, three thousand Atlanta laundresses organized and struck to demand a fairer pay rate of $1 per pound of clothing laundered. Though overwhelmingly Black, the newly formed Washing Society also organized the city's white laundresses through a level of cross-racial solidarity that was extraordinary for its time. The strike soon spread to other parts of the service sector, imperiling the city's entire economy. The English administration attempted to squeeze the strikers into submission on two sides: English's police forces arrested six of its leaders and charged them with "quarreling" and disorderly conduct, while his City Council proposed legislation that would capsize the Washing Society under heavy business fees.

The Washing Society ultimately won their demands, but major victories against the city's ruling class whites have remained rare. Elite whites feared that the poor, Black and white, would organize together to challenge the rule of the rich and gain mutual emancipation. They needed poor whites to embrace racial vitriol over the collective uplift promised by cross-racial, workplace-based campaigns like those advanced by the laundresses, the Knights of Labor, and the Communist Party.[8] As Hannah Riley details in this volume's chapter on narrative change, the white southern elite platformed rumors of Black violence to pressure-cook racist antipathy that exploded in rogue property destruction, torture, and murder.

Between 1890 and 1930, more than 450 people—almost all Black—died at the hands of racist mobs in Georgia. Most often, the victims were accused of violence against whites; in 1899, an estimated two thousand spectators gathered in Coweta County, Georgia, for the mob torture and killing Sam Hose, who had been accused of killing a white man.[9] In the Atlanta Race Massacre of 1906, sensational coverage of purportedly Black crime by the city's dueling newspapers bubbled over into a days-long violent white mob that claimed the lives of at least two dozen Black people and torched a major Black business sector. While on one hand, the city's white industrialists wielded police violence to renew their exploitative relations with the Black labor force, on the other, they wielded media narratives to deputize

poor whites into a performance of extralegal violence that cemented
social divisions among the working class.

Atlanta High Society

On May 8, 1886—four days into the general strike in Chicago that
would eventually bring about the eight-hour workday—Confeder-
ate Army veteran John Pemberton served the world's first Coca-Cola
at Jacobs' Pharmacy in Atlanta. His successors at the Coca-Cola
Company were notoriously ruthless in expanding the brand's footprint, from their invention and sale of Fanta in Nazi Germany to
generate profit despite the blockade, to their alleged involvement
in the disappearance, torture, and murder of union leaders by right-
wing thugs in Colombia in the 1990s.[10] Today, rather than gamble
on bids for higher office (a la James English) or hiring mercenaries
themselves, corporations like Coke—and dozens of others founded
or headquartered in Atlanta—triangulate with the city's paramilitary forces via foundation board membership and hefty donations:
The foundation of Robert Woodruff, president of Coke from 1923
to 1954, has donated $10 million to the Atlanta Police Foundation
(APF), while the Coca-Cola foundation pledged a cool $2 million
in 2018 and, until recently, held a seat on its board.[11]

Indeed, representatives of Atlanta's top-employing industries all
hold seats on APF's board or its board of trustees, from transportation (Delta, UPS, Norfolk Southern) and utilities (Georgia Power)
to education (Emory and George State universities) and finance
(JPMorganChase and Wells Fargo).[12] Those who don't hold seats are
found throughout the foundation's bankrolls: SunTrust, founded and
headquartered in Atlanta before its merger with BB&T to become
Truist, donated $3 million to APF in 2019.[13] Extremely wealthy pri-
vate individuals enjoy cozy relationships with APF as well. Arthur
Blank, Home Depot founder and part-owner of the Atlanta Falcons,

has contributed generously through his philanthropic foundation; a representative from Home Depot also holds a seat on the APF board. As well, Tony Ressler, part-owner of the Atlanta Hawks, is an APF donor. Two common interests tie these individuals and companies together: the need to exploit labor and an interest in projecting Atlanta and the State of Georgia as "good for business."

Good for business is bad for workers, and indeed, the unique depth of southern labor exploitation is what makes Atlanta's Cop City possible. Rates of worker organization in the State of Georgia remain at roughly half the national average, and with that comes lower wages, highly profitable but less safe working conditions, and record profits that corporations can perpetually reinvest into domination through their local police foundation.[14]

Rail companies like Norfolk Southern, an APF donor, often maintain private police departments that protect the operation of the railways from rogue interruption. When Norfolk Southern relocated to Atlanta in 2018, it also resettled the headquarters of its private armed forces, the Norfolk Southern Police Department.[15] In 2023, when railway operators rallied around the demand for seven paid sick days per year—which would have cost the railway companies roughly 2 percent of their annual profits—Congress intervened to kill a potential strike, holding steady the torrential flow of wealth upward from rail operators to the company's upper crust and into the coffers of its foundation. That same year, Norfolk Southern's philanthropic arm gave $100,000 to APF. APF intends to rent training space at Cop City to departments across the state and country, and it stands to reason that Norfolk Southern's police force would number among its lessees, reinforcing an allyship that will be critical for crushing the kind of working-class unrest railroad companies have historically taken on themselves.[16]

When first announcing its big move to Atlanta, Norfolk Southern's CEO cited Atlanta's Hartsfield-Jackson airport, the world's busiest airport and the central hub for Delta Airlines, as a major part of the draw to the city.[17] Delta, founded in Macon, Georgia, in 1925, is one of the big four major airlines and the pride of Atlanta's business community. It also boasts the lowest union density of any major airline; only pilots, the highest paid of the aviation professions, enjoy a guaranteed cost-of-living increases and other union-mandated benefits. At Hartsfield-Jackson, Delta offers workers in hospitality-oriented positions like baggage handling wages well below the national average and the metropolitan living wage of $25 an hour.[18] Meanwhile, the vice president of community and public affairs sits on APF's board of trustees. In 2019, the foundation took in a 45 percent increase in revenue; that year, Delta was the chief sponsor of APF's major annual fundraiser.[19]

Southern hospitality warmly welcomed Cop City to Atlanta. Waffle House and Chick-fil-A, both headquartered in the Atlanta metro area, are notorious for donating lavishly to right-wing political projects, including several million to APF in recent years.[20] Waffle House CEO and president Walt Ehmer sits on APF's board of trustees, while Waffle House servers earn a tipped wage of $2.15 an hour. The lead adviser to Chick-fil-A's chairman and CEO serves on APF's Young Executives Board; meanwhile, the Department of Labor has cited the company for tens of thousands of dollars in back wages and fines for child labor law violations in 2023 alone.[21] Depressed and stolen wages are good business for not only the company's elite but also for APF, which stands ready to violently disorganize the working poor.

The service industry purchasing the allegiance of the city's police is perhaps best exemplified with the Atlanta-based private equity firm Roark Capital, which owns Inspire Brands, the second-biggest restaurant company in the United States.[22] Inspire Brands invests mainly in fast-food franchises like Dunkin Donuts, Sonic, Arby's, and Jimmy John's, whose half a million employees produce $30 billion in sales annually. Even with such massive windfalls, franchisees operating under the Inspire flag have a well-documented history of labor law violation; since 2010, the Department of Labor has ordered the return of more than $4 million in stolen wages to sixteen thousand workers on the franchisees' payrolls. When one combines widespread underpayment with potential wage theft, the most wide-spread form of property crime in the United States, it is easy to see where the funds for Cop City come from.[23] Corporations reinvest the loot into the apparatus capable of enforcing the status quo of low wages and long hours—painfully, if necessary.

In 1934, forty-four thousand of the sixty thousand textile workers in the State of Georgia walked off their jobs on strike over low pay and code violations. Governor Eugene Talmadge declared martial law and flooded the state with four thousand National Guardsmen, who rounded up thousands of textile workers, strike sympathizers, and others suspected of association with the mill walkouts.[24] When Trion Mills in northwest Georgia exploded in violence in September of that year, local authorities hurriedly swore in nearly fifty special deputies to defend it against the combatant strikers. It made no difference, surely, that the vice president of Trion Mills was also the mayor of Trion.[25]

Today, corporate honchos need not gamble on bids for public office to ensure control over the cops. Instead, they slip plunder into the piggy banks of their local police foundations, whose sprawling training complexes and vast high-tech surveillance networks will ensure a workforce too certain of state violence and repression to dare rise up again—or so they hope.

Cries of fascism may seem overblown to outside observers, but for those living under the repression and who know fascism's signs, the present uncannily resembles an era in southern history that modeled for the world's most notorious villains how best to consolidate their power. As state legislatures attempt to make it more difficult, even illegal, to disclose information about police foundation donors, webs like those illuminated here may become more difficult to decipher, and so the work of skilled researchers may become even more critical to movement strategy around philanthropic accountability.[26] Indeed, throughout this book you will encounter strategies that Atlantans and their allies have applied to counter those who profit from cop cities and to resist the rule of the rich.

THREE

A Brief History
of the Atlanta Prison Farm

Atlanta Community Press Collective

Known today as the proposed Cop City site, the Old Atlanta Prison Farm, located at 561 Key Road in southeast Atlanta, operated as a city-owned jail where incarcerated people were forced to labor for the City of Atlanta from about 1920 to nearly 1990. Newspaper articles, letters, inspection documents, legislative records, and folk stories about the farm tell tales of overcrowding, "slave conditions," lack of health care, labor strikes, deaths, and unmarked "pauper's" graves. All of these reflect the racial and class dynamics at the heart of the carceral system, then as now.

We, a group of citizen researchers, pulled at one question—are there unmarked graves at Cop City?—and found hundreds more. We trace the straight line of carceral violence that runs through this land and the forest that surrounds it from its operation as a municipal dairy farm in the 1900s to the present.

The Elephant in the Tomb

"Maud, the deceased elephant and 280 inmates rest in peace at the City of Atlanta prison farm," reads a 1976 article in the *Atlanta Journal-Constitution*.[1] While at least two former Atlanta Zoo residents are interred at the prison farm, we suspect this line is a sick joke, as the rest of the article attempts to paint life at the prison farm as one of leisure and respite.

According to local resident and folk historian Scott Petersen, who has collected folk stories and oral histories about the land for over twenty years, a burial plot lies next to an old oak tree and a sunken-in structure that was once used to shade the warden during lynchings at the prison. There are records of "runaways" at another prison farm that were later discovered to have been killed and buried on-site.[2]

During our archival research, we attempted to find death and burial records for those who died while incarcerated at the prison farm. At least several deaths occurred. After the death of Robert Reynolds, a Black man whose death from head injuries prompted an investigation, 1953 mayoral candidate Charlie Brown declared that "approximately 10 prisoners [had] died in the jail in the last four years 'under mysterious circumstances.'"[3] In 1957, Samuel Baynes, a 36-year-old Black man, "dropped dead" shortly after a patrolman woke him up to get dressed.[4] In 1975, one man died after being sprayed with an insecticide, which the warden denied.[5] Despite these known deaths, we were unable to obtain official records listing either deaths or burials at the site. We do know, though, that a burial ground once owned and operated by the prison farm exists off Key Road. However, the tract of land that was originally the prison farm has been divided into many smaller pieces, only one of which is leased to the Atlanta Police Foundation to build Cop City.

Our findings were inconclusive, but we continued digging into the deaths of people detained there and along the way found records of horrible abuses, profiting off criminalization, and carceral expansion in the name of prison reform.

The Beginning of the Prison Farm

The Atlanta Prison Farm started out as a simple municipal dairy farm, producing various crops, livestock, and dairy. But accusations that the farm was losing city money, coupled with ongoing scandals at the city's stockade, opened debates within the city government from 1915 to 1920 about closing the stockade and moving some or all of the detainees to the municipal dairy farm. By combining the stockade and dairy farm, some city leaders thought they could save money on incarceration by making the new influx of incarcerated people work at the city dairy, and even generate revenue for the city.[6]

In 1918, the superintendent of prisons, T. B. Lanford, who ran the city stockade, was also put in charge of the municipal dairy.[7] Soon after, the *Atlanta Constitution* investigated claims of women incarcerated at the city stockade being tied to a chair known as the "bucking chair" and whipped with a strap for disobedience. Lanford at first denied these claims, saying that white women at the stockade were never whipped to his knowledge, and "Negroe women only seldom so."[8]

However, an investigation corroborated the abuse claims, and Lanford was ordered to stop the whippings.[9] In January 1920, Atlanta City Council passed a law banning whippings and offering a new reform: "solitary confinement on a diet of bread and water."[10] In response to this ordinance—and complaints that both the city stockade and dairy farm were losing money—Lanford suggested moving the whole operation to the dairy farm.

There was only one roadblock: It was not legal to build prison facilities on land outside the city limits, and the Key Road property, though owned by the city, was located in unincorporated DeKalb County. So the City Council simply passed a bill making it legal. By November, the proposal to close the stockade was agreed upon. The Key Road municipal dairy farm became the Atlanta City Prison and Dairy Farm, later simplified to the Atlanta City Prison Farm.[11]

The *Atlanta Constitution* (a precursor to the *Atlanta Journal-Constitution*) praised councilmembers bringing in the "largest number of prisoners at any one time in the past ten years, saving the city $20 a day on the cost of feeding prisoners and increasing dairy production by 250 gallons a week."[12] It was a win-win-win for the new property owners, the city government, and Lanford. But it was a huge loss for the most vulnerable citizens of the city, and for the residents of the surrounding DeKalb County area who had no way of consenting to the deal.

Maintaining Their Own Cages

Profiting off criminalization is not new to Atlanta, nor was it when the municipal dairy first opened. In the mid-1800s, enslaved people accounted for roughly one-fifth of the city's population.[13] Atlanta City Hall and many other iconic buildings and roads built in the early 1900s were built using convict lease labor from the Chattahoochee Brick Company, which was notorious for its brutal conditions and owned by a former Atlanta mayor.[14]

The people incarcerated at the dairy farm produced agricultural products for use in the city's jails and prisons, but were forced to build and maintain at least some of their own cages as well. In 1944, one of the older prison buildings was designated for use as a hospital for people with venereal diseases. This meant that if incarcerated people needed a new building, they built it themselves: "Most of the work was done with prison labor, with the city providing the materials."[15] They were also responsible for the cleaning and maintenance of the buildings in order to pass health inspection. According to an article in the *Atlanta Journal-Constitution* (*AJC*), "The dormitory [was] scrubbed daily by men and women whose drunkenness and traffic violations place them behind a mop or tractor for an average 15-day stay."[16]

In 1946, then superintendent of prisons H.H. Gibson bragged that he was cutting the city prison food budget in half and "furnishing the city 11,961 man-days of work on city streets by prisoners" within a six-month period.[17] This work heavily subsidized city operations and was considered crucial. By the 1970s, the farm "provided more than half the food and dairy products for inmates in city detention centers." By the 1980s, the prison farm had stopped growing crops, but still provided "42 percent of the pork and beef eaten by the prisoners, both at the farm and at the city jail."[18] Again and again, the city's jailers and elected officials congratulated themselves on the economic efficiency that coerced labor made possible—and prioritized this efficiency over health and safety wherever possible.

"An Ungodly Mess"

Leadership changed hands often over the course of the prison farm's lifespan, and each change of hands was said to be the dawn of a new, better era. In reality, conditions remained bleak throughout. Archival research shows that life on the farm was overcrowded, unsanitary, and virtually bereft of health care, such that in 1938, Atlanta mayor William Hartsfield described the farm "an ungodly mess" given the rampant spread of communicable disease.[19]

A police report from 1936 stated, "We find that all prisoners have separate quarters which are in sanitary condition, but overcrowded. We recommend that another unit be constructed for white female prisoners as well as white male prisoners."[20] By 1938, a new wing was completed to house seventy-five more prisoners, and another addition of the same size was expected to be added to the main building.[21] But only five months later, the prison farm's own superintendent again described conditions there as "overcrowded" and recommended another expansion and separate ward for "diseased prisoners."[22]

In December 1957, a DeKalb County grand jury presented findings from an investigation that found the prison farm to be severely lacking in health care. It recommended that sick people incarcerated at the farm be given examinations, that the farm maintain records about their illnesses and "employ a proper nursing staff," and that "some sort of sick quarters be put into effect so that prisoners who are ill can be held aside from the ones who are not sick."[23] The implication from these recommendations is, of course, that none of these practices were in place at the time.

Despite the construction of another new wing in 1958, in 1960 a grand jury found that the prison farm was still "exceedingly overcrowded," and "as a result, the health of prisoners is 'jeopardized.'" It suggested building a "work camp" to alleviate crowding.[24]

When journalist Dick Herbert went undercover at the Prison Farm for the *AJC* in 1965, he reported "tubercular, coughing, sickly men, waiting to die, society's discards, herded into an unwashed 'stockade' only to be turned out again without even a smattering of 'help.'" He found puddles of spit at drainage grills, wondered if many of the men had tuberculosis, and said that "it was not uncommon to find dead bugs or hair in food" which was "almost entirely a thin and liquid diet." According to Herbert, detained people often complained that "the best of the farm's produce and meats are reserved for the guards and hired help."[25]

Ten years later, another *AJC* article from 1970 stated that incarcerated people worked in the kitchen while infected with tuberculosis: "One man was sent to Battey State Hospital after it was found his tuberculosis was so advanced he started hemorrhaging. He had worked in the kitchen the night before." When asked about this, prison farm administrator R. F. Jordan admitted that "yes, some work in the kitchen, but only if their case is arrested."[26]

Recorded minutes from a meeting of the Department of Prisons and the Farm indicate that administrators planned to hire a full-time registered nurse in 1972 to assist the on-site doctor. An *Atlanta Voice* article from 1973 claimed there were "new" improvements including the "employment of a physician and two nurses" and "a humane approach to prisoner problems."[27] In 1976, this proposal was raised again in an inter-office communication at Grady Memorial Hospital; one of the officials suggested hiring out medical staff for the reason that it "will generate $125,000 in income."[28] Noxious living conditions at the farm persisted until its closure, and against a steady drumbeat of empty reassurances that expansion would alleviate human suffering.

Lawsuit in the 1980s

J. D. Hudson, the superintendent of the prison farm in its last years, was hyped by the press as a humanitarian reformer. He described previous conditions as "slave labor," but also said that detained people are "ridden with guilt about their lives, they want to be mistreated and abused, and they want to be denigrated as some sort of atonement for their sins." He bragged frequently of his intention to give people incarcerated at the prison farm "a measure of self-respect" so that they could "lead decent lives again."[29]

Upon his instatement at the prison farm, he announced, like many before him, his intention to end solitary confinement and forbid guards from hitting or abusing detained people. The great reformer himself was still in charge when the American Civil Liberties Union (ACLU) sued the city in 1982 for "illegal and unconstitutional punishments such as leg irons and excessive time in solitary confinement," along with unsanitary conditions. At the time, many incarcerated people were still being held alone in "a room seven feet long by four feet wide that is virtually without heat in the winter and without cooling in the summer" for twenty-three hours a day.[30]

The suit was settled in 1985 with a $4,500 settlement split

between the three formerly incarcerated people who filed the suit. The city never admitted guilt.[31] While the ACLU and those supporting the suit hoped this lawsuit would push the city to make changes, in 1987 the city tried to build twenty more solitary confinement cells at the prison farm. The project reportedly fell through due to allegations that the white contractors the city tried to hire were operating a front, taking job contracts intended for minority-run businesses.[32] Solitary confinement continues to be used as punishment in many prisons today, despite reports that it may fulfill all four elements of torture under international law.[33]

✳

This is not an exhaustive or comprehensive account. In fact, this version has been edited down for book format, and readers are encouraged to dig deeper into this history by reading the version hosted on the web.[34]

What we've laid out here is a history of a city cutting costs by extending slavery. We have uncovered six decades of physical and emotional abuse, torture, overwork, a lack of health care, poor sanitation and nutrition, and overcrowding. We have seen leaders in nearly every stage of the prison's history get caught breaking rules and laws while avoiding the same carceral fate as those they imprison. We have seen city officials reluctant to enact policies that would alleviate and repair these harms but eager to ensure the continuity of their own power. We have seen the Atlanta city government run over the rights of the residents of DeKalb County, who are disenfranchised from the city, time and again, and we see it continue today.

What we've laid out here shows that atrocious conditions persisted at the Atlanta Prison Farm for the better part of a century, despite claims at each stage that the bad times were behind us and a new era lay ahead. For the same reasons, it is prudent to take with deep skepticism the Atlanta Police Foundation's claims that the new training facility will allow us to "reimagine policing."

We have heard folk stories of unmarked graves from the community, and, given the rest of what we've uncovered, we believe these reports need to be taken seriously and investigated fully. Otherwise, the city risks not only erasing the history of the lives it has destroyed, but desecrating their graves in the process. Even if we cannot find the answers to the questions we began with, the City of Atlanta, as an institution, is responsible for untold violence and harm, for which it must take real responsibility and provide material reparations to the populations affected.

The Atlanta Community Press Collective is an abolitionist, not-for-profit media collective. ACPC's goal is to make the day-to-day workings of local government accessible to the public through explanatory reporting and to provide an investigative voice in a local media landscape increasingly dominated by corporate interests. Since 2021, ACPC has been at the forefront of investigative reporting on the Cop City project.

FOUR

Becoming External Enemies

From Occupy Atlanta to Stop Cop City

Kayla Edgett

In May of 2020, thousands of people rose up in Atlanta to challenge racist US policing practices. The uprising marked a tonal shift and revealed a new composition of protest in Atlanta. This was incidentally noted by an Executive Board member of the Atlanta NAACP, who, while condemning the first night of protest, told the media that the rioters were some "weird mixture" of the "AfroPunk/Antifa/Socialist/Anarchist crowd," from outside the city.[1] While the protests were undoubtedly composed of local residents from around metro Atlanta, this commentator observed a composition of actors that upset the traditionally imagined racial and class composition of movements for social justice in Atlanta.

Atlanta has variously been represented as the birthplace of the civil rights movement, the "city too busy to hate," an exemplar of the New South, and the Black Mecca. For decades, corporate and political elites have projected this image to make the city more amenable to elite consumption and corporate investment. Part of this "imagineering" has involved the denial of the longue durée of militant resistance to the violences of racial capitalism in Atlanta and the South.[2] If we are exposed to this history at all, we are made to believe that the postwar struggle for civil rights righted the wrongs born in the racist backlash to emancipation.[3]

If indeed Atlanta had laid to rest the worst of the racial terror

49

that has defined the South and the nation for generations, then how can we understand the emergence of a multiracial, multiethnic militant uprising of everyday people resisting the authority of the police, breaking into private property, and redistributing looted goods in 2020? How is it that those deemed as outsiders (those working-class Black and brown residents, those radical white youth who transgress whiteness by aligning themselves with movements for Black liberation) forced themselves onto the scene, forced themselves to be heard and seen, as the world witnessed in both 2020 and the movement to stop Cop City and defend the Weelaunee Forest?

In reality, Atlanta is the city with the highest income inequality and the most surveillance cameras per capita in the US.[4] Residents continue to face the violences of ongoing gentrification, a process that has shifted the city's racial composition so that the residential makeup in the "Black Mecca" is no longer majority Black. The "Atlanta Way" is touted as an effective strategy to avoid white supremacist violence, uplift Black residents, and bring capital investment to the city. In practice, this strategy involves elite upper-class collaboration to repress, mediate, and divide those elements of the long struggle for Black liberation led by the working class and poor.[5] Some Black activists, following the late Bruce Dixon, openly critique the class interests of what they call the "Black misleadership class" that came to power at the close of the postwar movement for civil rights and Black liberation.[6] In the face of these conditions, Atlantans have always resisted.[7]

The "weird mixture" noticed by the NAACP Executive Board member is the expanding networks of resistance, the unruly alliances that emerge through struggle, both in acute moments of crisis and in the everyday work of building abolitionist infrastructures.[8] A constitutive "outside" to respectable political engagement has reemerged, from the 2011 Occupy movement through the 2020 uprising.[9] Importantly, each moment of resistance emerges from the ongoing reproduction of the violences of enclosure, accumulation, exploitation, and criminalization; the boundaries and possibilities of each moment are defined, but not wholly, by the social and political imaginaries that precede them; and each moment births new understandings of identity based on the actors defining it. This is a story of revolutionary movement as iterative, creative, messy, and real, full of missteps and misunderstandings, of possibility and the discipline of hope.[10]

Troy Davis Park

In September 2011, a relatively small protest occupation with big ambitions was set up at Zuccotti Park in New York City. In the aftermath of the 2007 housing crash, the failed promises of Obama's first presidential term, and an economic "recovery" that left out most working people, Occupy Wall Street represented the rage of disaffected youth who had grown up watching the US government spend more money on permanent wars than social welfare. Inspired by global movements such as the Arab Spring, Occupy responded to the crisis of capital that had resulted in rampant evictions and foreclosures throughout the US, and its participants brought with them notions of racial justice, gender liberation, and systemic critique developed throughout the twentieth-century movements. Just as numbers began to dwindle to the very determined, threatening to disappear Occupy Wall Street into historical obscurity, a mass arrest on the Brooklyn Bridge catapulted the movement to cities across the United States.

Occupy Atlanta began in October of 2011 with an unlikely coalition of progressive students, anarchists, communists, crust-punks, frustrated working-class adults, unhoused people living downtown, and liberal activists. Some in this coalition had built trust through collaborating on campaigns, including fighting against Georgia State University budget cuts, admissions bans on undocumented students, and the execution of Troy Davis, a Black man wrongly convicted but ultimately murdered by the state. What began as "general assemblies" (large consensus-based meetings) turned into an encampment of Woodruff Park in downtown Atlanta, which the occupiers renamed Troy Davis Park. A small group of youth, largely white but multiracial, held down key components of the occupation, hosted anti-police marches, connected with families of police brutality victims, organized jail support, and attempted to bridge divides between long-standing Black radical organizing and the occupation.

Lasting only a few short weeks, the occupation encouraged the messy process of building political unity in place. Familiar disagreements between and among progressives and radicals about tactics and strategies abounded: Should we uncritically embrace nonviolent civil disobedience or respect a diversity of tactics, including strong language and property destruction? Are the police members of the working class or violent agents of the state? Do we want a reformed Wall Street or the end of the stock market, the end of capitalism itself? Should we allow John Lewis to skip the line to speak or oppose it on ideological grounds? If the mayor asks us to cancel an unpermitted concert headlined by rapper Killer Mike, should we oblige? Who is "we" anyway?

While these arguments spawned frustration, the diversity of demographics brought together through the movement was also its strength. Decades of neoliberal austerity—the destruction of public housing, Olympics-generated gentrification, the gutting of social support—had forced people out of homes and onto the streets of downtown Atlanta, where they had access to meager and dwindling resources. It was downtown, at Troy Davis Park, in the middle of the Georgia State University campus, that youth, many of whom were angry with their universities for budget cuts and student bans, linked up with unhoused folks who were fighting to defend one of the last homeless shelters in the US Southeast, Peachtree-Pine. This unruly coalition protested a downtown hospital for its role in a conspiracy to shut down the shelter. When the occupation was evicted by police a few weeks in, the movement moved its final meetings into the shelter before occupiers spread throughout the city to further develop movement infrastructure, pursue liberation studies, and organize against evictions, police, and prisons.

While the Occupy Wall Street movement as a whole fell short of anti-capitalist, abolitionist, and decolonial aspirations, largely sitting apart from Indigenous and Black liberation movements, Occupy Atlanta helped teach some of us to make freedom as a place through relationships with each other, connections across communities, and building what we need to survive and fight collectively.[11]

Hands Up, Fight Back!

In July 2013, the jury acquittal of George Zimmerman for the murder of Black teenager Trayvon Martin in Central Florida reignited abolitionist struggle nationwide, sparking the movement that would eventually come to be referred to as the Movement for Black Lives. For months leading up to Zimmerman's trial, mainstream media narratives focused more on the guilt or innocence of Martin than his killer. Across the United States, Black activists and co-conspirators elevated issues of racist media narratives, racial profiling by police and vigilantes, police brutality, and the devaluation of Black life. In Atlanta, like elsewhere, organizers connected Martin's death and its aftermath with national and local conditions: the ongoing recession and failed promises of an Obama presidency, as well as extreme economic inequality, racist policing, and ineffective reforms. Just a few years earlier, 92-year-old Black elder Kathryn Johnston had been murdered in her home by Atlanta's notorious Red Dog "anti-drug" unit serving a no-knock raid at the wrong address. The police community accountability board that was created after her murder had proven toothless. In 2012, in the Black Mecca, eighteen Black people were executed by police, security guards, or vigilantes.[12]

Fueled by ongoing murders by police and inspired by militant resistance in Ferguson, Baltimore, and elsewhere, the 2013–16 Atlanta movement for Black lives launched new rounds of critiques of the Atlanta Way, respectability politics, and the slow pace of change. The day after Zimmerman's acquittal, a group of multiracial organizers called for a march regardless of the verdict in the historically Black West End neighborhood. Organizers used the hashtag #HoodiesUp and the slogan "Hands up, fight back!"—a militant alternative to the slogan "Hands up, don't shoot!" The protest, numbering hundreds, bucked respectability politics as marchers skipped through the rain for miles, climbed onto structures, and faced down the police. In the months and years that followed, new organizations led primarily by college-educated queer Black youth would take turns with spontaneous formations calling for rallies, marches, direct actions, and symbolic die-ins.[13]

Activists deepened their grasp of policing and abolition, of trans and queer liberation, of intersectionality. We experimented with terrains of protest (the neighborhood, the highway, the train tracks). Youth openly critiqued the city administration and Atlanta's old-style civil rights politics; when civil rights leader and former mayor Andrew Young condemned protesters as "unlovable brats," some made T-shirts embracing the label.[14] And for three years, protesters preferred disruptive tactics to closed-door meetings with city officials. These choices marked a refusal of the Atlanta Way not seen since the Rodney King riots in 1992.[15]

But while this moment, far beyond Occupy Atlanta, accomplished the deepening and spreading of radical and abolitionist consciousness, the movement was caught between old forms of organizing and new ones not yet discovered—it was largely limited to street protests, to calls for education and mobilizing, and, eventually, to the leadership and formation of NGOs. Further, the movement faced an uphill battle as its slogans and critiques began to be co-opted, watered down, and channeled into calls for ineffective reforms at the national level. Locally, the state moved to identify leaders that could be negotiated with. Within these limitations, in the summer of 2016, the Atlanta movement largely lost its steam after well-meaning young organizers demanded a meeting with Mayor Kasim Reed that would turn out to be a dead end. A few organizations lingered, experimenting with organizational forms and sustaining organizing against police violence, but by 2020, most of those organizations had disbanded.

As is often the case, a massive revanchist movement grew in response to the national movement for Black lives. As street activity began to quiet in 2016, Donald Trump was elected to the presidency after running an openly white supremacist, misogynist, and xenophobic campaign. In Atlanta, white conservative Mary Norwood was almost elected mayor, a move that would have ended five decades of Black mayorships and that reflected the decline in the number of Black residents spurred on by gentrification.

Say His Name: Rayshard Brooks

The Trump years continued and exacerbated the crises preceding it, at times spawning national moments of insurgency, such as against immigration detention, and at times forcing people into defensive positions to fight for rapidly deteriorating civil rights. By early 2020, when the coronavirus grew to pandemic levels, Atlantans found themselves having to rapidly scale up mutual aid and advocacy projects. Food Not Bombs, a long-standing mutual-aid program that had expanded participation through Occupy and the movement for Black lives, grew almost overnight into Food4Life, which at its height saw hundreds of activists delivering food to hundreds of households a week. Car caravan protests targeted work conditions and prison conditions, as the most vulnerable were sacrificed by capital and all levels of government. Widespread sudden unemployment and the shift to "work from home" allowed masses of people, all at once, to critically examine the causes and exacerbations of the crisis, to see who was meant to live and who was made to die.

When the Minneapolis uprising ignited in May 2020 after the police murder of George Floyd, Atlanta quickly followed suit. What began as a large march turned into a riot downtown after police attacked protesters with chemical weapons. Over the course of two weeks, residents targeted symbols of wealth hoarding, such as the luxury Buckhead shopping centers, and gentrification, such as new pricey restaurants in Summerhill. Police violence, the deployment of the National Guard, condemnations by Mayor Keisha Lance Bottoms, Killer Mike, and T.I., a punitive curfew, and mass arrests initially fanned the flames of the uprising. Atlantans were asked to return to a normal that involved widespread poverty, police violence, and ongoing enclosures of formerly Black space.

Just as the local uprising began to hit the limits of spontaneity, Atlanta police officers murdered Rayshard Brooks, a Black father, brother, and friend, outside a Wendy's fast-food restaurant in South Atlanta. The neighborhood responded in real time, occupying the parking lot overnight, shutting down business operations the next day, and burning down the restaurant less than twenty-four hours after the murder. Occupiers set up camp and demanded that the land be handed over to the community to build the Rayshard Brooks Peace Center.

The uprising in 2020 was self-directed, lacking formal activist or nonprofit leadership, and propelled forward largely by working-class Black youth who were dissatisfied with the lack of material gains emerging from the 2013–2016 movement. A new layer, exemplified by motorbike crews, sideshows, and organized looting caravans, took initiative in the streets alongside new and old activists. The void created by the lack of NGOs allowed new questions to emerge about self-activity. Most notably, the occupation, which ended in the tragic death of eight-year-old Secoriea Turner, opened up questions about the role of armed defense.

The autonomous Left, taking lessons from previous waves of

struggle, embraced support roles—providing protective equipment, food, jail support, and medical aid during the uprising. With the lack of formal political organizations ready to bring in large numbers of newly radicalized people, these infrastructural projects proved to be the surest way to continue relationships when street protests quieted and demoralization began to set in.

The uprising ended as quickly as it began, but its effects reverberated for years. A constitutive "outside" of respectable politics had reemerged: This multiracial working-class and poor movement, disillusioned with the lack of meaningful reforms in response to the 2013–16 wave and willing to engage in militant tactics to secure freedom here and now, proved itself as a force to be reckoned with. If the uprising built new unity among formerly disconnected layers of the class, it would have the opposite effect on the state. The city government fractured under pressure as police revolted against the mayor's office. The police chief was forced to resign; the mayor chose not to run for reelection. This combination of working-class unity and capitalist and state fracturing set the stage for the corporate and political elite to rally behind the project we call Cop City. While the embers still burned throughout Atlanta, racist rhetoric and a manufactured "crime wave" began to proliferate through local media.[16]

We Are All Forest Defenders

In the spring of 2021, just months after the 2020 uprising, plans for Cop City were quietly announced by the city and Atlanta Police Foundation. Radical activists—abolitionists, anarchists, socialists, communists, environmental justice advocates, social ecologists— began to host public assemblies in the forest, build online infrastructures, and canvass the surrounding neighborhoods.

While neighborhood involvement was sparse at first, months into the movement a network of social justice–oriented preschools in the area joined forces with Mvskoke (Creek) activists and other radicals. In the forest, autonomous youth—mostly white and largely queer and transgender—set up camp, built tree-sits, and faced down construction crews. More and more anonymous communiqués emerged, claiming acts of property destruction in defense of the forest.

Through the occupation of the forest, people began to produce a new kind of place, a place for socialization, sharing, growing food— an experience and territory seen as worth defending. The term "forest defender" came to associate people with both an activity and a place—to be in the forest for any prolonged period meant to adopt the identity of a "forest defender" and be seen as such. Navigating the forest, knowing how to get to the grandmother tree or the riverbank, became a cultural act, an aspect of identification with the movement. Through their engagement with the land, through forest walks and festivals, children and their caregivers developed a connection to the forest, and therefore a connection to those defending it. Preschool students made banners for forest defenders, forging a bond between these two illegitimate political actors: children, who are excluded from political agency, and militant eco-activists.

Marches through the East Atlanta neighborhood became the most visible expression of children's protest, which garnered public support from other neighbors who under other circumstances may have rejected the militant tactics of the movement. In December of 2022, when the first domestic terrorism charges came down on the movement, a march snaked through that same neighborhood chanting, "We are all forest defenders," refusing the attempts at division by the state and projecting a unified identity.[17]

The domestic terrorism charges and police murder of a young forest defender named Tortuguita brought new social forces into the movement. University students who had witnessed the earlier phases of the abolition movement when they were children or teens came into the movement as students opposed to their universities' roles in Cop City. Their participation in the movement expanded beyond their campuses to include marching alongside preschool children, disrupting retail districts, and canvassing for the referendum initiative to put Cop City to a direct vote by Atlanta residents.

Since December of 2022, courtrooms and prisons have increasingly become key sites of resistance, bringing another social force into closer engagement with the movement. As movement participants have been jailed, they have forged bonds with "everyday" criminals—those incarcerated for so-called crimes of poverty, migration, and social deviance, at times resisting together inside or continuing relationships after their release.[18]

As Angela Y. Davis states in considering the commonalities between the terrorist, the criminal, and the communist: "All represent an external enemy against which the nation mobilizes in order to save itself."[19] The movement in Atlanta—and, because of the movement's reach but to a lesser extent, nationally as well—expresses a broadened identification with the criminal/terrorist/anarchist that recognizes Davis's insight and challenges dominant paradigms. As the state attempts to divide and defeat the movement, it actually forces an articulated unity of the movement and its participants as "external enemies of the state." When acts such as hanging flyers or attending a protest festival are criminalized, the state makes claims about who is in the movement that run counter to participants' understandings. In turn, those participants collectively construct an understanding of their subjectivation that crosses race and class boundaries. Middle-class families march in defense of poor trans youth sitting in jail charged with domestic terrorism. Local Black militants decry the severe repression faced by those the state would like to paint as "white outsiders." White activists give rides to Black neighbors to protests and meetings. Crust-punks cook meals for university students occupying their campuses. We all meet at a party to raise bail money for poor local residents who our comrades met in jail. These actions and other words and acts of solidarity reflect a re-articulation of the anarchist as criminal, the preschool teacher as Antifa, the clergy member as eco-extremist, and the criminal as comrade.

As historian Salar Mohandesi argues, building this kind of articulated unity, while accounting for material differences in experiences, may be rare, "but when it happens, the articulated unity substantially increases its capacity to realize transformational change."[20]

Abolitionist Infrastructures

As the movement so often reminds us, repression breeds resistance. If Atlanta is Cop City, it is also simultaneously a place of abolition. Ruth Wilson Gilmore defines abolition geography as "how and to what end people make freedom provisionally, imperatively, as they imagine *home* against the disintegrating grind of partition and repartition through which racial capitalism perpetuates the means of its own valorization."[21] To imagine and build this home, as both a place of immediacy and an aspirational place, movement participants are not only fighting against partitioning by organizing against the power of the state and capital, but are actively, intentionally caring for each other through weekly food distributions, ongoing free care work provided by movement healers, sexual assault survivor support, a Stop Cop City choir, and so much more.

There is still work to be done here. The movement to stop Cop City is a popular activist movement more than a mass movement. As the movement continues to "make freedom provisionally, imperatively" and its participants articulate a vision of "home," the self-determination of the most oppressed in our city, especially Black working-class and poor residents, will be key to realizing lasting transformational change.

The movement to Stop Cop City is the latest iteration of a long abolitionist movement that teaches us how to live together in radically reciprocal ways. This iteration, like others before it, will end, but, if we have done anything right, the strength of our unity, the lessons of our failures, and the abolitionist infrastructures we have built will persist for future rounds of struggle.

Kayla Edgett is an Atlanta-based community organizer and PhD student in the Department of Geography at the University of Georgia. Her activism and research focus on carceral geographies and resistance to racial capitalism in the US South. She is cofounder of the annual Atlanta Radical Book Fair at Auburn Avenue Research Library. Email Kayla at kayla.edgett@gmail.com.

FIVE

How the Black Misleadership Class Provides Cover to Cop City

Eva Dickerson

I'll never forget the day, during the spring of 2016, when I witnessed Atlanta's Black misleadership class firsthand. Members of the Housing Justice League, a resident-led organization borne of the Occupy movement, delivered public comment on the proposed development of an area surrounding a football stadium to the Atlanta City Council. City Hall was packed with students, elders, and families, many of whom had resisted the city's callous destruction of their neighborhoods for years. I watched my mentors Sherise Brown, Alison Johnson, and other elders speak with passion about their love for their community and the history of extractive so-called development that they endured. When Bertha Darden, who was in danger of losing her home to eminent domain, came to the mic and choked up with tears, the majority-Black City Council looked back at us with careless expressions of boredom. (Mrs. Darden passed away in August 2023; of the many brilliant activists I've known, she stood apart for her commitment to getting this city to do right by the people.) Keisha Lance Bottoms, who would become mayor in 2018, was on her phone when it was my turn to speak.

Far from being a glib insult, the phrase "Black misleadership class," popularized by journalist Glen Ford, is essential to understanding the dynamics playing out in Atlanta today.[1] While Cop City was schemed up via a collaboration between the Atlanta Police Foundation and the city's business class in the wake of the 2020 uprisings, who would sell Cop City to the people? First Bottoms, and then her successor, Mayor Andre Dickens, and other Black Democratic officials who have aligned with corporate interests and Republicans—Brian Kemp, Marjorie Taylor Greene, and Mary Norwood—to wage war against the multiracial, intergenerational, grassroots struggle to abolish Cop City. Cop City would not exist without the lie that the Black people who "run" this city are a part of my community.

But the movement challenges the Black misleadership class and the way it provides cover to Cop City. The protest technologies we built, borrowed, and shared among our comrades across the country and around the world in 2020 primed our imaginations for the strategizing required to destroy Cop City and transform Atlanta.

Atlanta's Black Democratic elites, committed to the so-called Atlanta Way, have proved to be an antagonistic, extractive force time and time again, from the local government's continued lies about the scope and cost of the facility to its bad faith "public engagement" efforts.[2] The phrase 'the Atlanta Way' describes the destructive collaboration between Black political elites and white economic elites in service of racial capitalism.[3] In exchange for their pacification of radical potential from the Black underclass and for championing projects and policies that harm ordinary Black people, Black political elites are rewarded with legacy political positions, backroom deals, and lucrative career advances. This collaboration lends respectability to racial inequality because Black political leaders are the face of it, helping endear Atlantans to a political ecosystem they would otherwise reject. For example, Keisha Bottoms was not just the mayor under whom Cop City was announced, but also as the mayor who tearfully scolded Black protesters on local television to "go home" in the midst of the George Floyd uprisings—while emphasizing her identity as a Black mother of four children in order to delegitimize the masses in the streets.[4] Similarly, as a councilwoman, Bottoms refused to establish a community benefits agreement that could have helped stop the dramatic gentrification of the Turner Field neighborhoods, and, in 2016, she voted to close Peachtree-Pine, which was the largest homeless shelter in the US Southeast.[5] Even as Bottoms betrayed Atlanta's Black underclass, the Black middle and celebrity classes continued to push the self-congratulatory title "Our Mayor Named Keisha" (an allusion to Bottom's culturally Black name).[6] After leaving office, Bottoms was rewarded for her years of throwing poor Black people under the bus, being hired as one of Biden's senior advisers and eventually named to the President's Export Council.[7]

Every Black politician in Atlanta is implicated by the Atlanta Way, because it is the only path to political success. Former mayor Kasim Reed—whose tenure was marred by corruption scandals—tweeted, "The Atlanta Way is alive and well," after the victory of his successor, Keisha Lance Bottoms, under whom the plans for Cop City would be announced.[8] As part of this collaboration, the Black misleadership class directs our anger back into "suitable" (read: ineffective) channels for "expression"—the voting booth, the entertainment industry, respectable public forums—in exchange for political and financial success.

After voting in favor of Cop City and against the hundreds of Atlantans who came to City Hall in June 2023 to oppose the complex, City Councilmember Michael Julian Bond (son of civil rights legend Julian Bond) told the *Atlanta Journal-Constitution* that the ensuing protest ran "afoul of 'the Atlanta way' that people are used to for protesting."[9] Whether it's Andrew Young calling us "unlovable little brats" in 2016 or John Lewis's "good trouble" identifying acceptable types of "protest," the Atlanta Way and the Black misleadership class's role in it prop up a city where the working class is under constant threat of police terror while corporations and upper-middle-class white communities enjoy the capital and social benefits of "the city too busy to hate."[10]

The Atlanta Way isn't limited to local politicians; it extends to anyone who benefits from the power of such a large Black voting bloc. Raphael Warnock's 2020 Senate campaign was framed as a monumental opportunity for Georgia residents to change the trajectory of our country. Warnock called Atlanta "the city too busy to hate" during his eulogy at the June 2020 funeral for Rayshard Brooks, who was killed by the police officer Garrett Rolfe. Warnock suggested that "rather than trying to destroy one another, maybe God wants us to use Rayshard's tragic story and this dark chapter to move us toward turning the page."[11] Although Atlanta is no stranger to protest, the uprisings after Brooks's killing, including the burning and occupation of a Wendy's, expressed decades of compounding hurt.

Still on the campaign trail, Warnock claimed that protesters wanted "police reform"—but the demand from the streets was abolition of the Atlanta Police Department. While he acknowledged that Rayshard Brooks wasn't just running from the police but rather "a system that too often makes slaves out of people," when it comes to Cop City, Warnock has little more to show than a statement opposing abolishing the police and some tepid criticism of the city's refusal to approve the Cop City referendum.[12]

Black Atlantans were told that we "saved" American democracy after grueling election cycles in 2020 and 2022, securing the US Senate for Democrats. That feat earned us a proposed police terror complex in a Black community made possible by the Black misleadership class in a stunningly undemocratic process.

As the movement against Cop City prepared for another week of action in the summer of 2022, Stacey Abrams, Georgia's most prominent Black Democrat, shared her plan to raise pay for law enforcement as she campaigned again to be the Black voice in the governor's office.[13] With the exception of a late, lackluster statement supporting a vote on Cop City in September 2023, Abrams had been silent about

Black Democrats' efforts to quash a referendum on Cop City's lease, even though Republicans wielded some of those same suppression tactics against her campaign when she ran for governor in 2018.[14]

The failure of Abrams, Warnock, Nikema Williams (John Lewis's successor), and other Black Georgia Democrats to oppose the facility is a slap in the face; but as the Black faces lending "respectability" to the Cop City project, they are simply performing their role in the Atlanta Way bargain. The fact that many of them fell over themselves to offer "solidarity" when Tennessee Republicans expelled two Black elected officials from the state legislature shows they play the game as they have been instructed for decades: Make only the most nominal of nods to the importance of justice and democracy, and nothing more.

Mayor Andre Dickens positions himself as both the spokesperson and arbiter of Black culture in the so-called Black Mecca. He and his administration have worked hard to present the militarization facility as something that Black Atlantans overwhelmingly desire. The mayor insists that Cop City answers Black Atlantans' demands that police stop killing them. To Dickens, the Atlanta Police Department needs the training facility to learn how to not murder us. We know that no training can transform the inherent nature of policing. City Councilmember Antonio Lewis cheered Dickens for uplifting the Atlanta Way after approving his 2024 budget, which allocated over 30 percent of the general fund to the Atlanta Police Department, despite voters' consistent calls to shrink the police budget.[15]

Through several hijinks—from giving a press conference with a group of Black men in ill-fitting suits in the background and honoring local elders with community awards to making videos exclusively featuring Black residents who claim to favor the training facility—the mayor has spun a false narrative that Atlanta's Black residents support Cop City. Most egregious of all the hijinks were the mass arrests at a music festival in the Weelaunee Forest on March 5, 2023. Activists on the ground noted that most Black people or people with Atlanta addresses were released, while many white activists were charged with domestic terrorism.[16] The mayor and other Black councilmembers falsely insist that mostly white people oppose the project. At one point, Antonio Lewis said, "If Black and brown people were out there, I'd be out there leading them. This is not that. This is anarchy."[17]

Black people recognize that their presence in this struggle disrupts the mayor's attempts to push Cop City through without resistance. That is why Atlanta University Center Consortium students and alumni from schools like Morehouse College and Spelman College, along with community faith leaders and organizations like Community Movement Builders and Black Voters Matter, have taken every opportunity to name the ways Cop City will harm Black Atlantans and describe how our most pressing interests (housing, food sovereignty, health care, etc.) are being pushed aside.

This was best demonstrated at one of the largest Black-led marches in the protest against Cop City, which Black radicals coordinated on March 10, 2023, in response to the strategically applied domestic terrorism charges; the murder of Tortuguita; and the incessant lie that white "outside agitators" rather than everyday Black Atlantans make up the movement. Kamau Franklin, founder of Community Movement Builders, called the mayor's bluff when he said, "Mayor Dickens, is this enough Black folks for you?" and added, "Do we have enough people from Atlanta here for you?"[18] That march and the many other actions led by Jasmine Burnett, Keyanna Jones, Mariah Parker, Matthew Johnson, and other Black organizers challenge Dickens's attempts to manufacture support for Cop City through false racial narratives about both the movement and Black voter preferences. We refuse to let him tell a story where Black Atlanta accepts his smooth gospel.

On July 27, Dickens complained about the "noisy people" who had already gathered thirty thousand signatures in support of a referendum to cancel Cop City's lease (more than the number of votes he received in the general election that led to him becoming mayor) and warned, "Atlanta is a group project where government, nonprofits, businesses, schools, faith-based organizations, and citizens all support the project or suffer the consequences."[19] Instead, the movement forces Black politicians to suffer consequences. What 2020 asked us and what the struggle against Cop City answers is: What if we took the mechanism of accountability for our democracy into our own hands? Now the tactics and strategies to stop Cop City can be used to challenge the power of the Black misleadership class and the Atlanta Way.

The frequency with which Black Democrats of Georgia weaponize the rhetoric of "the Atlanta Way" and "good trouble" suggests a fear of the legacy of the 2020 uprisings. It threatened the Black misleadership class's comfortable position within the power matrix of this city. The fact that the fervor of protest from 2020 has flowed into and focused the organizing against Cop City is an escalation of that threat. The uprisings also signaled that the era of viral videos and hashtags was coming to an end, and from those ashes we could usher in a new era of spontaneous, tactical, and protracted engagements with the state to demand much more than "Hands up, don't shoot."

We got some early practice at a decentralized resistance strategy in 2020, scattering the Atlanta Police Department's ability to respond to the number of disruptions across the city. We developed and strengthened mutual-aid networks for everything from jail support and bail funds to rideshares and homeless support that spanned the state, country, and beyond. Collectives came together to research and then teach strong protest strategy, drawing on support from comrades in Chicago, Baltimore, Palestine, Chile, and Hong Kong. Elements of that work have shown up in the many efforts against Cop City—the result of careful and intentional efforts among our communities to connect the current moment to all the ones that led up to it.

In *Big Brick Energy*, a report analyzing the 2020 uprisings across cities, the communist collective Unity and Struggle argued: "By popularizing militant tactics, maintaining infrastructures to sustain resistance, and hampering law enforcement's ability to coordinate, we set ourselves up for tactical successes. By keeping factions of the state at odds, cultivating citywide collaborations across different communities and class layers, and defending the legitimacy of Black street militancy, we lay the basis for strategic momentum."[20]

Yet the collective also notes that gains have been lost. Most cities failed to reduce police budgets, much less abolish them. And the liberal institutions that grandstanded about racial justice have all but walked back their commitments while attempting to co-opt the energy and fury from the streets into the Democratic Party machine. In other words, the shift toward electoral democracy weakened the protests.

It was unbearable to be in Atlanta in the fall of 2020. That October, I got a text from an unfamiliar number: "Hi, I'm a volunteer w Black Lives Matter. George Floyd and Breonna Taylor can't vote, but you can. From the protest to the polls, find where to vote here." A friend showed me a screenshot of a text message from another organization that read "Black lives won't matter unless we vote." In Atlanta, the institutions that make endless bids to steal power from us—nonprofits, civic society organizations, and of course the Georgia Democratic Party— shifted from promises of transformation to demands that we get out of the streets and fall in line at the voting booth. (Throughout the hours of impassioned speeches on June 5, 2023, demanding that the mayor and the City Council reverse progress on Cop City, people alluded to the fact that should the people we elected not bend to our will, they would be replaced. Yet the current City Council and mayor are already just replacements for the previous City Council and mayor.)

Now the movement has added another tactic: gathering signatures for a referendum. While this made opposition to Cop City more accessible to those who had yet to find a place for themselves in this struggle, it has not yet stalled construction. Meanwhile, the talented coalition behind the referendum has had to jump over hurdles placed in front of them by Black Democrats who otherwise fetishize the right to vote. When we are closer than ever to cohering a mass of people who understand that we are at war with the state, the effectiveness of sabotage over all other tactics cannot be overemphasized.

As my friend Micah Herskind has written, the constellation of tactics employed by radical Atlantans includes everything from encampments and agitprop to direct sabotage of the facility. These tactics are not only in line with a long legacy of strategies against environmental destruction; they have also led contractors to drop out of the project and delayed construction by over two years.

The movement against Cop City has forced the Black misleadership class to push its claim that state-sanctioned protest is the "true" Atlanta Way while decrying sabotage and direct confrontation. But how could the destruction of construction equipment or the occupation of a forest ever compare to the killing of our comrade Tortuguita? How could confrontation with the police compare to disappearing our people into the bowels of jails and prisons for indefinite amounts of time? The struggle against Cop City is an opportunity for Atlantans to flex their own power and build mechanisms for reclaiming influence and social capital from our Black misleaders, and redistribute not only our wealth but our collective power among the people.

A version of this piece was originally published in Hammer and Hope *in summer 2023.*

Starseed eva (they/themme/baby girl) believes in a freer, greener future and is on a journey alongside their world-expanding friends to get there. The apple of their eye is the city of Atlanta, where they live, work, play, and experiment with others about how we might practice a more compassionate way of being together. Their abolitionist ideology comes to life through childcare collectives, neighborhood farmers' markets, community gardens, popular education campaigns, and earth-based projects. When they're not organizing against GILEE or Atlanta's lecherous leadership, they're probably riding their bike or stealing flowers from a gentrifier's garden.

Timeline of the Movement

The following is an incomplete timeline of events in the Stop Cop City movement. Many events listed are merely reflective of many more similar actions, protests, and tactics.

October 2017: Atlanta Police Foundation (APF) presents initial Cop City plans, proposed for 160 acres of Weelaunee Forest.

December 2017: Atlanta City Council formally incorporates plan to preserve Weelaunee Forest into city charter.

May 2020: Minneapolis police murder George Floyd, sparking nationwide uprisings.

June 2020: APD officer Garrett Rolfe murders Rayshard Brooks outside a Wendy's in southwest Atlanta, reigniting nationwide protests and leading to the burning of the Wendy's. After Rolfe is charged, 170 police officers organize a sick-out. APF pays each officer $500 to boost morale.

March 2021: Mayor Keisha Lance Bottoms publicly announces Cop City plans.

May 2021: Over two hundred people gather at Weelaunee Forest for informational night and barbecue. Later that week, activists destroy seven unguarded construction machines in the forest.

June 2021: Residents speak against Cop City for nearly four hours of public comment at a City Council meeting. Coalition forms to canvass residents, build a public pressure campaign, and organize protests throughout summer. First Week of Action takes place.

August 2021: Neighborhood associations representing twenty thousand Atlantans pass resolutions opposing the project. City Council votes 8–7 to delay Cop City legislation and reduces proposed acreage to 85 acres.

September 2021: Residents speak for over seventeen hours of virtual public comment at City Council meeting, with over two-thirds opposing Cop City. Council votes 10–4 to approve Cop City legislation while activists protest outside councilmember homes during the vote and are promptly arrested.

November 2021: Forest defenders begin camping in the Weelaunee Forest, garnering national and international attention. Andre Dickens wins mayoral race, and second Week of Action takes place.

January 2022: Four forest defenders are arrested during a March for the Forest. A Bank of America branch in Minnesota is vandalized in solidarity with those arrested. Forest defenders repel multiple initial construction efforts.

April 2022: Activists convene two-day gathering in the forest to discuss rematriation of forest lands with Mvskoke leaders. Cop City subcontractor Reeves Young drops out of the project after public opposition and increasing acts of sabotage. Activists continue to target contractor executives and offices. Children and families host rally at Brownwood Park in East Atlanta.

May 2022: Third Week of Action takes place, with hundreds pouring into the forest.

June 2022: DeKalb County Planning Department posts a "stop work" order at Cop City site to stop unpermitted demolition efforts. Work stops for five months. Activists kick off a nationwide Stop Cop City tour to galvanize national opposition to Cop City.

July 2022: Movement convenes its fourth Week of Action, including a music festival attended by hundreds.

September 2022: South River Watershed Alliance writes letter to DeKalb County detailing an environmental case for denying construction permits to APF.

December 2022: Police raid forest encampments, arresting and charging six forest defenders with domestic terrorism. Days later, developer Ryan Millsap sends a crew to demolish the park entrance to the Weelaunee Forest.

January 2023: Joint police task force raids the Weelaunee Forest, arresting seven forest defenders on domestic terrorism charges and murdering Tortuguita while they reportedly sat with their hands raised and legs crossed on the ground. A cop car is burned and windows of APF donors are smashed during a protest in the days following, and activists engage in retaliatory sabotage across the country. More domestic terrorism arrests follow and Georgia governor declares state of emergency, activating National Guard.

March 2023: Fifth Week of Action opens with a march to reclaim the forest following January raids. Police raid a music festival in response to a nearby direct action, charging twenty-three mostly out-of-state protesters with domestic terrorism. Black organizers hold a mass march from the King Center to the Atlanta Police Foundation.

May 2023: Police raid the home of Atlanta Solidarity Fund organizers, who are charged with money laundering. A bombshell investigation by Atlanta Community Press Collective reveals widespread deception about Cop City's true costs. City Council introduces legislation to authorize $67 million in public funding (over twice the initial projection).

June 2023: Atlanta residents speak at City Hall for record-breaking fourteen hours of in-person public comment against Cop City. City council approves $67 million in funding. The next day, a new coalition announces referendum effort to put Cop City on the ballot.

July 2023: Referendum organizers sue the city of Atlanta to ensure residents living near the forest in DeKalb County are allowed to collect signatures on the petition. A judge issues an injunction that temporarily lifts the residency requirements for signature-gatherers.

September 2023: Organizers announce over 116,000 signatures collected for referendum effort. The 11th Circuit Court of Appeals issues a stay on the temporary injunction, leaving the counting of petition signatures in limbo. The City refuses to begin verifying submitted petitions. Georgia attorney general announces 61 person RICO conspiracy indictment of Stop Cop City activists, alleging that activists constitute a criminal enterprise.

October 2023: Block Cop City action draws five hundred from across the country to stop the construction on the site.

February 2024: National coalition to stop cop cities across the United States begins to form.

PART 2

NO COP CITY

SIX

Mvskoke Migrations

Mekko Chebon Kernell

It has been a few years since I began walking with the movement to Stop Cop City, a movement taking place in the ancestral domains and territories of the Mvskoke Creek people in the colonized State of Georgia and the city of Atlanta. Over the past decade, I have been a part of numerous initiatives that have worked to protect the rights and self-determination of Indigenous people of North America and across the world. Many of these nations across Turtle Island have had periods of migration and movement over the centuries, but have resided in areas amenable to a high quality of life for nearly twenty thousand years. To put this in perspective, in 2024 the settler-colonial nation of the United States will only be 248 years old if we select July 4th, 1776, as its starting point. It is a country that should be understood as only in its infancy compared to the Indigenous nations that saturate the continent. However, despite this country's relatively short existence, hundreds of tribal nations have suffered immensely from efforts of racism, colonization, assimilation, and dispossession of lands since encountering these colonizing entities. Many of the experiences of these nations are just now becoming a part of modern academia, with numerous publications documenting our collective stories e from the perspective of Indigenous people. Tribal nations, such as the Mvskoke, have suffered immensely during this time and have only recently begun to reconstruct the fractured history and cosmology that informs contemporary Indigenous existence.

Physical and Spiritual Migrations

As I entered my career and vocation committed to interfaith conversations and protecting the cosmology and religious structures
of Indigenous communities, I realized over time that any efforts for
long-term healing, recovery, and cultural stability will always be
connected to one's ancestral homeland and the ability to exist on
the very earth that gave birth to one's language, clan system, and
communities. Cities that we now refer to as Atlanta, Jacksonville,
Tampa, Macon, St. Louis, and countless others reside on top of the
very places where modern Indigenous people situate their stories of
creation and existence regarding when they first came to set foot on
this Earth Mother. Unfortunately, with the dispossession of land,
we too as Indigenous people have been displaced from our original
relationship with this earth and all that call her home, all of creation. We have been displaced from the reverence and intimacy that
once was inherent in daily life, and have been working to reestablish
an existence that once was prevalent throughout the world.

Because of this epiphany, for the past ten years, I have led and been
a part of numerous journeys back to this ancestral territory located in
the states of Alabama, Georgia, Florida, and Tennessee. With the guidance of family, elders, and other traditional practitioners of our ancient
spiritualities, I began to make intentional trips back to our homeland's
lands that were not accessible or even talked about throughout my childhood. These journeys back to our Indigenous homelands have been an
endeavor that I have called "Mvskoke Migrations." It is my opinion that
the ability to migrate from one's ancestral conception to contemporary
places of residence and vice versa is a sovereign right of contemporary
Indigenous people. It is a right that must be protected, with all its associated complexities. This process of migration has been an effort to engage
in a life-altering process of reconnecting and bringing dispossessed
people back to the physical locations of one's ancestors. But it is much
more than just a physical return to a specific location; it is a spiritual and

cosmic decolonizing initiative to return to the understanding of how deep the roots of existence go back in the ancestral domains of Indigenous people, specifically the Mvskoke people. Throughout this time, I have brought my family, my children, members of the Helvpe Ceremonial Grounds, and now members of the broader Mvskoke Nation to these ancient lands to begin the process of rematriating our existence back to the places on this earth that call us home.

Coming Home

In fall 2021, as the world still worked to understand the global pandemic in our midst, I was invited by community leaders to return to a certain part of Mvskoke homelands located near Atlanta because the area was under threat of being destroyed. Having heard of my work defending our Earth Mother and the rights of Indigenous communities worldwide, they sent emissarial messages to see if I would be willing to talk to them about what was happening to this country's largest urban forest. At that time, the forest was still known as the South River Forest.

These community leaders' actions were the primary reason I became involved with the movement, alerting me to the real threat of environmental damage to these ancestral homelands. The leaders came to my home community during one of our gatherings of the ceremonial community. In this setting, situated in my open-air camp in Oklahoma, they shared with me the horrors of the proposed destruction of the forest. As we ate together that evening, I sat and listened to what had transpired in the previous weeks in Atlanta as the proposal for Cop City began to surface. I remember this night very well, as my family and my eldest children sat nearby listening to our discussions. After this time of sharing, the leaders asked me to get involved or share some words with the local community in Atlanta in hopes that my presence would strengthen the land defenders who had already been providing resistance in the forest. Speaking plainly, they asked: "Can you help us?" It meant a great deal to me for people to come to my home, and specifically to my encampment, and ask for this type of assistance face-to-face. In our Indigenous culture, it is understood that if something is important enough, it can only be spoken about in person. There is only one way to elevate the importance of such conversation and that is to fast, refraining from food and water, and communicate it in the Mvskoke language.

However, despite the linguistic limitations, I took this request as seriously as possible. It did not take but a few moments to agree to assist. After a few more minutes of conversations and becoming even more acquainted with the resistance that was taking place, I suggested that we could perhaps engage in a multidimensional action that would draw attention to the forest and to the fact that this area is Mvskoke homelands, and also serve as a moment for a broad community of Mvskoke people to journey back to the area to continue our reintroduction to land that already knows us. In addition, as it was almost wintertime, I suggested that we could have a stomp dance in the forest that could also serve as a counter-narrative to the thanksgiving holiday.

In November 2021, after much conversation and fundraising, the Weelaunee Forest heard singing and speeches in the Mvskoke language for the first time in nearly two centuries and possibly even longer. Members of the Mvskoke Nation and the ceremonial community from Oklahoma, most of whom were from the Helvpe Ceremonial Grounds, descended on central Georgia to participate in the stomp dance and cultural teach-in planned for the Saturday evening following the holiday. During discussions about the planning of this day, we decided that it was necessary and even compulsory to pay homage and visit one of the many sacred sites of Mvskoke people that saturate the states of Georgia, Alabama, and Florida. We spent the first half of the day making offerings and singing at the Ocmulgee Mounds, which is said to be the birthplace of the Mvskoke people. Elders, ceremonial members, and children from the delegation made footprints for the first time in this ancient homeland that gave birth to the clans, languages, and families that persevere in modern Mvskoke communities. After hearing some of the history of the site and breaking bread together, the delegation departed to Intrenchment Creek Park, which at the time was an entry point to the forest, for the stomp dance and cultural teaching moment.

The delegation arrived at a park filled beyond capacity awaiting the start of the cultural teach-in and dance. Over the course of the day, I learned the full extent of the city and APF's plans to turn the forest into Cop City. From my experience with Indigenous communities internationally, including having toured refugee camps across the world, I knew that the proliferation of any weaponry or militarization of local police forces could never establish a more peaceful society, especially for marginalized communities. This quickly became a rallying point for our night in the forest. As we scrambled to begin our work that night, we realized that over five hundred people from all walks of life came to hear from contemporary Mvskoke people and to see the dancing. This was our first effort to begin education on the importance of protecting every tree and all green spaces from the dangers of Cop City. It was also a strategic moment for contemporary Indigenous people, as it was an opportunity to educate the broader community about the modern-day existence of Native American people and our desire to be in relationship with our ancestral domains. To this day, this moment has remained one of the largest events of the movement.

Singing Ourselves Back Together

Following the stomp dance, leaders of the Oklahoma delegation realized that we needed efforts to continue decolonizing Indigenous identity and educating internally among modern Mvskoke people about our homelands and our understanding of the natural world. In response to this collective revelation, conversations emerged around the need to involve more Indigenous people and specifically more

Mvskoke people. A primary challenge for a community that has been forcibly separated from its homelands for over two centuries and has withstood numerous attempts at forced assimilation to a foreign identity is that we as Mvskoke people today have become somewhat distant from our cosmological understandings of our relationship with this Earth Mother. This is one more component of the many ways—more than can even be acknowledged—in which the Indigeous people in various tribal communities are just now recovering from the intergenerational/historical trauma they have epxerienced..

In spring 2022 we held a conference, entitled "Singing Ourselves Back Together," in the same park that the stomp dance took place in. The gathering intended to bring scholarly Mvskoke voices together to think about and cultivate a Mvskokean worldview concerning the environment and the violence being inflicted upon the earth. Respected professors and community leaders, some Indigenous and others not, came to Intrenchment Creek Park for a two-day gathering of singing, dancing, eating, and learning. Once again, several hundred individuals attended and began learning about this part of Georgia's horrific history.

The land that is home to the South River Forest was originally in relationship with the Mvskoke people and their ancestors before it was illegally sold to the State of Georgia and distributed to settlers in a land lottery. After this sale, the land was broken into several plantations where people were enslaved for decades until the twentieth century, when it then became a prison farm. The militarized police training facility is being built on this same land where centuries of colonial violence against creation has taken place. As time has gone on, we have witnessed the continuous infliction of violence upon the community by the same systems of so-called governance that we have seen throughout history. During the conference, Black, Indigenous, and other community members paused for a reading of the names of enslaved people in the area that were uncovered by scholars who participated in the conference. We also discovered that this forest area was once called "Weelaunee," which refers to the water that flows in the river system along the forest. Ever since this moment, people throughout the world have commonly used the name when referring to efforts to protect this area. Through this conference, we not only brought together a broad range of Mvskoke voices but also demonstrated to the world the unity that can be found between Black and Indigenous voices and the broader community.

Hope

Since this conference, the movement to Stop Cop City has worked to include Mvskoke and Indigenous voices—voices that represent a people who have for centuries worked to protect our homelands and their inhabitants. Voices that represent a people who have worked through every societal structure imaginable in hopes of protecting a race of people and lands they have inhabited since the beginning of time. Multiple delegations of Mvskoke, Seminole, Cherokee, and Euchee citizens have come to central Georgia to learn about resisting efforts such as Cop City but also about educating the world on how to live in reverence with our Mother the Earth. They each have also expressed the dream of what it would be like to once again be in relationship with this territory, as they had for thousands upon thousands of years without harming this earth and each other.

Since the stomp dance and the Singing Ourselves Back Together conference, these representatives have participated in television interviews, radio interviews, webinars, teach-ins, cultural presentations, podcasts, Atlanta City Council meetings, weeks of actions, rallies, spiritual moments, migrations, bookstore conversations, and other activities. We hope to alter the trajectory of Mvskoke homelands to the point of eliminating violence and violent training facilities on the land and embracing a reverence for the natural world where all the biodiversity of life lives in harmony and wellness.

During the first stomp, we experienced joy and shed tears. I watched Indigenous children dance with non-Indigenous children who now live in the Atlanta Metropolitan area. I witnessed for a few moments the potential of what society could become if we remove the violent systems of oppression that we have inherited. I told the audience that we always think about our homelands. I departed that night with one thought in particular: "I hope there will be a homeland to migrate back to when my grandchildren walk on this earth." Today, we continue to share our story, offer solutions, and pray and conduct ceremonies in our ancestral home in hopes that one day we will reside again full-time in the domains that gave birth to our people.

Mekko Chebon Kernell is an enrolled member of the Seminole Nation of Oklahoma and is of Mvskoke Creek heritage. He received his bachelor of arts in political science from Oklahoma City University and a master of divinity from Phillips Theological Seminary. He is a cultural practitioner and member of the Helvpe Ceremonial Grounds. Chebon is an executive in the United Methodist Church and has worked all throughout the world defending the rights of Indigenous People.

SEVEN

Eviction Notice from the Mvskoke People to Mayor Dickens and Cop City

Mvskoke Organizers

In March 2023, a group of Mvskoke organizers traveled to Atlanta to deliver the following eviction notice to the entities involved in building Cop City on ancestral Mvskoke land. When they attempted to deliver the notice to Mayor Andre Dickens at a meeting of the Atlanta Regional Commission, Dickens fled. The organizers read the notice anyway.

Contemporary Mvskoke People are now making the journey back to our homelands, and hereby give notice to Mayor Andre Dickens, the Atlanta City Council, the Atlanta Police Department, the Atlanta Police Foundation, the DeKalb County Sheriff's office, and so-called "Cop City" that you must immediately vacate Mvskoke homelands and cease violence and policing of Indigenous and Black people in Mvskoke lands. We also ask for an independent investigation into the assassination of our relative Tortuguita and that the trumped-up charges be dropped against Weelaunee Forest defenders.

According to the history of Mvskoke Peoples, we originated in so-called Georgia near the Ocese Creek in the valley of the Ocmulgee River. As individual Tribal Nations, we lived as stewards and in relationship to this land for more than 13,000 years until the illegitimate "state" of Georgia negotiated with the tyrant Andrew Jackson for the militarized forced removal of Mvskokes and Cherokee relatives to Indian Territory in Oklahoma. The State of Georgia has been operating illegitimately and without the consent of its original peoples ever since.

Georgia is the birthplace of oppressive policing, originating with Indigenous genocide and the Trail of Tears and the capture and enslavement of African descendants seeking freedom. Our ancestors who are buried here continue to suffer while the City of Atlanta and the State of Georgia deploy the very same escalated militarized tactics against Black, Indigenous, and people of the global majority that were used in Indigenous genocide and Black enslavement. The state and the City of Atlanta have a historical, moral, and legal obligation to cease the clearing of trees and land and to cease developing militarized weaponized policing.

Since the 1832 Trail of Tears, where nearly half of our people were brutally murdered by the predecessors of the very same entities seeking to establish a massive "Cop City," the colonial presence of the state and local governments of Georgia and police have unjustly denied Mvskoke people access to our homelands. As ceremonial people, we have come home to gather medicines, have ceremony, and be welcomed by our ancestors. This is impossible for us when Atlanta and DeKalb County undertake plans to build a massively oppressive militarized policing facility within what is known as the Weelaunee Forest (paying homage to the Mvskoke description of the South River, Ue Lane or "yellow water"). For us as Mvskoke peoples to have a safe homeland to return to, the "Cop City" project must immediately be stopped. Cop City cannot be built in the Weelaunee Forest, in the city of Atlanta, in the State of Georgia, or anywhere in the Mvskoke homelands. Cop City cannot be built at all.

As the original relatives of this land and as ceremonial Mvskoke people, we stand in solidarity with the Black residents of Atlanta in opposition to continued genocide via Cop City.

EIGHT
The Saboteurs

Paul Torino

In the beginning, there was fire. In May of 2021, several pieces of heavy equipment belonging to Reeves Young Construction, a key Cop City contractor, were torched in the Weelaunee Forest. This action was taken after a few presentations and large assemblies covering the proposed development laid out the project's basic parameters, its protagonists, and their weaknesses. Not even a month later, the replacement machines were burned. Between then and May 2024, around eighty-five pieces of equipment, cars, trucks, tractors, trailers, annex buildings, offices, or assets have been burned. About half of these incidents targeted machinery left in or near the Weelaunee Forest. Others targeted assets, machinery, or property belonging to law enforcement, or to contractors and subcontractors working with the Atlanta Police Foundation.

Over twice as many actions have occurred that do not involve incendiary devices or the use of fire, such as breaking windows, pouring bleach into engines, gluing locks, cutting down poles, smashing cameras, or otherwise disabling machinery. These actions have occurred across the country with astounding frequency: After the murder of Tortuguita on January 18, 2023, acts of sabotage and vandalism were reported every single day for a month. In 2024, these actions continued and even accelerated. Actionists have continued to torch and destroy contractors' machines, police vehicles, and Cop City funders' property.

Few can deny the courage and determination of those committed to frontline defense of the Weelaunee Forest. Although their actions may spread uncertainty and even fear, there is no question that the anonymous groups and individuals who inaugurated this movement—the saboteurs—are brave and intelligent. Their bravery is a component of their intelligence, because those who act without certainty about the outcome (which is how we should define bravery, I believe) have correctly understood their own role in the construction of reality. That is already a significant realization. Still, their intelligence is more than a testament of courage. It is expressed in theories and ideas that have observable hypotheses and limits. I have been asked to explain some of these hypotheses for the purposes of this publication.

Those who engage in acts of sabotage are not irrational. They are community members acting according to their analysis of the situation, their specific proclivities as individuals, and a bit of intuitive sense. There are economic and political considerations for sabotage, and most or all saboteurs are aware of them in one way or another. Another way to say this is that there are direct (economic) as well as symbolic (political) arguments to make about the timing and means of a specific attack or action.

The technical ethos that underwrites these actions, irrespective of their direct and symbolic meaning, is best expressed in a simple formula: Minimize time, minimize effort, minimize risk, maximize damage. Occasionally, activists dedicated to other frameworks complain that this kind of action is "easy" and that other forms of organizing take lots of hard work. For the most part, the saboteurs agree. And that's the point.

The Economic Considerations

Sabotage is conducted by activists against economically incentivized projects in order to cause economic damage. The theory of many is that if the project or industry becomes more expensive than the foreseeable profits or benefits, it will be canceled. In the absence of other considerations, this one alone could be seen as a form of militant reformism. All who endeavor to change policies, halt developments, or punish unethical or oppressive forces could initiate a similar strategy, even if they do not believe in the radical reorganization of society.

There are other ideas built into this framework, however, that protagonists of our movement have developed further.

Cop City is the brainchild of the Atlanta Police Foundation, a nonprofit organization that raises millions of dollars a year and claims to represent the interests of the police. In reality, it is a real estate company that holds many properties. Regardless, it is not a construction company capable of building this facility. For that, it needs contractors. The contractors need subcontractors, architects, lawyers, insurers, and so on. The entire scheme requires donors, lenders, and legislators to provide legal clearance, ordinances, and political will. Finally, the project needs advertisers and spokespeople.

The entire project is vulnerable, then, at its point of production (in Weelaunee, in warehouses, construction sites, etc.), its point of consumption (contracts, board meetings, etc.), and its point of "assumption" (in public relations, the media, fundraiser events, or anywhere the idea is being made popular or legitimate). If activists are able to disrupt or destroy the point of production, to fragment or derail the point of consumption, and to disorganize and demoralize the point of assumption, they can conduct a full-scale operation against the project.

For over two years, this is exactly what has happened. Specifically, by targeting contractors and subcontractors of the Atlanta Police Foundation, the movement has caused substantial delays to the project and has cost the foundation entire projects and partners. Insofar as these contractors have a means of reorganizing their companies away from APF, sabotage and direct action can encourage them to do so. When activists showed up at the home of a high-level Atlas Technical Consultants employee, they were informed that "Atlas is no longer involved . . . because you guys are fucking nightmare and you broke all of our fucking windows." Other contractors have similarly dropped the project.

As of January 2024, every firm and company working on the construction or financing of Cop City are board members of the Atlanta Police Foundation. Only their behind-the-scenes allies, such as the architects, lawyers, landlords, and asset managers, are not already embedded in APF in some way. Everyone else has fled or avoided the project, despite its lucrative contract offerings. Whether or not the movement can convince APF board members to step down or break away is yet to be seen.

The Political Considerations

Direct action of all kinds, sabotage or otherwise, empowers people. It does so at every scale: Crowds, movements, workplaces, communities, departments, affinity groups, and individuals can all make use of direct action. Direct action is a simple concept: Those who will perform an action do so without mediating institutions or structures, targeting their concerns directly and immediately, without respect to official political channels. When parishioners and clergy link arms in front of a bulldozer that they want to stop working, this is direct action. When a young student climbs into a tree in order to prevent a chainsaw from cutting it down, this is direct action. When a neighbor places an improvised incendiary device beneath a row of police vehicles in order to destroy their ability to continuously patrol the forest, this is direct action.

The politics of direct action are well known in social movements in the US and elsewhere. Direct action is intuitive and indispensable for those at their wit's end. Those drawn to direct action value participation over representation, and value results over further delays. Moreover, by directly engaging with private companies or government institutions in the field of active and live real-time conflict, activists challenge the legitimacy of government in a very specific way. In modern democratic states, myriad bureaucratic institutions, associations, and civil society organizations are cultivated, funded, and maintained to address the problems or grievances of society, especially those of the lower classes. These bureaucracies are slow, confusing, and inefficient. When activists direct their ire straight at the heart of a construction project, engaging construction companies and their boards of directors—in person, at their homes, at the job site, at church—they bypass an incredible amount of civic infrastructure. Doing so leaves governing authorities with no real mediation potential. Their last recourse, their only true power, is to send in the police.

By continuously sabotaging Cop City infrastructure and directly challenging the right of the contractors or APF to conduct this project, activists have forced the local authorities time and again to send in the police. By engaging the police in physical conflict, by using direct action against them (including by throwing stones, fireworks, and Molotov cocktails at them, but also by running away from them, hiding from them, disobeying their orders, etc.), activists have also challenged the right of the state to govern. By provoking the police into a spiral of paranoiac militarization around the Old Atlanta Prison Farm, the movement has overextended the police and harmed the ideological pillars they stand on: The police no longer appear as mediators between hostile forces, the thin blue line of "civilization" ensuring peace between rival classes, or, in this case, between activists and construction companies. Instead, they have been dissolved into the conflict completely, as participants in a hostile campaign against a civilian population.

Fig. 1. Untitled photograph of a police cruiser set on fire following a march organized in January 2023 in response to the murder of Tortuguita. (Courtesy of *A City in the Forest*, a film by Lev Omelchenko and Nolan Huber-Rhoades.)

This forces the situation to develop in a specific way, well charted by history. Either the movement collapses under the weight of repression (probably experienced by its protagonists as a web of "interpersonal conflicts" or some kind of convoluted "betrayal" of one segment by another); or the internal pressure inside the state is too high to support this kind of escalation, and the project is frozen or canceled in light of public outrage; or, finally, the civilian population slowly adapts to confront and support militant and serious actions against the project and its frontline defenders: law enforcement. At the far end of that second potentiality lies the path of widespread mass radicalization. If the movement can avoid becoming a private grudge match with the authorities and can cultivate opportunities for widespread participation and self-organization in society, the potential for an insurrection—an attempt to overthrow the government by way of popular upheaval—becomes thinkable, even if it does not currently seem realistic. At the very least, it is the correct orientation of activist campaigns and social movements moving forward.

Anyone who seriously advocates for the abolition of the police, the carceral system, the racial state, and its capitalist organization must appreciate that between their dreams and reality lies a small ocean of riots, sabotage, strikes, upheavals, revolts, insurrections, raids, explosions, occupations, and more. This movement is one more baby step forward into the water. It's not so cold.

Fighting Like Winning Matters

It is not possible to say in advance that a plan, proposal, or strategy will fail or succeed. If it were, taking action would be much simpler. Since the future cannot be distilled by quiet introspection or ideological debate, serious people must think about their aims and the methods they could use to attain them, and then they must proceed to the action in short order, lest the circumstances change without them. The "wait and see" pathology that predominates is not only erroneous from the perspective of action—it is also catastrophic for the development of theories, since our ideas about the world emerge from specific conditions, which are forged in part by the actions of real living beings.

Nothing guarantees that reality conforms to the clever insights and rhetoric of those taking action. More often than not, their means and their intentions drift apart in unpredicted ways, since the variables are infinitely diverse and impossible to control. Certainty is not an adequate threshold for people who want to change the world. Preponderance and plausibility are the only assurances serious people can offer one another in the flux of high-stakes, fast-moving events. Therefore, activists and creative people must be capable of self-awareness, flexibility, and humility. More than anything, they must be brave in the face of such uncertainty.

There is no strict division between "aboveground" and "underground" forces. In reality, people who do criminal acts of subversion, such as joining an encampment in the forest or sabotaging a piece of machinery, are normal people. They live regular lives, for the most part. There are some cases in which semi-professional activists dedicate months or even years to a struggle in a format that must be completely subsidized by their comrades and mutual-aid structures. But this is rare. Some of the "underground" forces, or people who predominantly act in secret, also participate in legal and public activities in a campaign. Some activists refuse to do so. I presume the reader can intuit the reasons someone who has been doing criminal acts of sabotage may be hesitant to join mass assemblies full of strangers or to go on the news.

Other activists only participate in aboveground actions. They do not know how to do acts of sabotage, they are opposed in principle, or they are scared. Perhaps they believe their specific skills are better exploited in public positions within the movement. Aside from those who are systematically opposed to the use of direct action or sabotage, all of these other reasons are perfectly understandable.

Those who dedicate their efforts to donning masks, throwing stones, building tree houses, breaking windows, erecting barricades, and setting fires, and those who dedicate themselves to drafting press releases, going in front of news cameras, facilitating public meetings, and knocking on doors probably have a little bit of overlap in participation. But it is impossible to prove this definitively. Because of the different types of action and the various methods of applying leverage, people engaged in different tactics develop a different consciousness about the situation they are living in. Without proper political discipline and theory, underground activists may become paranoid and skeptical of public-facing forces and organizing. They may become cynical about the need to interface with non-participants of the movement, or to explain events to the corporate media. On the other hand, public-facing organizers may become terrified of sabotage. They may blame all their difficulties on the very people who are risking the most to assure the campaign is successful. They may wish that anonymous and secretive militants were more like a detachment of the outward-facing, public face of the movement, a weapon or pressuring force that can be used in negotiations, for example. This is how armies relate to governments within democratic states. Regardless, this is not how real movements are developing today. What is in fact developing is worth looking at from a slightly broader lens.

Autonomous movements are reaching a crossroads in the United States. In the past twelve years, tens of millions of people—primarily the working and middle classes of the downwardly mobile urban intelligentsia—have participated in episodic outbursts of popular rage. These movements, these outbursts, are becoming more frequent and more aggressive. A complete analysis and comprehensive strategy built around the long arc of anti-racist resistance from the 2009 Oscar Grant protests in Oakland, California, to the 2023 Eddie Irizarry riots in Philadelphia is overdue. If we limit our ambitions to just what is most well known and compare the 2014 Michael Brown revolt (first in Ferguson, Missouri, then everywhere) to the historic 2020 George Floyd Rebellion, the pace of escalation is almost comically simple to chart. Through that limited lens, in just six years we have seen a completely linear escalation of tactics, by way of several intermediate or localized protest movements. In 2014, residents of Ferguson burned a gas station down and looted dozens of stores. This was the high point of a nationwide movement that took place in hundreds of cities. In Baltimore, Milwaukee, Charlotte, Minneapolis, New York, and elsewhere, popular responses to racist killings of Black men by police catalyzed small revolts and protest movements, and exposed more people of all backgrounds to the urgent and combative methods of real resistance. In 2020, the activity restricted previously to just the apex of a local eruption took place in nearly a thousand municipalities. The high point of the 2020 movement was the siege and burning of a police precinct in Minneapolis.

In 2026, or 2029, or 2035, what will struggles look like? Will the subversive actions and unique combination of above- and underground resistance common to the movement to Stop Cop City become the new grammar of struggles, the baseline of resistance from which social eruptions proceed? What would it look like for the burning of precincts to take place in dozens or hundreds of cities, and for something an order of magnitude bolder to form the new high-water mark of the next popular eruption?

This is not a rhetorical question. Saboteurs, forest defenders, aspiring revolutionaries, and underground activists in this movement are taking the question of the revolution at face value. It will be a literal and actual series of events culminating in millions, tens of millions, of invisible acts of care, of transformation, of love and generosity. It will also be a physical confrontation between the carceral forces and their paramilitary foot soldiers, and liberation forces probably led by the segments of the population that have been participating in social movements since 2014.

Aboveground activists must take this seriously as well. It is up to them to continuously build the communications and media infrastructure necessary to challenge conspiracy theories and repressive narratives about bold and destructive acts. It is up to them to frame debates and assemblies not in contrast to illegal and insurrectional activity, but in combination with it. It is up to them to rent meeting halls, to make documentaries, to organize first aid, and to raise funds. This does not mean that the militant minority controls everything as an anonymous vanguard that others must obey. In the final instance, it is up to everyone to care for others, to participate in the reproduction of movements, to give and receive criticisms and feedback in responsible and intelligent ways.

But aboveground activists must accept that the theory of starting from a mass orientation, of slowly building campaigns to more and more militant confrontations with power, does not necessarily equip society to take the steps necessary to actually do so. As long as some people are well known to journalists, to local police, to politicians, they will always find small ways to delay the moment of physical conflict. This is not because they are liberals, and it is not because they are untrustworthy. It is because they are vulnerable. They are taking a necessary risk in showing their faces, in being someone people identify with. But if they want to be taken seriously, they also have to rely on the courage and ferocity of people who nobody knows, who cannot speak to cameras safely, who may not have dedicated their politics around convincing assemblies, generating consensus, mobilizing diverse networks, or providing legal aid to others.

Move fast to change a few things right away. Move slow to change many things in the long term. Only the combination of these attitudes can secure the real transformation of society.

Paul Torino is an artist from Atlanta. He has participated in uprisings and revolts across the country and world for over a decade. Occasionally, he writes, sometimes alone, usually with others.

NINE

Base Building to Stop Cop City

Successes, Failures, Reflections, and Lessons for Future Organizers

Ashley Dixon

The oppressors do not favor promoting the community as a whole, but rather selected leaders.
—Paulo Freire, *Pedagogy of the Oppressed*

Base building is about more than just outreach. It's more than recruiting people to attend events and sit in the audience passively receiving information. Instead, base building is a method of building power. Specifically, it is building grassroots leadership to take ownership of or create a campaign; to deliver a speech at the front of the room, to begin recruiting one's own neighbors, to interview with the media, and to organize events. It is about the unsexy work of creating meeting agendas, coordinating phone banks, making difficult or uncomfortable asks, and bringing other people on board to do the same. It is about genuinely meeting people where they are and trusting them. It is about understanding and tapping into the fabric of the community that already exists where you are trying to build. It involves cultivating relationships and trust with those who are closest to the issue, and making our society's severely limited avenues toward political action as accessible as possible. Base building demands that an organizer remains an organizer, not a leader, and commits to building a network of leaders and organizers around them to build the movement.

Base building is a critical but often underappreciated part of movements. We need it in order to win. It has been central to Stop Cop City's sustainability, from how we created infrastructure, built leadership, and conducted outreach, to our security practices, data-sharing practices, and planning of community events, to how we handled conflict within the movement and sought to understand lessons for future organizers.

I came to the Stop Cop City movement on the heels of the Close the Jail ATL campaign, an effort led by Black formerly incarcerated women with Women on the Rise to close the Atlanta city jail and transform it into a community resource center. I am a white abolitionist from a working-class background in rural Kansas and a resident of unincorporated DeKalb County. I have spent over a decade in both paid and unpaid positions as a labor and community organizer, and am currently a staff organizer with Showing Up For Racial Justice (SURJ). I joined the five-year struggle to close and transform the jail after the campaign had technically already "won." Former mayor Keisha Lance Bottoms, the same mayor who announced plans for Cop City, had already signed legislation to close the jail in 2019, but after the pandemic decimated the existing base and political winds shifted, the jail never actually closed. This reinforced my belief in the necessity of base building: Despite a solid "insider strategy" and relationships with key politicians, our coalition ultimately did not have the power to defend our victory. In seeking to build that power, and at the request of Women on the Rise, SURJ targeted white folks in the wealthy neighborhood of Buckhead in our door-knocking. Over the course of about a year, we began to build up a base of white people, developing six committed volunteer leaders trained to base build: to run phone banks, canvasses, and textbanks; have 1-on-1s; and make a solid ask.[1] This infrastructure later became critical in our efforts to base build around the Weelaunee Forest.

From "Close the Jail" to "Stop Cop City"

In June 2021, as the City Council fought our demands to follow through on its jail closure promise, SURJ volunteers were increasingly drawn to the burgeoning Stop Cop City movement. Angry at city leaders for their betrayal, motivated by the growing momentum around the campaign, and passionate about abolition, we began attending Community Movement Builders affiliate meetings, brainstorming with CMB about potential campaigns, and coordinating with the advocacy organization Color of Change to learn more about police foundations and their funding. We also knocked on the doors of white folks around the city to turn them out for public comment at the September 2021 vote on the Cop City lease.

As we continued to canvass for jail closure, our base also became fully committed to stopping Cop City. In CMB affiliate meetings, we decided our first target for divestment from APF would be Coca-Cola. We turned out volunteers to protests targeting Coca-Cola, hosted art-making parties, dropped banners around the city, and organized local and national call-in campaigns demanding that Coca-Cola step down from APF's board. Through these collective efforts, Coca-Cola agreed not to renew its APF board seat: a major victory that sparked further enthusiasm among SURJ volunteers and the broader movement.

Our base-building and divestment campaign also served as political education for both residents of the neighborhoods surrounding the forest and volunteers. One of our lead SURJ volunteers, Lily Ponitz, an environmental engineer who lived near the forest, shared this reflection after beginning to canvass:

> When I started canvassing . . . I found out so few people were aware that Atlanta City Council was investing time and money in a militarized training facility. For some, this project was basically in their backyard. I had already been

thinking about Cop City from the environmentalist perspective, and canvassing challenged me to think about it from an abolitionist perspective. Because when folks asked me for a solution, it was easy to say that they can put the facility at another site—one that is already paved, and not healthy forest. However, this would only delay the inevitable, or move the problem to another neighborhood, one that has already been impacted by industry development that created that paved area. Like anything natural, this is a cycle. We cannot keep stoking this cycle with concessions, we have to resist any increase or continuation of police and prison budgets. We need to push the City Council to spend their time building alternative supports for people of the city, as that is the only real way to improve safety here.[2]

Ponitz later joined the city's Community Stakeholders Advisory Committee in October 2021, a committee purportedly designed to solicit community input on Cop City. From the beginning, she publicly critiqued the project both as a resident and as an engineer, and was harshly censured by committee members, exposing the undemocratic nature of the committee itself.

Summer Shake-Up

As the movement went on, it became clear during the summer of 2022 that on the whole it was not base building in communities most directly affected by Cop City. Canvassing formations that existed prior to the September 2021 vote had broken down, and it did not make sense for an organization that organizes white people to lead base-building efforts around the forest, which was home to majority-Black residents. At the same time, there were already criticisms that even in a majority-Black city, white people were most visible at events, protests, and City Council public comment sessions. It was obvious that base building around the forest was desperately needed.

Around this time, I began to hear whispers of another multiracial canvassing effort. With several SURJ volunteers, I began attending meetings to talk about base building. Though initial meetings drew over forty attendees, they eventually broke down due to different ideas about how to base build, different political philosophies, interpersonal conflict that mostly played out virtually, racial tensions, and the frustration of some attendees over the movement's lack of structure. This moment's key lessons included the importance of having some structure even in an autonomous movement, the need for relationship- and trust-building, and handling interpersonal conflict face-to-face.

In August 2022, the new formation's originator stepped away and asked for a volunteer to step up in their place. I accepted the invitation, but knew that as a white person I should not embark on these efforts alone. So, we reached out to CMB and invited Kamau Franklin to join and help co-facilitate initial meetings. He agreed, and although meeting attendance at this point had been greatly reduced to between five and ten people, together we worked through some of the remaining conflict and began canvassing.

Creating Base-Building Infrastructure

Various iterations of canvassing efforts have arisen during key moments of the campaign. Many of these efforts involved canvassing for one key event with a specific goal in mind—for example, the September 2021 effort to turn out hundreds of Atlanta residents for public comment. In addition, various nonprofits, grassroots organizations, and networks of individuals have canvassed and flyered neighborhoods around the forest, usually inviting residents to events in the forest and weeks of action, or encouraging residents to host their own house parties to inform neighbors about what was happening in their backyard.

I understood that handing out flyers to working folks who are struggling to pay rent, struggling to feed their children, dealing with major health issues with no health insurance, or trying to find their next paycheck often does not result in them coming to an event, let alone organizing one themselves. Even if they show up to the event, their involvement may likely stop there. Even as folks who have experienced negative or life-threatening interactions with police, or who simply do not want to see the forest in their backyards obliterated, their attention is understandably often drawn to other daily struggles they experience.

We wanted working-class residents to attend events, but we also wanted them to tell their stories to the media, to join us for canvassing and phone banking, to talk to their neighbors, and to help craft the story of the movement and why it was important to stop Cop City. Ultimately, we hoped they would become the dominant voices of the movement itself. Although this has yet to occur, we did have some successes, and have learned many lessons along the way.

The team that showed up to canvass twice weekly consisted of me, the six SURJ volunteers who had been trained through the Close the Jail campaign, newer SURJ volunteers with little base-building experience, a Black CMB volunteer who would later be trained to lead canvasses, and five to ten mostly white volunteers from the broader autonomous movement. We agreed that, true to the group's original intent, this would be a largely autonomous effort since we were organizing in majority-Black neighborhoods and no one organization would be claimed as a political home for all the canvassers. We used an organizing model I brought with me from union organizing called CCR: commit, confirm, remind. First, we obtained a commitment from residents to attend a town hall or meeting. Then, we called them to confirm they would attend. And finally, on the day before the event, we texted reminders.

Our canvassing script first asked for people's thoughts on the construction of Cop City and allowed them to ask questions before we asked our key agitational question: "How do you think these millions could be better spent—what would you like to see changed in your community?" Then, we listened to the residents, who usually had a lot to say. We ran a thirty-minute training at the start of each canvass that emphasized the importance of making a strong, confident ask (i.e., "will you attend an upcoming town hall about Cop City at X date at X time?") and, most importantly, collecting phone numbers. Many less experienced canvassers were worried about privacy and data collection, or wanted to just collect email addresses. But every experienced organizer knows that a phone number is key to getting—and keeping—someone engaged.

In the beginning, we canvassed mostly in the parking lots of establishments in areas surrounding the forest: Kroger, Walmart, Dollar General, and locally owned small businesses such as barbershops. We walked with folks to their car, and sometimes even offered to help load their groceries. Eventually, particularly when preparing for a resident-organized block party, we also canvassed neighborhoods directly surrounding the forest. On average, seven out of every ten people we spoke with were strongly against the project, and about half signed up to join the struggle.[3] Among the minority who were not firmly opposed, many expressed wanting to hear or read more about the issue. At the end of every canvass, we debriefed to discuss what went well, what we could do differently, how we should consider adjusting our approach or script, and any security concerns that arose.

We also created a remote phone-banking infrastructure. Because this effort was autonomous and not financed by any one organization, we did not have access to any expensive speed dialers. Instead, we created a phone-banking Signal chat through which we regularly coordinated remote phone banks to residents before events. For security purposes, we asked the initial cohort of volunteers to only add people they knew in person. Volunteers hosted these remote phone banks, conducted training on a script, and asked volunteer attendees to answer residents' questions about the movement and confirm their attendance to upcoming events.

Finally, we created a secure text thread. This was an excellent way to not only send reminders for big events but also to communicate with the broader movement when rapid mobilization was required. In addition, we sent each person we canvassed an article highlighting the major issues surrounding Cop City. Everyone who attended our town halls and signed in was added to this list and consequently received invitations to movement events.

While the rest of the team held this work down, I focused on 1-on-1s with residents in which I made a specific ask for them to take on a leadership role at the next event: either making a speech, giving public comment at City Hall, hosting a meeting at their house for other residents, or speaking to media. Many had never given public comments at City Hall, written a speech, or designed an agenda, and I often helped them develop their plans every step of the way, just as I had done with SURJ volunteers during the Close the Jail campaign.

None of this adequately captures the very real-time commitment or emotional toll it takes to hold so many relationships and genuinely try to help people when possible—a direct consequence of a society that refuses to provide adequate resources for our people. In many cases, our work took the form of dropping off meals at people's houses, helping them find housing due to an impending eviction, or talking folks through a mental health crisis at midnight.

Because the environment of the movement is rife with paranoia due to heavy police intimidation, and because canvassing days were well publicized, we were also often concerned about police infiltration. On several occasions, people attended canvasses or messaged on Signal solely to critique the work while refusing to contribute to it, stating that we were doing it incorrectly, or that white people should not be doing it at all. If these individuals were not police, they nonetheless succeeded in disrupting the work just as the police would.

In addition, sometimes there was more explicit police harassment. This ranged from police regularly showing up and ordering canvassers to leave, to more extreme examples such as uniformed police following canvassers to their car, recording their license plate numbers, and demanding their IDs and phone numbers. One time, an undercover officer approached canvassers in parking lots and asked them for "help" by requesting that they call a number in order to reach someone inside the shopping center, only to later reveal that she was a police officer. We were unclear about what the police were hoping to accomplish from this: possibly they sought to obtain our phone numbers. In any case, we regularly debriefed security situations that arose, made sure all canvassers had a lawyer's number to call, and strategized on how to deal with similar scenarios.

Creating this infrastructure also taught us valuable lessons about how to foresee and reduce potential conflict going forward, particularly when it comes to data sharing. When you build a list, you build power. At first, people may not care about canvassing, but as you grow a list, they take notice. By the end of our base-building efforts, our list had grown to about one thousand residents who opposed Cop City.

As we canvassed and built our list, questions over how we would use the data quickly arose. Many from across the movement would request access to the list to promote events, including those who did not participate in canvassing. Data requests from all corners of the movement put us in quite a predicament. There was no clear structure for data sharing, but our small group of weekly canvassers felt that we had built trust with and were accountable to residents around the forest. We wanted to be intentional and strategic in our outreach, ensuring that residents were fully informed about arrest risks for any protests (especially when we didn't know who was planning events), and also that we did not overwhelm people with communications. Even still, tensions continued to rise. I share this experience in hopes of demonstrating both the importance of building decision-making structures early on and of ensuring that, if the base you're organizing is multiracial, that the organizers are too. I also hope to highlight the difficulty of creating collective infrastructure and accountability structures in a largely autonomous movement. In the absence of such infrastructure and organization, the whole movement suffers.

Key to our success in creating the (however imperfect) infrastructure that did exist was the rare willingness of SURJ, a national nonprofit, to let me as their staff member be accountable to a local movement. Although there were times I felt pressured in my work role to shift volunteers into electoral work, ultimately I was able to continue doing the work that residents, our local volunteers, and local partners deemed most important at the moment. This kind of flexibility within well-resourced national nonprofits will be key in the success of future movements. Getting politicians elected is meaningless without the existence of a base to hold them accountable. Imagine what the national nonprofit industry could help local organizers accomplish on a larger scale if we invested more resources and trust in local movements, and in the people who know best what their communities need. The possibilities are endless.

Town Halls

Our first community town hall was proposed during an outdoor meeting of a loose network of activists across the movement: multiracial, spanning different political orientations, and including autonomous actors and representatives of various organizations. We had just started scheduling and running neighborhood canvasses twice a week, and formed a breakout group at this meeting to brainstorm for a neighborhood town hall. Enthusiastic about creating a space for our small but growing list of residents, I developed an initial agenda for the town hall and received feedback from others in the group.

I knew that we would eventually want to see residents doing this work, but our canvassing efforts were revealing how little people knew about the proposed project. What people most wanted was to learn more about the project and plug into efforts to stop it. At the same time, I wanted to avoid creating an event where informed activists talked "at" residents, so in addition to carving out a portion of the town hall for an open mic session, I committed to finding and preparing three residents to speak during the open mic about why this issue was important to them. While this may sound easy, it involved hours of intensive labor: phone-banking our list of over a hundred residents, getting to know them, asking for a face-to-face meeting, driving to their apartment, expressing urgency of the issue at hand, and asking them to momentarily set aside other pressing real-life concerns and take the brave step of publicly telling their story. Once they accepted, it meant addressing their fears and concerns about having never given a large public speech, and meeting again to help draft their speech.

The work paid off. Three residents committed to sharing their stories, and when we held the town hall, even more residents would be inspired by seeing some of their neighbors share their stories, and would stand up to do the same.

Fig. 2. Constitution Road apartment complex resident Jimlia Ruffin speaks at our first town hall in October 2022: "I have been here thirty-three years, and I have seen a lot of police brutality. And the more I see it, the more I hear about it. I am definitely going to play a role. Whatever I fit in, I'm gonna get in. . . ." (Photo courtesy of *A City in the Forest*.)

Resident-Led Block Party

After turning out residents to several town halls and large events such as the March 2023 march from the MLK center to the Atlanta Police Foundation, we wanted to see what residents would do themselves, and be more hands-off with event planning. A very skilled Black organizer had arrived on the scene who was canvassing frequently and wanted to help organize an event in the actual neighborhood of the forest. We switched gears from canvassing in parking lots and started knocking doors on Key Road, right next to the forest. We began holding weekly meetings with residents and a few organizers. It was a truly multiracial effort: Latinx organizers helped us phone-bank residents

Fig. 3. Key Road resident Vicky speaking to a reporter with local media at a March 2023 town hall: "We need playgrounds, we need our streets fixed. We do not need a police academy in our neighborhood." (Photo courtesy of Ashley Dixon.)

we met who did not speak English, and a relatively equal number of Black and white organizers and residents worked together to plan the next big event. A few residents who were activated by previous town halls also frequently joined to knock doors.

These efforts culminated in a beautiful event in Glen Emerald Park. Stretching over a full afternoon, the party included entertainment and performances by residents, a lemonade stand and bouncy house for children, a DJ, a local face painter, and other fun activities. In contrast to other events, the publicity for the party was modest in order to ensure it remained an event that was truly organized by residents, for residents. Although the event garnered minimal media coverage, it gave neighbors the opportunity to connect and resulted in sign-ups, rideshares, and mobilization for two important record-breaking public comment sessions in May and June of 2023, at which hundreds of people turned up to speak against the funding of Cop City.

The event at Glen Emerald Park was our last before the referendum campaign began, brought on by a newly formed coalition of nonprofits that took a more hierarchical approach to the work. Certainly, not all organizers on the ground welcomed this decision, as many felt it would distract movement participants from building power in other capacities. Many also felt the effort was futile, as the Atlanta establishment would never allow a vote to happen. In addition, the vast majority of those who lived around the forest would be ineligible to sign the referendum since they lived just outside the city limits. For better or worse, the referendum shook up the movement's infrastructure and largely autonomous structure, and brought new leaders into the mix. At this point, with many people on the brink of burnout, SURJ volunteers and many others switched their focus to referendum canvassing.

Hero Worship

In a culture that rewards people for becoming social media stars, being spokespeople, and writing articles and books, the left must prioritize collective over individual advancement. This means prioritizing base building. A mentor taught me that if I was speaking in front of a room, even if what I was saying was important, what I was doing *was not organizing*. To be an organizer is to hand the microphone to someone else. We must adopt this philosophy on the left as a whole if we want to grow.

The reality is that there are plenty of charismatic leaders around the forest, in our movements, in our communities, who have not even been given the microphone. These folks need an opportunity to be trained and mentored. That requires leaders to step back and move other working people who are not paid nonprofit staff into leadership. While there are different necessary roles in the movement, base building can result in residents themselves taking on those roles. The question becomes: How do we change the culture of celebrity and individualism embedded in everything we do? The answer is that we must intentionally build up the people around us, instead of stepping into the spotlight ourselves. And we must acknowledge that no matter what we do, we cannot win if we do not bring our communities along with us.

Ashley Dixon is from a working-class background in rural Kansas and currently a lead organizer at Southern Crossroads living in unincorporated DeKalb County, Georgia. During the Stop Cop City struggle, she worked as the Atlanta organizer for Showing Up for Racial Justice (SURJ). Prior to SURJ, she spent years as a union organizer and at a low-wage workers' center in Nashville, Tennessee, where she also fought to end city and state private prison contracts.

TEN

Is This Enough Black Folks for You, Andre Dickens?

Curtis Duncan and Kamau Franklin

Community Movement Builders (CMB) was formed in 2015 as a mass-based Black organization, advancing radical politics with a build-and-fight strategy. By "build," we mean we must examine history to determine what is needed for our survival and create models based on our politics that begin to meet some of our needs, such as mutual-aid/liberation programs, cooperatives that employ people from the community, sustainability funds for both community and organizational members, and land trusts. By "fight," we mean to lead with resistance. We must challenge the oppressive systems of the state as we build power with Black poor and working-class communities. CMB-Atlanta is based in the Pittsburgh neighborhood of southwest Atlanta, a community founded in 1883 by formerly enslaved Africans. Pittsburgh is where our struggle against police violence and Cop City began—where CMB's political and community grounding allowed us to play a leading role in the streets and in fighting against the narrative of the Black misleadership class as we sought to revive the Black radical tradition and grow the movement in Atlanta and beyond.

The Rayshard Brooks Peace Center

The murder of George Floyd on May 25, 2020, ended the isolation brought on by the COVID-19 pandemic. During the pandemic, CMB created mutual-aid programs to provide food and toiletries to community members, but physical contact was limited. After the murder of Floyd, we went from quarantine to a petri dish. Thousands of people hit the streets to take part in the uprisings against police murders. In Atlanta, as elsewhere, these generally nonviolent but militant demonstrations with minor property destruction were often met with an extreme police response.[1] The outsized police response demonstrated once again that the role of the police was to terrorize Black and working-class people and to safeguard the property of the rich.

Within three weeks of Floyd's murder, the police in Atlanta added to the violent streak of murders of Black people across the nation. On June 12, 2020, Atlanta police shot Rayshard Brooks in the back at a Wendy's parking lot that was less than a mile away from the CMB organizing house.[2] The next night, the Wendy's restaurant was burned to the ground in a militant protest. By June 14, an organic takeover of the Wendy's site began, as people who lived in the community joined forces to create a liberated space on the grounds where Rayshard's blood was spilled. It was not an activist takeover, but a neighborhood takeover. The local community wanted to preserve the scene of the crime so that others could come and bear witness to where Brooks was gunned down, and Brooks's sister and others called for the creation of the Rayshard Brooks Peace Center at the Wendy's site. People immediately set up tents for sleeping, places to cook, and guard posts to keep the area open and to stop valuable pieces of evidence from being destroyed.

CMB members were asked to come to the site by those already working with the community. We offered resources and support for those holding down the area, joined in the struggle to create the

Rayshard Brooks Peace Center, and participated in an organizing campaign to win public support. The stated goal was community control of the space to support youth projects rather than the pouring of more resources into violent policing. We engaged in canvassing, petitions, rallies, and marches to demand that Wendy's negotiate in good faith with the community to turn over the land. This campaign served as a training ground for many community members and activists, and it also set the framework of the community determining where and how resources are allocated, centering the community's voice, and solidifying our narrative regarding the role of police in Black communities. However, after weeks of negotiations, the tragic killing of eight-year-old Secoreia Turner outside the Wendy's was used as an excuse to halt negotiations. As time passed, the community's demands remained unmet, unrest continued to grow, and city leaders openly called for more policing. The scene was set for a larger struggle.

The Early Fight Against Cop City

In March 2021, then mayor Keisha Lance Bottoms in her State of the City address announced the building of a new police training center.[3] Soon after, details of the size and scope of the project and of the military-style training and tactics to be practiced on-site emerged. After a May 2021 rally in downtown Atlanta protesting the continued forced evictions and bombings used to advance Israel's ethnic cleansing of Palestinians in Sheikh Jarrah, CMB and others took the opportunity to begin a conversation about the proposed plans for the Cop City site.[4] We understood immediately (as others did) that this center was not about training to fight crime, but rather about further militarizing against Black working-class and poor communities to prevent and squash resistance movements.

CMB members and other organizers jumped into action and began organizing demonstrations against Cop City. The movement against Cop City started as an activist and organizer movement. It was mostly led by politicized groupings and did not originate in a single specific community. We jumped into the fight with anarchists, socialists, environmentalists, a variety of social justice leaders, and others. The organizations, collectives, and individuals were hyper-local organizers who had been a part of the city for years. We were one of the few organizations or collectives that had a legal structure, and at the time the first explicitly Black organization taking on this fight.

Between late summer and early fall of 2021, CMB and allies organized some of the earliest protests at City Hall against Cop City, and we began canvassing in south DeKalb County and southwest Atlanta to inform the community of the proposed threat of Cop City that would continue to over-police Black residents. This work developed the skills of the diverse multi-tendency organizers and activists and the communities in which we worked. Organizers developed stronger relationships, processes, and structures as issues of race, tactics, decision-making, hierarchy, and class emerged and were navigated throughout the campaign. Students at various institutions began to participate and organize on their campuses, reviving the historical role of students in Black liberation movements. Some collectives and organizations were created, some were revived, and some grew, and a movement infrastructure emerged.

The burgeoning movement against Cop City was not without its challenges for us. In the Pittsburgh community where CMB is based, we ran up against roadblocks from the neighborhood association, whose membership included Black homeowners pushing for more police. Some of the community associations enjoyed having the police come to their meetings to rattle off crime statistics with the pretense of being "guardians" of the community. It is no coincidence that even in a working-class community like Pittsburgh, there were property owners who saw the police as protectors of their real estate, even if it meant supporting the people who pushed our neighbors out in support of gentrification. Joyce Sheperd, the City Councilmember who sponsored the Cop City legislation, was a Black woman who represented the Pittsburgh community. Atlanta's Black Democratic misleadership has perpetuated the same scare tactics that white Republican politicians have used to manufacture support for police and jails.

In response, we worked in the community to shift the position of those we could and mobilize those who already were clear that they never asked for Cop City and that they wanted a neighborhood to live in where cops and developers would not push them out. Individual members of CMB engaged with larger coalitions on a targeted online and canvassing effort that highlighted Sheperd's support for Cop City and the continued overpolicing of our community. Joyce Sheperd's defeat in the next City Council election was a small but mighty victory for CMB and the Stop Cop City movement.[5]

Fighting a Black Democratic Narrative

Part of our role was to communicate that Cop City was a danger to the Black community *no matter where it was built*. We knew that projects like this usually get built in poor and working-class Black communities. In this case, the neighborhood adjacent to the Weelaunee Forest is 74 percent Black and Latino.[6] The fact that the only new city funding to be poured into this community would "train" the police was a slap in the face to the real needs of the community. Black politicians continually put out media messaging that more police and more police training are needed to increase safety. This narrative is used over and over again to justify spending upwards of 25 to 40 percent of municipal budgets on policing, while also funding developers who come into working-class and poor Black communities to gentrify them.[7] This is why the so-called Black Mecca is no longer majority Black.[8] CMB had to make sure that the larger public, particularly the Black public, understood that more police does not mean a crime reduction but instead an increase in incarceration rates, more stops, more arrests, more fines, and more Black deaths. CMB had to serve as a counterpoint to Black politicians telling our people that more training would solve the problem of overpolicing, when we know that the Atlanta police already receive 90 percent more training hours than required by the State of Georgia.[9] We had to make sure people understood that although we represent less than 50 percent of the population in Atlanta, our people still account for nearly 90 percent of the arrests.[10] One of CMB's and other Black organizers' most important contributions to the struggle against Cop City was making sure that our central narrative emphasized the dangerous role that police and Cop City played as an occupying force in Black communities.

Furthermore, CMB worked with our allies by canvassing and door-knocking to continually counter the city's countless lies about what Cop City was, how much it would cost, and who it was being built for: The truth was that Cop City was going to be a privately owned military training ground and playground for police to boost morale and increase recruitment.

The Struggle for the Hearts and Minds of the People

Throughout the struggle, the city's Black Democratic leadership, white media, and state Republican leadership attempted to paint protesters as white "outside agitators" coming to Atlanta to unleash anarchy.[11] Although many on the ground were indeed white, we did not see that as an issue. The lack of participation from the Black community given the legacy of Jim Crow and ongoing police terror, socioeconomic factors, and the fact that many Blacks have been appeased by Black faces serving white power was something we had to acknowledge and struggle against. The issue was how were we going to bring more Black organizations and community members into the struggle. From our view, this was our role in the struggle, not anyone else's. If there was a lack of participation from the larger Black community, and sometimes there was, then we should be critiquing our organizing methods as a Black organization—not pushing against non-Black support.

We increased the level of canvassing in Black communities to bring more people into the struggle. As we increased our canvassing and organized town halls and speak-outs, we also began to challenge more mainstream Black organizations to be more vocal in their stance against Cop City. We reached out to our personal contacts and engaged in public shaming and information sessions to make sure more mainstream Black organizations took a public stance against Cop City. While we were not able to bring out the numbers that we desired, we succeeded in visibly increasing the participation of the community and Black organizations, bringing them to the forefront of the struggle. Though our mobilizations were never equal in size to those taking place after police murders of unarmed Black people, we kept going because we understood that even if the turnout within Black communities was not as large, it would still help spread the word that the purpose of Cop City was to continue targeting Black communities for overpolicing.

Black organizing against Cop City reached its apex in March of 2023 when we organized a Black-led rally and march from the Martin Luther King, Jr. Center to the Atlanta Police Foundation (APF) offices.[12] Most major social justice and voting rights groups, many of whom had previously stayed out of the struggle, sponsored the rally. Noticeably, the Atlanta NAACP decided not to endorse the march because it claimed that "violence" might take place, pointing to past occurrences of property destruction and the possibility of white nationalist counter-protesters. The rally was a high point for participation by Black organizers and groups from across the city.

We were conducting a careful dance with the hundreds of Atlanta police in attendance looking for any reason to break up our march. It was an electric evening of cat and mouse—we would occasionally take the streets but then go back on the sidewalk to avoid arrest. We ended up at APF's offices in high winds and intermittent heavy rain, but with a joyful spirit of resistance as we surrounded the entrance and blocked people from entering or exiting for several more hours. The police surrounded us on the sidewalk in front of the building as some in the crowd spilled into a lane of traffic in the streets. Cars honked in support as they drove by, further lifting the spirits of the protesters. Black students, community members, and fellow Black organizers took turns at the mic chastising APF, Atlanta police, and the mayor. The idea that Cop City was not an issue that the larger Black community and Black organizations cared about was put to rest.

At one point, Kamau directly called out the mayor, who had claimed that the movement was made up mainly of white people, asking, "Is this enough Black people for you, Andre?" Apparently, it was, because on the way home from the march, Kamau got a call from a mayor's aid, who yelled, "Why are you protesting us? You have access! You have access!" But something that Black elected officials fail to understand is that access means little—what the community demands is power.

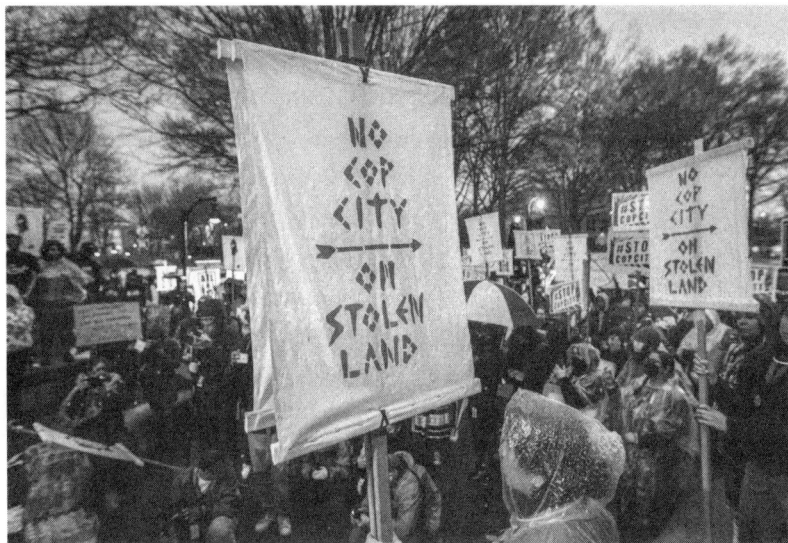

Fig. 4. Hundreds of Atlantans gather for a Black-led rally and march from the Martin Luther King Jr. Center to the Atlanta Police Foundation. (Photo courtesy of David Decker.)

The Role of Black Organizations

In response to our action, Mayor Dickens put together a shameful press conference filled with the Black bourgeois. Former and current Black elected officials, clergy, and business leaders stood outside City Hall to praise the police, claiming that those gathered were tired of crime, and to denounce organizers as outside agitators.[13] They felt compelled to respond because every day, more Black people and organizations were joining the movement.

As a Black organization on the ground, we were positioned to push back against the myth that Black mayors or Black preachers were the only voice of the community. Instead, we were able to center the Black organizer and their counter-narrative, which articulated the real desires of the larger working class and poor Black community.

We ridiculed the prevailing notion that the Black elite were the inheritors of the civil rights mantle or the Black struggle. The hypocrisy of invoking Dr. King while employing the language of southern segregationists in calling organizers "outside agitators," along with supporting voter suppression tactics against the referendum, exposed their alignment with white conservatives in wanting the same thing: the supremacy of Cops and Capitalism.

Proof of our success in fighting against Cop City emerged in a 2023 study by Emory University, which found that a majority of Black residents did not support Cop City.[14] Without an organization like CMB at its center, the movement against Cop City would not have been successful in countering the white conservative and Black misleadership class's "outside agitator" narrative, and it would not have convinced the majority of Black residents that Cop City was a danger to the Black community.

The movement collectively supported the leadership of Black organizers and organizations like CMB, and as the movement grew, so did the participation of Black organizations. By 2023, most local Black-led, voter rights, and civil rights organizations had come out against Cop City. National Black organizations began to get involved by providing resources and developing the threadbare infrastructure that the movement had survived on for two years. Capacity and know-how moved the struggle forward in unexpected ways, including initiating a referendum process in which the Movement for Black Lives played a pivotal role. Through the referendum process, we succeeded in collecting 116,000 signatures from Atlanta residents demanding to vote on Cop City directly.[15]

By the end of 2023, the "white outside agitator" narrative had almost completely disappeared, as Black organizations' opposition to Cop City became undeniable. What started as a small movement had grown into one where there could be no question that Black organizing was now at the center of the struggle against Cop City, uplifting the Black radical tradition in Atlanta.

Curtis Duncan is an anti-civilization anarchist, environmentalist, and advocate for Black lives. He attended Hampton University with a concentration in marketing and received an MBA in marketing from Clark Atlanta University. He is originally from a suburb of Philadelphia and currently resides in Atlanta.

ELEVEN

Protecting the South River Forest

Jacqueline "Jackie" Echols,
interviewed by Matt Scott and Mariah Parker

The following interview took place in October 2023. It has been edited for clarity.

Matt Scott (MS): As president of the South River Watershed Alliance for thirteen years, you are probably one of the best people to speak to about this forest. Why is it important?

Jackie Echols (JE): Well, it's important for a lot of reasons. The community is about 76 percent people of color. Along the river, you have copious amounts of trees and green space. The river is daylit, above ground, all the way from South Atlanta to Jackson Lake, including the Cop City site. That's unprecedented for an urban stream, which is usually piped somewhere. It's the largest remaining—*was* the largest remaining—contiguous parcel of green space in Atlanta. Add those 300 acres with the 136 acres in southwest DeKalb, across Intrenchment Creek, and you have 500 acres.

Mariah Parker (MP): Those 136 acres—that's Intrenchment Creek Park, right? Can you talk about the "Stop the Swap" movement?[1]

JE: The Intrenchment Creek Park swap, initiated in 2018, predates Cop City as an example of how predominantly Black communities in southwest DeKalb are being systematically destabilized and the natural environment destroyed. Intrenchment Creek Park was created in 2002 to meet the need for green space otherwise absent in this area of the county. DeKalb did nothing to improve the park for eighteen years except build a gazebo and a parking lot. The physical condition of the park, for which the county was directly responsible, was then used as justification for swapping 40 of the 136 acres to Ryan Millsap of Blackhall Studios in 2020. Millsap planned to use the site to expand the footprint of his existing film studios across Constitution Road.[2] The South River Watershed Alliance (SRWA) and four DeKalb County residents filed a lawsuit in February of 2021 contesting the swap. That's around the time the plans for Cop City also happened.

MS: How did you get into protecting the South River?

JE: Oh, that started in 1997 with the Atlanta consent decree. I was teaching at Clark Atlanta University. It doesn't take long for the word to get around about environmentalists—and particularly if you're Black. I was introduced to some folks and we started meeting. Do folks talk about frontline? We did frontline thirty years ago. The grassroots organization I became affiliated with, Clean Stream Task Force, was specifically formed to promote sewer separation. Participants were Bill Eisenhauer, Sherrill Marcus, Vivian Steadman, Harry Leon, Richard Bright and a few others. Most are deceased. Only Bill Eisenhauer is still in Atlanta.

Atlanta's combined sewer system used to cover approximately eighteen miles radiating from Peachtree Street in downtown Atlanta outward. Most of the combined sewer outfalls or discharges were in predominantly Black communities. When it rained, stormwater mixed with sewage flooded streets, communities, and streams. It only takes one-tenth of an inch of rain to trigger a combined sewer overflow.

When we got started, our goal was to force Atlanta as part of this consent decree to separate the combined sewer system—sewage in one pipe, stormwater in another—and be done with it. To raise visibility, we used to gather on the corners of the streams that were impacted by the combined sewer with our signs; one of them I used to love was "Cut the Crap."

MP: Ay! That's brilliant.

JE: We had one guy—I have a photo of him—that created this toilet mascot. He was actually a toilet. We would get together on street corners along Peachtree Creek. Sometimes we'd get people to join in. People would honk their horns. It was a lot of fun. We'd just walk up and down the street and protest—that got visibility and got the word out. Eventually we were able to orchestrate this huge meeting with the EPA about the sewer system and sewer separation. The fact that most of the sewer outfalls were in predominantly Black communities was an environmental justice issue, no doubt about it.

Eventually, the Clean Stream Task Force got a meeting with the EPA. I've never seen so many Washington bureaucrats in my life. We had this all-day meeting, they listened, and a couple weeks or three weeks later the final line was, "Yes, this is an environmental justice issue." The EPA agreed there were negative impacts, but no action was taken. Fortunately, the Department of Justice sided with this ragtag group of twelve folks and told Atlanta that they would separate at least nine miles of sewer in predominantly Black neighborhoods.

The city of Atlanta entered into this consent decree with the EPA in 1997. A consent decree is a once-in-a-lifetime opportunity, because the EPA is stretched thin, there are numerous violations nationwide, and it can take a long time and a lot of money to address combined sewer system violations.

MS: How has your experience of fighting these environmental struggles changed in the last decade and a half?

JE: You'd think with the ability to elect a Black mayor, and for a very long time now a predominately Black council, the environmental issues would have gotten better, and they haven't. Sometimes I think communities would have made better with white leaders that we had before, because at least you could embarrass them. You could call them a bigot and a racist and get something out of them. That's what we see with Andre, too, with Cop City. The only thing that got his ire up was when those Morehouse students called him a sellout.

MS: Yeah, the Morehouse students were asking, "What can we do?" And Matthew [Johnson, of Beloved Community Ministries] was like, "You've already done more than we collectively on this stage have done to make Andre Dickens respond."

JE: I know that's his weak spot. He used to live in my neighborhood, around the corner. I was president of the neighborhood association and he was vice president. We used to be friends, but probably not so much anymore. Once I sat and talked with him for three hours. I said to him, "You know about the impact on the trees and water, the impact on the community." He said, "Well, where are we gonna put all these buildings? I mean, there's only one big spot."

I said, well, the idea is you don't need eighty-five acres of it. Because nobody wants an eighty-five-acre police facility in their backyard. So no, I'm not saying my solution to this is moving it somewhere else. I said, you need to think a little more strategically about just what kind of training you actually want to provide and how much space it actually takes to do that, given the impact it will have. This is not a NIMBY issue. This is not an "in anyone's backyard" issue. You would not want a gigantic police training facility in your backyard. It's wrong. It's racism. It's environmental racism.

He had a flippant comeback and a pushback for everything I was saying, but he did not and could not address the issue of environmental racism.

That's why I hammer him on it. You choose your strongest point and hammer it. Don't go off into tangents that he ducks and dodges.

I come at it from the angle of improving the water quality in the river. In 2019, I ran across an aspect of the Clean Water Act that requires states to manage waterways based on recreational use. It's called the "Triennial Review." During this three-year ongoing regulatory process, an organization can submit documentation of the [river] recreation that you've been engaged in. I started the Beyond the Bridge kayak canoe outings and the South River Water Trail program in 2011. For what, eight years, after that I collected all of this data on public recreational use via kayak and canoe outings on the river and submitted it as part of the Triennial Review process for 2019 through 2021.

During that period between 2015 and 2018, there were only about fourteen miles approved for the entire state. During the 2019–2021 review, SRWA nominated all forty navigable miles of the South River. Thirteen miles were approved.

MS: Doing the math here, you more than tripled—

JE: It was a huge increase, going from none to thirteen.

MS: What would you say to someone who may be coming into the fight to save the South River Forest—a forest that has been cleared?

JE: [*Sighs*]. For the longest time I didn't go out there. I couldn't. I cried the first time. I actually felt sick. And I still do when I see it; the only thing I could say to myself is that we can replant. Nature is resilient. It regenerates. You have to have the mindset of being with it for the long haul. I work all day, I go to bed, and I get up the next morning, and I do it all over again. It's not always you stand up and can point to a big win. Sometimes it's a little more subtle than that. But it's enough to keep you going.

We do a lot for such a small organization. The progress that the SRWA has made is amazing. From the city of Stonecrest down to Jackson Lake, folks are investing in put-ins and take-outs, and now the Nature Conservancy, the National Oceanic and Atmospheric Administration, and the National Fish and Wildlife Service are interested in improving downstream fish passage into the South River. My big effort now is to expand passive water trail recreation upstream, where people live. My goal is to cultivate passive recreation on the upper ten-plus miles of the river in communities where change is needed. Better water quality comes from people using the river to enjoy nature, bird-watching, eliminating stress, or just enjoying the river. Recreation, even passive, builds a connection to the river. What is passive recreation? The type of recreation doesn't matter. They just have to care.

MP: When we arrived you said, "I don't usually go to these, but I'm going to the RICO protest on Monday."3 So, why are you going?

JE: I want to hear what the judge says. I want to be there to hear it. It's almost surreal that we would end up with what, obviously, are made-up charges. And it's impacting so many people. I don't know, it's something that hit me. I said, I'm going to go and hear it for myself.

MS: Your opinion originally of the forest defenders and the people occupying wasn't that great, right?

JE: I think they get caught up in the moment, and what's needed is longevity. It was destined that something bad was going to happen. There's too much tension too close. You know. And when I heard that morning that the young [person] had been killed, for two days, I couldn't even function. But I knew something like that was going to happen.

You know, we filed a lawsuit over the Intrenchment Creek Park land swap in February of 2021. Then Cop City happened. At first, protesters were camping on the Cop City side. The police pushed them off there, and they ended up on the Intrenchment Creek Park side. Then, Blackhall [CEO] Ryan Millsap got into it with all his bulldozing.

My point being, when we got to court on the Intrenchment Creek Park issue, Blackhall and DeKalb County had days of depositions to drive up the cost of it, hoping that we would get out of the game. One of the main issues that they were making to the Superior Court judge was that we were responsible for the occupation. It's like the RICO thing: Throw spaghetti at the wall and see what sticks. We have spent thousands of dollars on depositions that went nowhere, defending the fact that we are not part of the folks who occupy the forest. It could have been so much simpler and cut-and-dry, the way it was with Blackhall, DeKalb County swapping this land against state law. But instead, we ended up having to fight the claim that we were part of this Cop City movement.

I know they want to help. I know they mean well. But nothing they're going to do is going to change Andre's mind, and that's where we have to put the pressure. Protesting out there is not the way. Everyone goes home, and then what?

MP: The SRWA filed a federal lawsuit in August 2023 to halt construction of Cop City under the Clean Water Act. Can you tell us about that lawsuit and how you see SRWA moving forward?

JE: In August 2023, the South River Watershed Alliance filed a federal lawsuit against the City of Atlanta and Atlanta Police Foundation for the violations of the Clean Water Act they've committed for the construction of the police training facility. Intrenchment Creek is already "impaired" due to stormwater-laden sediment flowing into the creek from Atlanta's combined sewer system. Georgia's Environmental Protection Division is required under the Clean

Water Act to set limits on how much sediment can enter the creek without violating water-quality standards. States can't adopt or enforce limits that are less stringent than existing standards developed by the Georgia Environmental Protection Division—and yet that's exactly what the City of Atlanta and the Atlanta Police Foundation have done in order to build Cop City. By not enforcing the standards in the existing water-quality permit issued by the state, Atlanta is being allowed to discharge additional sediment from the construction site into an impaired creek in violation of state water-quality standards. We hope that the courts will issue an injunction to halt the project's construction, at least for a time.

....

Editors' Note: In January 2024, a federal judge ruled against the South River Watershed Alliance's request for a preliminary injunction against further construction, though the Clean Water Act case against the City of Atlanta and APF continues as of March 2024.[4]

Dr. Jacqueline Echols has been actively working to address environmental injustice in the South River watershed for more than two decades. She has been at the forefront of the fight against what she describes as the "rollback" of environmental protections by the federal government and the escalation of environmental racism in Atlanta as demonstrated by the construction of the 171-acre police training mega-facility (aka "Cop City") in the middle of predominantly Black marginalized communities in southeast Atlanta.

Matt Scott is the editor of the Atlanta Community Press Collective, which was founded in 2021 to address a lack of critical coverage regarding the Cop City training center. His reporting largely focuses on the Atlanta City Council and the Cop City project, and he hosts a docuseries on the sixty-one individuals charged with a racketeering conspiracy related to the Cop City protests. He lives in southwest Atlanta with his girlfriend and their dog Frank.

TWELVE

A New World in the Forest

Anonymous

The following is an oral account of life in the Weelaunee Forest during the days of the forest defense, which lasted roughly from November 2021 to March 2023. It has been edited for clarity.

Hundreds, if not thousands, of people, sojourned from around the country to occupy the Weelaunee Forest, leaving their lives behind to go to a forest in a city unknown to them because they believed a new world was possible. They came to the forest, setting up infrastructure that made for a resilient and creative way to resist where the people took care of each other in community. They faced many raids, but they remained steadfast in the belief of the righteousness of their struggle and peace in knowing that one day the future that they fought for would come to fruition.

Another world was made in the Weelaunee Forest. There was no use for money when you entered. The forest defenders were primarily queer and neurodivergent people who could not be satisfied by the worlds that they left behind. We taught and learned from one another the skills we needed to create a world of our own. We put together wooden planks and wire to make suspension bridges across the creek from Intrenchment Creek Park to the Prison Farm. We built tree houses by chopping up downed trees in the area—we could have purchased lumber, but who had the money? Forest defenders set up a kitchen with a couple of stoves and sinks where you could wash your dishes. There were ice packs to keep food cold. We had everything we needed. Community volunteers brought 250-gallon tanks of water in. I was known for carrying five-gallon jugs all around me, on my front, on my back, often totaling roughly eighty pounds of water.

Maybe, in retrospect, the repression was inevitable, but my God, we were able to do the most amazing things. In the Weelaunee Forest, I thought everything was possible. And in many ways, it was.

You got that feeling of possibility at the July 2022 Week of Action, when developer Ryan Millsap's bulldozers rolled in to destroy the park where many gathered, and they were instead burned by forest defenders. Piling up hundreds and hundreds of tires, people could keep out construction equipment for days through sheer grit. There were tree houses built where people were capable of staying for days with all their needs met. Gates that were booby-trapped with poop so if you opened the gate it would fall on people. It felt like we were capable of anything.

In the forest, you could become whoever you wanted to be and be loved for who you were. I saw a lot of people who had never been accepted where they were from finally find and make community.

Life in the Forest

I got involved with forest defense in early 2022. I had been doing logistical work to support the defense at the beginning of that year. There were nighttime activities that required significant resources and labor to get through the woods, and I was willing to put in that kind of work to stop the construction. The first time I got really involved was when we were creating blockades to make it more difficult for the police to get into the forest—using wooden stakes, concrete, and other materials to inhibit materials from getting into the forest. I got close with people by the spring and stayed that way through the occupation's end toward the end of that year.

The terrain itself could be kind of treacherous. There were camps on the Old Atlanta Prison Farm side of the forest (owned by the city) and camps on the Intrenchment Creek Park land (owned by DeKalb County). After the suspension bridge that connected the two sides was cut following one of the weeks of action, making sure people got supplies on the Prison Farm side required traversing the creek and carrying a lot of heavy supplies. Before that point, the forest defense was at its infrastructural height, because the raids hadn't gotten that bad yet. We could actually build sustainable things.

I'll walk you through what a day looked like during weeks of action: You would have people from all across the country come together and begin to develop the infrastructure weeks in advance, bringing in enough water for hundreds of people to last a week. People would stow away camping equipment in case others came who needed a place to stay. Some people knew each other from previous actions—there was a lot of overflow from different pipeline defenses and other mass occupations to protect lands. You had people creating cultural experiences ranging from sweat lodges to developing BIPOC camps.

A day would start with somebody waking up, starting a fire, and boiling water for breakfast. People would show up to chop the vegetables. There was a kitchen crew that would show up to make sure there were meals for everyone. The atmosphere was usually joyous. There'd be a little ribbing between people because they knew each other well.

One activity was moving massive amounts of tires at the Old Prison Farm to be used as barriers. We would have work parties that went late into the night where people would move these massive stacks and stacks of tires to build a mountain of them someplace else. I wish that you could have seen it. People had a hive mind, working completely in tandem. You'd have someone standing on top of a mountain of tires, throwing them down to people who'd lug them away in the night. People were doing it all night and would show up for breakfast with massive streak marks across their arms from the tires.

I only spent a few weeks' worth of nights in the forest, but I spent my days there to make sure people's basic needs were met because we needed their support. I would go around dropping off water and checking on people, making sure people were alright and their spirits were up so they could keep up the occupation. I would help people set up their tarps and secure their tents. We needed folks' presence on the ground to sustain things because that made it difficult for the Atlanta Police Foundation to continue construction. It was a year-long occupation!

In the forest, we took care of each other. During the day, there would be different actions planned. You would have people doing skill shares, informational events, wellness events, daily yoga classes, and different forms of cultural exchange such as dancing. There would be people that were scouting the territory to make sure the forest stayed safe and clear, that there weren't any trucks coming in to do work on the land. Different teams made sure that supplies continued to come in, that food was getting to the right places, and that water was being brought in to provide for people.

In terms of decision-making, it often felt like things just kind of happened. In a lot of cases, there would be meetings that were announced the day before. Morning meetings were a thing—sometimes weekly. They weren't as welcoming as people would have liked. People would decide on the sharing of duties, who would do what, and how. People would bring up grievances or ideas. It depended on what was going on at the time. Morning meetings would happen in a meeting space called the "Living Room." There'd be unlimited peanut butter and jelly sandwiches—your five-year-old self would say, *This is exactly what I want when I grow up!*

One of my favorite memories is from the May 2022 Week of Action. People were so free and happy. There were so many smiles and so much joy. People were just doing it and making it work. It was a festival of sorts. There was music and concerts throughout the weeks of action. People just read, talked with each other, and played songs around the campfire. There was one person who would skate-board through the forest, grinding on roots and shit—the most wild surreal shit you could conceive of. They ended up breaking their leg. But they just laughed it off and went to the hospital. It was funny because all of us, especially the older folks, were like, "Man we should have said something but it looked so *sick*."

There were so many moments of collective joy in the forest. During the July 2022 Week of Action, we had a pretty good showing. Hundreds, maybe even more. They had a music festival that drew a significant crowd. People brought generators and a stage. All that shit was built, and they'd have music all day. There was just so much labor that went into everything. It was just such a beautiful showing of labor.

We never thought that it would end. We thought it would keep going forever. We didn't know what we were going up against, how brutal the repression would be. When you're living in joy like this, it's hard to believe how evil the forces you're fighting are. We had no idea what we were walking into.

The Forest Chaplain

There would at times be conflict in the forest. We would have medi-ations throughout the day attempting to deal with conflict. Some-times it was racial conflict: White people with dreads are always going to come up at a certain point. I'm thinking of the May 2022 Week of Action, where there was a big conflict between the hippies and Black folks. Those were conflicts I had to mediate, and some-times people were racist. I heard things like "racism isn't a thing anymore." Sometimes, there were conflicts between people man-aging the camp who felt that others weren't doing enough to pro-vide support—like helping with the food and prep. Some were just hoping that it would be more communal, but the workload would usually end up falling on the same people over and over.

Then there were just general conflicts—interpersonal beefs, lovers' quarrels, and so on. But we had to address them. You need these people to get along, because a movement depends on them. It's not like people can just fall out like they usually do. This actually kind of has to work.

I became a chaplain in the forest. My presence was valuable for healing tensions where possible. Many people of many different faith backgrounds, beliefs, and ethics came together to stop Cop City. For me, I come from the African American Baptist tradition. I believe that our God is universal, the ultimate power from which all life emanates and all blessings flow, and that by observing the people that our God chooses, when and where God chooses to act, and the example of Jesus Christ, we catch a glimpse of God's character.

I've especially reflected on this ever since Tortuguita was murdered. Jesus taught that we have to create a world of our own. We have to generate the power within ourselves to change things and transform this world through renewing our minds, and all other things will follow. And Jesus, like others before him, was ultimately killed by the state. Jesus encouraged others to live into the fullness of their life and potential, in the face of a world that told them they were not worthy. He believed in radical redeemability. He healed people, fed people, and challenged the power structures of his day, chasing money changers out of the temple. And despite his message of peace and good works, he was still ultimately killed by the state.

If you stay in the forest, you get killed. If you burn it down, you get killed. If you try to start a new world, simply by transforming yourself, you still get killed.

The Raids

Raids of the forest were an occupational hazard. There had been raids throughout the forest defense. People would get picked up when the police came through the forest, but it was a public park, so they couldn't get anybody on much. People would go to jail, but they'd get released. That was the cadence. You'd get picked up sometimes for criminal trespass, misdemeanor—nothing big, nothing crazy, just big enough to be a bit of a hassle.

Space Camp was the main camp where the kitchen and the fires were set up. We remained there for most, if not all, of 2022. Space Camp was kind of the home base for the Intrenchment Creek Park side of the occupation—the Prison Farm side was where the tree houses were. They experienced a lot more police incursions, so they had to stay in tree houses to stay safe. All the tree houses had names. One had a retractable ladder. One time, when the cops were chasing them into the tree, they just pulled the ladder up like, "Nope!"

The raids increased, but people got smarter about hiding. They found more remote places in the woods to camp. It was easier for them to be off the beaten path so they couldn't be found. The police didn't find Space Camp, a standing camp with all our infrastructure, for months. There was nothing comparable to the raids we started to see in December 2022, where people were charged with domestic terrorism. That just hadn't been on the radar before. It was a sharp escalation. By then, people were also exhausted from having to hide from the police, and from trying to get others to come and help when there was a raid. The supply lines were definitely disrupted by the repression. It got harder for people to get what they needed.

Infrastructure had been completely destroyed and completely rebuilt several times. But people were always willing to go back and build again, and the people who stayed stayed because they believed that much in the righteousness of their struggle and felt so sure that history would absolve them.

There was a big influx of people in early January 2023. They came to paint pieces of rubble that Millsap's bulldozers had torn out from the path in an act of symbolic protest. A few days later, Tortuguita was murdered. It took a while for people to come back after that, but they finally did in March 2023, ahead of the sixth week of action. After that, when we could no longer access that park, it did something. Things were never quite the same.

My takeaway from my time in the forest is that another world is possible if you're willing to build it—and *only if* you're willing to build it. It took so much labor and sacrifice to maintain, but there was a certain magic about being in nature that much and being part of a living movement. If you met the people, if you saw how much living-giving energy there was and how much hope it inspired in the people there, you couldn't help but be inspired yourself. This movement has been called many things, but I do not think that we should shy away from calling ourselves children of God, because the way we cared for one another in the forest was one of the greatest examples of Christian love that I have ever seen.

THIRTEEN

Students vs. Cop City

Narek Boyajian, Dr. Andrew Douglas, Oren Panovka,
Daxton Pettus, and Jaanaki Radhakrishnan,
interviewed by Kamau Franklin and Mariah Parker

The following interview took place in October 2023 with students and faculty from various universities across Atlanta who have been involved in the fight to Stop Cop City. It has been edited for clarity.

Kamau Franklin (KF): Thanks everyone for participating. We thought it was important to highlight the role of students and faculty in fighting against Cop City and the larger role of students in radical movements—what ignites students and, at the same time, what elements hold them back from full participation in movements. To start, do you recall the moment you decided to take action to stop Cop City?

Jaanaki Radhakrishnan (JR): It was funny. I had a big crush on someone in a climate coalition on [Emory's] campus. They'd asked me to do things, and I'd be like, "Yes, whatever you want." I was supposed to be leading a climate strike for them. I assumed that their demands would at least mention Cop City. The closer it got to the strike, the more that I realized that they were not planning on discussing it at all. In fact, they were planning to celebrate the university's climate accomplishments, which I found to be completely absurd.

I sat in a meeting with a group of student organizers who do good work and listened to them tell me that Cop City was not a climate issue, and there was not room for it in their platform. I was floored. I realized the lack of awareness on campus. How scared people were to engage with this issue. And that's when I decided, okay, I'm gonna put myself behind this.

Daxton Pettus (DP): After Tyre Nichols's death, I did a lot of research into the case and came across information on Cop City. Morehouse released a statement about the Tyre Nichols killing that uplifted the mayor [Andre Dickens] and his actions to build Cop City. I and many students felt this was preposterous. In my research, I found out that the presidents of Morehouse, Clark Atlanta University, and Spelman are all part of the Atlanta Committee for Progress, who were some of the original supporters of Cop City in 2021. I brought my research to a teach-in, and in that meeting we agreed to organize an event and to have a list of demands for the school. That was my first action: At the next "Crown Forum" event—which is mandatory for all Morehouse students—Morehouse, Spelman, and Clark students lined up in the front and took over the end of the event, demanding that our schools be against Cop City and against the system of policing.

KF: Andrew, how did you, as a professor at Morehouse, get involved in organizing against Cop City?

Andrew Douglas (AD): My timeline is similar to Daxton's. The murder of Tyre Nichols in Memphis in January 2023 prompted a statement from the Morehouse administration, but no statement about the police murder of Tortuguita right here in Atlanta. Many of my faculty colleagues and I didn't want the administration's statement to speak for us or our students. We wanted to go on record with a stronger statement that we thought was truer to the social justice legacy of the college and the teachings of Martin Luther King Jr., our most famous alumnus. So we wrote up a statement: "There is no Cop City in the Beloved Community." About fifty-three faculty members signed on to that, more than a third of our full-time faculty.

Before that, some colleagues and I had organized a teach-in on Tyre Nichols and connections with the Stop Cop City movement. Students just took over that space and started organizing. That led to the protest at the Crown Forum maybe a week later. We had our faculty statement ready to go right when that student protest went viral on social media in the Atlanta area. That was a really beautiful moment of synergy between students and faculty. I think that moment helped some faculty members who were a little more cautious about getting involved. There was a growing sense that we're here to support the students and we need to speak up.

KF: That protest at the Crown Forum became a seminal moment in the Stop Cop City movement, because it was a historically Black college and challenged the mayor's narrative that the movement was all white people. Later, it led to Mayor Dickens staging a meeting with students on campus. How did you feel knowing that that action generated a response from Dickens and the college president?

DP: Well, first to take a step back, in our demand letter we gave the Morehouse president until 5 p.m., that Sunday, to address the student body. But before even addressing us, he invited the mayor to come to address us. So we did feel some sort of way about that.

His real purpose in coming was very clearly to promote the facility, and to tell students why the reservations that they have are wrong and we should support it. They only gave five minutes for one student to speak; the rest of the ninety-minute program was for the mayor to talk about the facility. Students came with very critical questions that needed answers, but the mayor could not give those answers. It was ignorant to come unprepared to an institution of Black students talking about a system that significantly oppresses Black people.

KF: Oren and Narek, do you want to talk a little about your origin stories?

Oren Panovka (OP): I got involved after the murder of Manuel "Tortuguita" Terán. I went to the protest happening outside of Morehouse while Andre Dickens was speaking, and that's how I got connected with movement folks. I would say my first action was the march to retake the Weelaunee Forest on the first day of the March 2023 Week of Action after police raids had closed it.

Narek Boyajian (NB): The school I attend, Georgia State University, plays a significant role in prison-industrial complex expansion in Atlanta. The university is represented on the APF Executive Board by GSU professor and millionaire Deepak Raghavan; GSU president Brian Blake sits on the board of the Atlanta Committee for Progress, which expressed its full support of the facility the same day it was publicly announced in 2021. The GSU Foundation and Criminal Justice Department are donors to the APF. The most disturbing connection, however, is through a program called Georgia International Law Enforcement Exchange (GILEE), housed in GSU's Andrew Young School of Policy Studies. GILEE trains thousands of US and Israeli police in topics like "border policing," "urban policing," and "drug interdiction." There is substantial evidence that shows GILEE teaches racial profiling, mass surveillance, arbitrary detention, and brutal violence against protesters.[1]

Seeing these connections, as students, forest defenders, and community members, we made the following demands of GSU: One, end all investment in Cop City and sever ties with the APF; two, end all institutional involvement in GILEE; three, reinvest in student needs, determined by a student-led community benefits agreement.

KF: What has it been like to organize on campus?

DP: At Morehouse, there's a collective consciousness when it comes down to policing. It's still difficult, because while Morehouse has been the center of movements, the administration has historically been against the conflict that comes with political action. But the student and faculty support was clearly there in the beginning. It's clear that there's an appetite for more knowledge.

JR: It's interesting to listen to Daxton talk about organizing at Morehouse. That collective consciousness piece is so critical, but we do not have it here [at Emory] at all. It's a very white, very wealthy, vaguely liberal in a "these are my liberal years, so I can piss off my Republican parents" way.

If we hold a rally, we could get numbers pretty easily. But when it comes to building the capacity to do the work, it's much more of an uphill battle. Privilege plays a huge role. We have a lot of very wealthy students, and a lot of low-income students of color. Early on, we were operating under the assumption that, as students, we had a certain level of protection. So when we occupied our quad in 2023, and our own university called eleven APD vehicles on a group of ten to fifteen students, it was jarring. For some people, it created commitment and investment. It pissed a lot of people off, it certainly pissed faculty off—I think that is what got most of our faculty members involved.

But this serious threat further alienated some students of color. That's something that we struggle to hold more than anything: How do we create a system of community care and trust that allows people to take the risks? For me, and for a lot of students from marginalized backgrounds—low-income, first-gen—there's that piece of like, what is my responsibility to my parents? To protect my future? I am on a full scholarship with money from Coca-Cola, which has invested in Cop City. There have already been questions of what my organizing means for my scholarships. With the retaliation from the state, what does it mean when you're nineteen years old and involved in work that could shut down your capacity to organize for the rest of your life? How do you evaluate your impact in this movement, versus your impact for the next, fifty or sixty years? Is this the hill that I want to die on?

Mariah Parker (MP): You mentioned occupying the Emory quad in 2023. Can you tell us more about that?

OP: The organizing was pretty ad hoc. A month or a month and a half before this, it was really just me and another Emory student doing stuff. I connected with some other students and somebody sent a message in a really big Emory group chat like, hey, "Emory Stop Cop City really needs more involvement, this fight is really pressing." A friend of mine sent a message in the Black Emory student group chat, which led to one of the students holding a Stop Cop City teach-in at the Emory Black Student Alliance House, which is where I met Jaanaki and some others.

It was a lot of freshmen and sophomores—I was a sophomore at the time, Jaanaki was a freshman. There were some juniors and seniors, but most of us were younger. I'd say it was about eight to ten of us who did stuff to make the occupation happen. We'd never organized a direct action before. We didn't really think through the possibilities. It's very easy to look back and say we weren't prepared and we shouldn't have done it because the repression could have been very bad for us. But I want to push back on that. There's always going to be reasons to not act. Oftentimes, even if people don't feel fully prepared, it's actually better to act. And the repression can be really scary, but the repression is actually good for the movement. It helps us grow. Organizing around the police being called on us has been one of the best ways we have connected with more students and faculty members. It drew a lot of attention to Emory's involvement in Cop City and the genocide of Palestinians.

MP: What's a struggle your collective has faced and how have you overcome it?

DP: There's a lot of difficulties when it comes to, like capitalism. Students come here, and they get funneled into political positions. They get put on boards, and they're tokenized. In the movement, there are reformist people and abolitionist people. That's the big conflict with organizing the AUC [Atlanta University Center Consortium]: We're going back and forth. Students saying "abolition" and students saying "reform," but both saying "no Cop City." It's difficult to navigate that and to maintain relationships with those two different positions. But our current Student Government Association (SGA) president spoke at the original protest against Cop City. Many people in SGA are against Cop City, the majority of the people in the chapel for the Crown Forum protest were against Cop City. The level of consciousness is still there, but unification still needs to happen to really push things forward.

NB: We've struggled with repression and particularly how it impacts students who are relatively new to organizing. It can leave us wondering how we move forward. We echo the words of Mariame Kaba, who says, "Let this radicalize you rather than lead you to despair." Throughout every disappointment, we encourage students to turn their frustration into mobilization. And we study the lessons of many movements that came before us together, hoping to build on the creative transgressive actions of our comrades who have experienced similar responses from education institutions and the state.

MP: What's been a high point in your organizing and what did it take to make it happen?

NB: A high point in our student organizing has definitely been a broader recognition of the need to end the GILEE program and its direct connection to Cop City. People have organized to end GILEE for decades, but recent years have marked a clear shift of energy to Stop Cop City, I think particularly because it is a site-based struggle.

I believe our campus organizing helped bring GILEE back into focus within the Stop Cop City movement. We also revived the broader off-campus campaign to shut down GILEE.

KF: We often talk about how organizing on campus is transitory. It's something that you do for a few years. Then you go on to other things. What would you like to leave behind in place for new students?

OP: Even though our time on campus is transitory, I don't think that our time in this movement is transitory. There have been graduate students or non-student organizers who have been crucial to the work on Atlanta campuses. We can also fill those roles.

DP: I agree. What that looks like to me is connecting with organizations that are already doing work in the community. There's a group, Midnight Riot, who does community service in the West End, and I'm hoping to build a relationship with Community Movement Builders. It's about breaking down the barriers that the institution has put before us.

JR: What I hope to do is combat the entire culture of transitory work. None of us should be irreplaceable. We're all thinking about how we can make sure that each student leader that emerges is actively creating more student leaders. We almost hope to eliminate the concept of leaders entirely, and have this autonomous space where people feel ownership, and like they have the necessary support to act in whatever way they see fit. That's a big goal for me. It's none of my concern what students decide to do once I am gone. It *is* my concern whether or not they have the ability to decide.

I'm interested to hear what Andrew has to say about this because we look to faculty to continue this work and, I won't lie, dealing with the faculty coalition drives me crazy! Those meetings, oh my God. But those are the people who are gonna stay around.

AD: Yeah, in terms of sustaining and growing organizing over time, I'll point out three challenges. One is that we need to develop some consensus around the role of the faculty. Is it largely a support role? Is the idea that we ought to use our position and status to defend students' rights to organize? Or should we try to teach and educate students and ensure that they're seeing things as we think they need to? This is tricky, because oftentimes, especially around issues of policing and carcerality, it's the professors who need to be educated. In any case, lecturing students is not what they need or want in this moment. That was the approach that Dickens took when he came to speak at Morehouse; he and his staff came with PowerPoint slides and promotional materials and treated the students as if they just hadn't been educated on massive new investment in policing. We cannot replicate that orientation toward our students. We need to figure out how to create an environment where we're both supportive and edifying.

We also need to complicate this entrepreneurship and leadership culture that has saturated higher education. This is very acute at a place like Morehouse, where the administration leans into a kind of "Great Man" theory of history and really promotes the idea of the entrepreneur, the founder, the heroic leader figure. We don't always need to focus on starting new organizations and initiatives. Oftentimes this can detract from more important work of building onto existing movements. It's encouraging to hear what Daxton said about getting involved with organizations that are already afoot.

The final thing I'll say is we need to get better about connecting on-campus struggles with off-campus concerns. If a junior or senior in college is organizing to address financial aid issues on campus, that work is organically tied to bigger issues around the funding of public goods, the nature of financialized capitalism. That campus organizing becomes a foundation for, say, sustained debt abolition work after graduation. If a student is working on campus housing issues, that becomes a basis for gentrification and tenant organizing off campus. One of the beautiful things about the Stop Cop City organizing is that it has helped students get out of the bubble of campus, helped them see that the campus is a microcosm of our larger society. My sense is that drawing these kinds of connections can help sustain organizing campaigns as students come in, cycle in, and cycle out.

KF: Is there anything else you'd like to add?

OP: As a student in non-student spaces, it's definitely better to first listen a lot, and do a lot of things that might not seem exciting, but are still important, like bringing supplies or going canvassing. The generational knowledge of Atlanta organizers has been by far our best teacher, because universities are not going to give us the tools with which to dismantle them.

And also, the most successful organizers take feedback well and are not going to insist on their viewpoint every time. Even if they feel that they're right, they're still gonna go with what the group says. "I'm still gonna do what you think is best, I'm willing to be wrong on this." That is a crucial thing to preserve one's organizing community.

JR: The world conditions us to think that when you are asked a question, you have to know the answer. As organizers, we are trying to build a world that is nearly impossible for us to conceptualize, because we are all conditioned by capitalism. We have no idea what we are doing generally. We occupy this space of uncertainty constantly. And so, I would like to encourage all students to lean into that. In order for us to build a world that is radically different, that is truly liberated, we have to be okay with having no idea what we're walking into, with making the best-informed guesses that we can, and being ready to pivot if we make a bad choice.

AD: I just want to flag maybe three things. One is that we've been focused on undergraduates, and at Morehouse, of course, we only have undergraduates. But graduate students have been such a huge part of this movement, some of whom have been caught up in some of this state repression with these bogus domestic terrorism charges. This is tied to the resurgence of the academic labor movement, where graduate students have been at the vanguard. There's a lot of work to do to build on the resurgence of the academic labor movement across faculty ranks; to bring undergraduate students into that organizing; and to connect it with the organizing work around police and prison abolition, around debt abolition, and so forth.

I also want to highlight the national faculty coalition that's been built up around Stop Cop City. The Stop Cop City movement dovetails with the national Cops Off Campus Coalition. We've had faculty from all over the country write op-eds in support of Stop Cop City. We've had professors travel to Atlanta during some of the weeks of action. We've really seen a national faculty coalition, which has been absolutely crucial to this movement.

Finally, I think it's important to stress how this movement, specifically the student organizing within this movement, has exposed how colleges and universities operate, and this has had such tremendous educational value. Perhaps greater educational value than whatever students are formally taught in the classroom. To see firsthand, for example, that the university is run like a hedge fund, with administrators and trustees concerned to protect asset values rather than promote any moral principles or vision, to really understand why no university president will align with students and campus workers and denounce this repressive policing paradigm, is such an edifying lesson in the contradictions of our capitalist society. Students really ought to be proud of the education that, as it were, they've given themselves.

KF: Somebody said this earlier, but there is no real movement without students. When y'all got involved at various levels, it changed the game. The work that you all did made the city notice and made them concerned in ways that they weren't before. Once they felt they lost the campuses, that became a huge deal. And that shows the power of student organizing, the work that you do, the impact that you have. Thank you for your work and organizing.

Narek Boyajian is a queer Armenian American graduate student and community organizer based in Atlanta. They are committed to abolitionist, anti-colonial, anti-imperialist movement work.

Andrew J. Douglas is a professor of political science at Morehouse College. He is the author of several articles and three books, including *W. E. B. Du Bois and the Critique of the Competitive Society* (2019) and, with Jared Loggins, *Prophet of Discontent: Martin Luther King Jr. and the Critique of Racial Capitalism* (2021).

Oren Panovka is a lifelong Atlanta resident and student at Emory University. He became involved in the movement to Defend the Atlanta Forest / Stop Cop City in January 2023, following the assassinations of forest defender Tortuguita by the Georgia State Patrol.

Daxton Pettus, a student at Morehouse College, is pursuing a bachelor's degree in philosophy with aspirations to further his education with a law degree. With over nine years of organizing experience, he has galvanized communities on issues like overpolicing, gentrification, and the general marginalization of Black people. Currently, he's focused on empowering student advocates in Atlanta, particularly on concerns like Cop City.

Jaanaki Radhakrishnan began organizing in middle school, inspired by her older brother and a long line of Black mothers. Currently an undergraduate at Emory University studying anthropology and religion, she's continued her troublemaking tendencies on campus and hopes to pursue a PhD. Jaanaki is deeply grateful to her family, friends, partners in this work, and the communities that built her up and continue to support her, especially the Detroit organizers who raised her.

FOURTEEN

There Is No Cop City in the Beloved Community

An Open Letter from Members of the Morehouse College Faculty

Over forty Morehouse College faculty published the following letter against Cop City in February 2023. Faculty from other universities, including Spelman College, Georgia State University, and Emory University released similar letters. Signatures have been omitted.

As members of the Morehouse College faculty, we have grown accustomed to consoling and counseling our students as they attempt to grapple with cycles of police brutality. Year after year, as Black people continue to be abused and killed at the hands of the police, jailed and surveilled in barbaric ways, we struggle to make sense of it all. We struggle to help our students determine where we go from here.

But events that have transpired in Atlanta in recent months—specifically, the City's initiative to build a $90 million police training facility, commonly known as "Cop City"—give us a clear indication of where we need to direct our energies. Atlanta, our home town, has become the epicenter of the struggle over the future of policing in America. Now is the time to STOP COP CITY.

The proposal for a new police training facility was publicly announced in 2021, at a time when the nation was still reeling from the killing of George Floyd and a broad coalition of concerned citizens demanded that cities and states defund the police. Last fall, the Atlanta City Council formally approved the project, what amounts to a massive new investment in the police, despite widespread public opposition. In a city that is rapidly losing its famed tree canopy, the project is also environmentally disastrous; it would require the clearing of 85 acres of Atlanta's lush South River Forest. Plans call for shooting ranges, spaces for militarized drills, a Blackhawk helicopter landing pad, and a mock city complete with buildings and roads to allow the Atlanta Police Department—as well as other police agencies drawn from all over the region—to practice urban warfare tactics along the lines of the SCORPION unit in Memphis or the TITAN squads in Atlanta. There is an undeniable and direct relationship between the fate of Michael Brown and George Floyd as well as Tyre Nichols and the pending plan to build Cop City.

Let us not delude ourselves: Cop City, if built, will result in more death and destruction at the hands of the police. Indeed, the Cop City project already has blood on its proverbial hands. On January 18, 2023, as authorities conducted a sweep of the forest site, police shot and killed protestor Manuel Terán, known among friends as "Tortuguita," under very suspicious circumstances. Details of the tragedy remain sparse. As we mourn Tortuguita's death, we call for an independent and transparent investigation of the incident.

In times like these, the name of Morehouse's most famous alumnus is often bandied about, typically in an effort to tame a groundswell of rage, to channel the righteous frustration of Black and working-class people into nonviolent modes of protest. But we must not sanitize the legacy of Dr. Martin Luther King, Jr., who sought to expose and challenge the "triple evils" of racism, militarism, and materialism; taken together, King opposed the commodification of Black bodies and he understood that police violence was a pernicious because systemic problem. "Armies of officials are clothed in uniform," he said in 1964, "invested with authority, armed with the instruments of violence and death and conditioned to believe that they can intimidate, maim or kill Negroes with the same recklessness that once motivated the slave owner."

It is telling that Cop City is slated to be developed on the site of the Old Atlanta Prison Farm. Before the site was sold to the City of Atlanta after the Civil War, it was a slave labor camp. And before that, the Weelaunee Forest of the Muscogee Creek people. The trail of tears is not a thing of the past.

We must listen to and learn from this history. We must study how state violence directed against Black, Indigenous, People of Color (BIPOC)—as well as working-class people of all colors—reproduces itself in different ways over generations. We must listen to the voices of those most affected by police violence and abuse. Our civic leaders have not done this. On the contrary.

Georgia has the highest rates of correctional control of any state in the nation by far, twice as many as almost every state, at 5,143 per 100,000. Only New York City's police foundation raised more money in 2020—and that was before Atlanta's fundraising roughly tripled in 2021. Atlanta is the most surveilled city in America. It is the most economically unequal major city in America. King said in 1967 that "a nation that continues year after year to spend more money on military defense than on programs of social uplift is approaching spiritual death." Today, we say that a city that continues year after year to spend more money on policing and urban warfare than on programs of social uplift is approaching spiritual death.

King claimed in 1966 that "only a refusal to hate and kill can put an end to the chain of violence in the world and lead us toward a community where men [and women] can live together without fear. Our goal is to create a beloved community, and this will require a qualitative change in our souls as well as a quantitative change in our lives."

Strangely, we tend to celebrate Atlanta—and the so-called

"Atlanta way"—as a Black Mecca. As an alumnus of Morehouse and a luminary of Atlanta, Dr. King articulated an inspiring vision of the beloved community. The dream has become a nightmare: There is simply no place for Cop City in the beloved community.

We, the undersigned members of the Morehouse College faculty, call upon our civic leaders and fellow educators in Atlanta to denounce Cop City, to take immediate action to cancel the project, and to respond to the will of the people—and not merely the wealthy and well connected—in determining the character of our communities and the conduct of those who claim to serve and protect us.

FIFTEEN

The Roots of Resistance

Building Narrative Power

Hannah Riley

> Over the last few weeks, I've started hearing from friends
> outside ATL . . . both from people in the national media and
> "civilians." It's clearly getting more national attention but
> people outside of ATL really still don't get the issues at play.
> At all. I think we can help inform people. . . . I think doing a
> proper sit down on tape . . . will help get your message out in
> the right way locally and nationally.

If you don't know who sent this email, it reads like a fairly standard
pitch from a public relations firm to a politician dealing with a particularly sticky scandal. The nature of the relationship is clear: We
take you on as a client, and help ensure the exact message you want
the public to hear gets out.

The author, however, isn't someone at a PR firm. The missive was
written by the publisher of the *Atlanta Journal-Constitution* (*AJC*)—
the paper of record for a metro area of six million people—to the
head of communications for Atlanta's mayor, Andre Dickens.[1]

The email was sent in March 2023, roughly two years after the
public first heard plans for Cop City. Two and a half months earlier,
police murdered Tortuguita in the forest. After the murder, the Stop
Cop City movement burst into the mainstream. After over a year of
the *AJC* and other corporate outlets being the authoritative voice

on the topic locally, national publications were starting to pay closer attention, new local outlets were gaining traction, and the greater public perception was drifting away from the state's narrative.

From the beginning of the Stop Cop City struggle, organizers knew that corporate media was not going to report accurately or favorably on opposition to a policing project that the city power structure had coalesced around. Indeed, the city's mainstream media, with the *AJC* at the helm, had been successfully manufacturing consent for unpopular policies and fearmongering for decades. Winning the narrative war would require not just engaging with existing media, but building new infrastructure that went around mainstream media entirely. This is what organizers did.

The Cox Media Empire and Cop City

Each item of news we consume has been laundered through multiple peoples' brains, and at every turn, it has been edited, consciously or unconsciously, slightly or dramatically, to fit readers' understanding of the world. Good journalists serve as interpreters, taking what they hear from sources who have their own agendas (and are not infrequently state aligned), and then giving their readers the appropriate context so that they can make their own assessments.

Atlanta has just one prominent newspaper—the *AJC*—owned by a billionaire family company. Like most major American newspapers, the *AJC* claims in its mission statement that it holds power to account, uncovers hidden stories, and highlights a diversity of perspectives.[2] In truth, while the *AJC* has some excellent journalists on staff, its political coverage often functions as PR for the city.

The *AJC* is owned by Cox Enterprises, which is owned by the Cox family (America's eighth-richest family, in fact). Cox Enterprises' ownership spans Autotrader and Kelly Blue Book to Cox Communications, which is the third largest cable provider in the United States, as well as a plethora of media outlets, including TV, print, and radio.[3]

The Cox media empire's original patriarch, James M. Cox, came up through local Ohio media before launching his political career and eventually becoming the governor of Ohio, in 1913. His political ambitions and his media ambitions were two sides of the same coin—to become truly powerful, you have to control the narrative. Despite never living in Georgia (the ultimate outside agitator!), Cox purchased the *Atlanta Journal*, the *Atlanta Georgian*, and WSB Radio in the 1930s, garnering his family considerable political sway in the state. In the coming decades, the Cox Media empire would only grow.[4]

Like many legacy American newspapers still in circulation, the *AJC* has a dark history. Over a century before the *AJC* began manufacturing consent for Cop City, both the *Atlanta Journal* and the *Atlanta Constitution*—which merged in 2001 to create the *AJC*—fomented anti-Black violence. In 1905, for example, as the two papers' publishers ran against each other for governor of Georgia, they used their newspapers to fan the flames of white fury, through imagined Black political gains and fabricated stories of Black men raping white women. The papers' coverage led to a mob of angry white people laying siege to historically Black neighborhoods in the city, murdering at least twenty-five Black Atlantans—some stabbed, some shot, some hung from city lampposts.[5]

Today, the *AJC* maintains its power throughout the city not just through its printed words but through its influential relationships. Alex Taylor, the CEO of Cox Enterprises, was the chair of the Atlanta Committee for Progress when the Cop City proposal came to light, and volunteered to lead the project's private fundraising campaign.[6] The *AJC* regularly omitted this conflict of interest from its editorial coverage of Cop City until public backlash prompted a belated acknowledgment of the conflict. Because the Cox empire owns so many outlets and stations (whether outright or partial), and because their executives (to say nothing of the family themselves) are so wealthy, it's hard to overstate—or even accurately calculate—their influence over matters civic and journalistic.

On June 12, 2020, less than a month after the murder of George Floyd, Atlanta police murdered Rayshard Brooks. Atlantans took to the streets for weeks after the killing, demanding that Atlanta Police be defunded and resources reallocated toward social programs that help people thrive. Walking in lockstep as they have for decades, the local corporate media apparatus and the Atlanta Police shifted into joint-crisis communications mode. They fell back on all the classic talking points trotted out when police are in hot water. (*Axios Atlanta*, which is owned by Cox Communications, ran a story titled "Low Morale Hinders Atlanta Police Recruitment." The use of this line won cops a sympathy prize from the Atlanta Police Foundation in the form of $500 checks for every on-duty officer.)[7]

This was the media milieu into which Cop City was born. As a broad array of Atlanta residents registered their opposition to Cop City in the summer of 2021, the corporate media ecosystem wasted no time in its attempts to manufacture public consent for the unpopular proposal. The week after a City Council vote on Cop City was postponed, the *AJC* ran a relatively rare editorial, entitled "Crime Wave Should Spur Action on Center."[8] In it, the editorial board disingenuously connected the nationwide increase in murders (something criminologists linked to the trauma of a massive pandemic and the sharp increase in gun purchases) to the need for Cop City.[9] The same day, the *AJC* published another op-ed, this one by Robert Loudermilk Jr., the board chair of the Atlanta Police Foundation, speculating about whether or not the City Councilmembers who had voted to table the vote cared about public safety, and urging Cop City be built.[10]

Throughout 2021, the steady stream of pro-police op-eds kept apace. In just the first six months of the year, Atlanta Police Foundation president Dave Wilkinson had two published opinion pieces in the *AJC*. In January, months before plans for Cop City were released to the public, he penned a piece titled "City's Crime Rise Can Be Reversed Once More," wherein he extolled the virtues of public-private partnerships, bemoaned the "soaring murder rate," and, with a seemingly straight face, wrote the words: "The sustaining foundation of success in fighting crime requires a motivated and enthusiastic police force."[11] Thematically, their stuff is pretty stale. Like the interview with Mayor Dickens that came out of the *AJC* publisher's emailed pitch, Wilkinson's op-eds didn't make much of a splash; they didn't course-correct the state's story or bring more people around to its side. It was just another opportunity for the state to spotlight its narrative—and, as it turns out, just doing that alone really matters.

When you control a newspaper, you don't just control news, you decide what *is* news. If on a given day the mayor is giving a speech and an activist is chained to Cop City construction equipment, the choice of which event to cover and which to give primacy to is incredibly influential, with political implications. When the *AJC* or WSB Radio or FOX 5 uncritically parrot a city press release or feature wall-to-wall "crime" coverage fed to them by police, it shapes how people understand their own safety and the state interventions that would make them safer. It helps manufacture consent for projects like Cop City.

The Georgia Ewoks

In the winter of 2022, police violently raided the Weelaunee Forest multiple times, arresting forest defenders and destroying their homes and belongings. Organizers used the ramped-up repression and state violence to further expose Cop City for what it was to national media. When police killed Tortuguita in a barrage of gunfire in the forest, the narrative escaped the clutches of the state permanently.

Although Atlanta's local corporate media had been in control of the narrative up to that point, organizers had already begun to build new infrastructure that would force national media to tell a different story of the movement: that of a diverse group of concerned citizens who had raised their fears and voiced their disapproval for a project destined to suck up untold public dollars, with vanishingly little public input and at the expense of critically important forest land, to give Atlanta police a deadly playground. And they were being met with violent state repression at nearly every turn.

The Guardian, the *New Yorker*, the *Los Angeles Times*, the *New York Times*, *USA Today*, and functionally every other large mainstream outlet in the United States covered the story with depth and inquisitiveness. National independent outlets, such as *The Intercept*, *The Appeal*, the *New Republic*, and *The Nation* also covered it. Journalists from Spain, Finland, the United Kingdom, France, and others reported on the repression of Cop City activists. A friend sent me a photo of Stop Cop City graffiti in Mexico City. Another sent me one from Berlin.

This coverage was no accident. Organizers in Atlanta steadfastly refused to allow reality to be bulldozed by the local state narrative. The news agenda was no longer being decided upon by the business elite that run Atlanta, or in the PR offices of police and politicians. Instead, the state found itself in a very unusual position: a defensive one.

For coalitions fighting on the front lines, there is often scant free time to do media work. Journalists work on tight turnarounds; if you don't return a call asking for a quote or clarification within hours, the piece is likely to go to print without it. Constant pitching, relationship-building, and press list–building—which is time- and energy-consuming—is essential if you want to get good (or even just neutral) news coverage. Organizers in Atlanta recognized that from the beginning. Learning in part from Chicago's #NoCopAcademy movement that it was critical to label your target with a more accurate name than what the powerful had dubbed it, the movement coalesced around calling the training center "Cop City," as well as using the phrase "Defend the Atlanta Forest." It's impossible to overstate the importance of shifting these terms from the outset.

Doing media work can be particularly challenging in a struggle like the Stop Cop City movement, which is autonomous and decentralized. There are no clearly appointed leaders; no legacy nonprofits running narrative strategy or communications; no development department. As with so many other aspects of the movement, organizers saw the existing corporate media infrastructure and decided they needed to build a new one. Instead of relying on mostly hostile mainstream outlets, the people created their own methods of disseminating information and crafting narrative.

Organized and structured through various Signal and Telegram chats, people opposed to Cop City created loose media formations and became responsible for a litany of things (some of which people came into the movement knowing how to do, and a good amount of which was learned on the go.) The ad hoc media groups would work on responding to requests from journalists as well as reaching out and pitching stories, seeking corrections when needed, drafting press releases and media advisories, keeping an up-to-date press list, connecting reporters with a variety of sources, and conducting internal media trainings. In and out of the forest, varying groups of activists regularly held press conferences to set the record straight.

There was no time for rest. The steady stream of propaganda and lies coming out of City Hall required constant, real-time response from the movement. When Mayor Dickens announced the State of the City address (typically a self-congratulatory speech given to a room of sycophantic politicos), organizers immediately responded by creating their own event—the People's State of the City—in a conference room in the same hotel. Knowing that members of the press corps would already be assembled for the mayor's address, organizers invited them to come hear the people's response as soon as the mayor was done speaking. The action made the *AJC*'s and other outlets' coverage of the State of the City—with the demands and reactions of the people of Atlanta counterposed against the mayor's canned lines.[12]

Organizers were fighting the narrative war on all fronts. As the movement consolidated relationships with movement-aligned journalists and made inroads with less friendly ones, it began shifting from responsive to proactive media strategies. Activists coordinated with journalists to arrange tours of the forest, painting a picture drastically different from the *AJC's* portrayal of scary anarchists. In 2022, *The Daily Show's* Roy Wood Jr. visited the forest, highlighting forest defense and the proposal's impact on the surrounding Black community. When some Atlanta police officers show up mid-interview, Wood chooses to follow the defenders into the forest, saying, "I'd rather take my chance with the Georgia Ewoks than the cops." This coverage—and many stories like it—painted a decidedly different picture of the movement, a David-and-Goliath story of peaceful, tree-loving forest defenders against an armed-to-the-teeth police state.[13]

When police murdered Tortuguita, the movement's various media formations were already relatively established and prepared to respond. Knowing that the state would immediately set out to demonize Tortuguita, organizers jumped into action to tell the story of who Tortuguita really was; to tell stories of their commitment to their loved ones, to the forest, and to a world free of police. As organizers repeatedly caught officials in lies surrounding the circumstances of the murder, the state's disingenuous narrative of Tortuguita as a violent extremist fell flat.[14]

In the following months, organizers were ready to respond and proactively shape the narrative, at every turn. When the state called Stop Cop City activists "outside agitators" and selectively arrested white people from out of town, the movement responded by showing the depth of Black opposition to Cop City, exemplified perhaps most clearly in a march led by Community Movement Builders, Movement for Black Lives, and Black Voters Matter that proceeded from the Martin Luther King Jr. Center to the Atlanta Police Foundation headquarters.[15] Months later, organizers launched a campaign to put Cop City to a direct vote by the people of Atlanta, using the slogan "Let the People Decide"—a direct challenge to the city that claimed to save democracy via the 2020 presidential and Senate elections while refusing to honor its own citizens' input.[16] When the state announced its 61-person RICO indictment of activists, a group quickly released a parody video called "The People's RICO," which turned the state's conspiracy charges back on itself and illustrated the networks of powerful actors behind Cop City.[17] Again and again, the decentralized movement has outflanked the state, putting city leaders on the defensive and forcing them to respond to its framing.

A New Media Ecosystem

While engaging in and shaping corporate media narratives locally and nationally, the Stop Cop City movement has also helped to strengthen a nascent alternative media landscape. When the plans for Cop City were announced, the Atlanta Community Press Collective (ACPC) was composed of only a few volunteers building a research and open records clearinghouse. Today, it's an abolitionist nonprofit newsroom whose findings and investigations have shaped the discussion around Cop City at City Hall and in the press corps more broadly. ACPC has held the city's feet to the fire through its investigations, forcing other local outlets to become more critical in their own reporting. Its work exemplifies one part of the *AJC's* stated mission: "functioning as a watchdog on government." This is a pillar of movement journalism: Whether it's done through consistent open records requests or attendance at even the most obscure-seeming subcommittee meeting, demystifying local governance is critical. If enough residents continue to feel that local government is opaque and untouchable, journalism will remain largely a conversation between politicians and the media.

ACPC's diligence in shining a light on even the most mundane city business has paid out in bombshell stories. A breakthrough story revealed the actual public cost of Cop City—Atlanta officials had said it would cost $30 million, but ACPC's investigation revealed that number to be closer to $50 million. When the piece was picked up by a broader press, the city admitted it would cost far more than initially proposed.[18] ACPC has also put out a series of interviews with the defendants in the RICO case, giving them a platform to tell their own stories. Other southern movement outlets like *Mainline* and *Scalawag* have committed entire weeks of coverage to correcting the narrative on Cop City. All of these stories are steadily promoted on social media, playing a critical role in the dissemination of the movement's narrative.

The success of the Stop Cop City movement's narrative work has bewildered and angered prosecutors and politicians in Georgia. In the sprawling RICO indictment (which attempts to criminalize the building blocks of leftist organizing, such as mutual aid and "anarchist zines"), the movement's media savvy is brought up multiple times. And, honestly, absent the clearly antagonistic slant, it's a decent summation of the perfectly legal media tactics: "Defend the Atlanta Forest uses websites, social media, and statements to traditional media . . . to promote its extremist political agenda, legitimize its behavior, and recruit new members." "In an effort to de-legitimize the facts as relayed by law enforcement . . . members of Defend the Atlanta Forest often contact news media and flood social media." Or, the best one of all: "Defend the Atlanta Forest holds media-attended press conferences to control the story and promote their own narrative. Anarchists publish their own zines and publish their own statements because they do not trust the media to carry their message."[19] A broken clock is right twice a day.

Delegitimizing the dominant state narrative is, indeed, exactly how movements like this succeed. From the beginning, Stop Cop City organizers, in real time, juxtaposed the violence of the state with their own actions: What's more harmful to the community, they asked, burning one bulldozer, or allowing that bulldozer to tear down a forest that helps keep the nearby land from flooding, lowers the overall temperature, and serves as a home for hundreds of species? What's more violent, building a sprawling complex devoted to training people in various forms of violence and surveillance, or opposing the complex by living in a tree you're hoping to save? One side kills people, the other side burns police motorcycles. That's the story.

Hannah Riley is an Atlanta-based writer, communications specialist, and community organizer. She has worked at the intersection of the criminal legal system and media for over a decade at various nonprofit law offices, including the Southern Center for Human Rights and the Innocence Project, and she is on the Board of Directors for the Atlanta Community Press Collective and The Appeal. Hannah currently works as a strategist and consultant supporting newsrooms in producing journalism that equips people with the information they need to build safer communities.

SIXTEEN

Let the People Decide

Mary Hooks and Kate Shapiro

On June 6, 2023, many hundreds of Atlantans flooded City Hall to protest legislation that would allocate $67 million in public funding for Cop City. When police claimed the building had reached capacity, hundreds more spilled into the streets, chanting and waiting to be let in the building.[1] Just three weeks earlier, Atlanta residents had spoken against Cop City during seven straight hours of public comment, shattering the local record for in-person turnout.[2] On this early June day, they doubled that record, speaking for over fourteen hours. Despite the overwhelming opposition, the Atlanta City Council, the majority of whom are Democrats, voted to allocate $67 million to Cop City.

The City Council, Democratic mayor, and Atlanta Police Foundation likely hoped and prayed that this was the end of a two-year fight that had already included civil disobedience, street protest, forest defense, corporate targeting, and mass citizen lobbying. But for the organizers against Cop City, as with so many other moments in the movement, we knew it was time to pivot and explore a new tactic—one that reflected our belief that given the massive repression, the people of Atlanta have the right and responsibility to decide the fate of Cop City. Two days after the June funding vote, a broad coalition would stand in front of City Hall and announce a new mass-base strategy to put Cop City on the ballot in a citywide referendum.[3]

Launching the Referendum

In April 2023, a handful of lawyers and activists began floating the idea of getting Cop City on the ballot. The movement had long employed a diversity of tactics to delay and defeat Cop City, and we saw powerful potential in a referendum effort not only to overturn the Cop City legislation through a direct vote, but to strengthen the fabric of the social justice movement in Atlanta by providing mass entry points for new organizers, directly engaging hundreds of thousands of Atlantans, further shaping the narrative, and consolidating popular opposition to Cop City.

We didn't know much about how to get a referendum on the ballot, as there had only been one citizen-initiated referendum nearly a century ago in Atlanta. The rules and regulations surrounding local referenda in Georgia are incredibly restrictive. The Georgia referendum statute allows only sixty days from the filing of the petition to collect signatures from 15 percent of the total number of people registered to vote in the previous municipal election. The law also required those who *collected* signatures to be Atlanta residents. This presented massive obstacles: First, it disenfranchised thousands of Atlanta residents who had moved to the city after 2021 or were not registered to vote in 2021; second, it meant that DeKalb County residents who lived close to the Cop City site but outside city limits could not vote on the proposal; and third, it severely limited the pool of people who could collect signatures. Residents closest to the site could neither sign the petition nor ask others to sign it. All of this is, of course, by anti-democratic design.[4]

All told, we would need to gather over 58,000 signatures. Because we knew the city would try to throw out as many signatures as possible, we set a goal of collecting over 75,000 valid petitions. This meant we would strive to collect 120,000 petitions, based on the advice we received from others with more experience with the tactic. We also learned that to get on the November 2023 ballot, we would need to file our petition and begin collecting signatures in early June—leaving us hardly any time to prepare.[5]

We knew it would be an uphill battle. But at that point in the fight, we had nothing to lose and even more public support to gain. We especially drew inspiration from Camden County, a rural area in South Georgia, where residents had recently won a referendum overturning their county government's decision to build a massive commercial launch pad to send rockets into outer space.[6]

There was some disagreement within the movement over whether to pursue the referendum, especially from those who knew, like many of us, that democracy is a sham in this country, that the electoralization of issues can be employed to squelch social movement activity, and that those in power will do all they can to stop a vote. But, in the spirit of a multi-tactical movement, we resolved to use all the tools at our disposal to halt Cop City in its tracks—hoping that, even if we could not vanquish Cop City through the referendum, we could use the effort to stall the project and further build the movement.

ψ

When we filed the referendum petition on June 7, 2023, we had a team of enthusiastic volunteers, but no money, no offices, and no Georgia-specific ballot initiative experience. But organizing is what we do. So we organized, building most of the infrastructure *after* launching the campaign. We put out a call for volunteers to join our Field, Communications, Legal, and Fundraising teams. We began hustling to acquire resources, knowing we would need to pay canvassers to hit our daily signature goals. Before we had the money to hire paid canvassers, we began sending out teams of volunteers to every corner of the city to hit high-foot-traffic areas of town. We held weekly Monday night calls for partners and volunteers to share updates, coordinate, and align. We recruited neighborhood captains as leaders to organize their networks and communities.

People across the city self-organized bar crawls, cookouts, petition signing parties at supportive businesses, and more. One business gave free ice cream to anyone who came into its shop wearing the "Let the People Decide" canvassing T-shirt. It became a summer staple to see petition collectors on Atlanta's Beltline (a walking path), at parks and grocery stores, in cafés, and at concerts and drag shows. Some rank-and-file firefighters and emergency medical technicians gathered signatures, making clear their frustration at being used by the city to provide cover to overfunded police. Our people rode MARTA trains and buses to get signatures. We hit arcades, gaming shops, tattoo shops, schools, roller skating rinks, salons and barbershops. When the *Barbie* movie made its debut, a group of folks made shirts and a whole plan to be at the opening weekend to gather signatures. We posted up at churches, and when some of them didn't let us in, we walked with parishioners to their cars and got them to sign while we sang freedom songs.

We said from the start that "everyone knows their people and where they are, so go find them." And we did just that. Despite it being Atlanta's hottest summer on record, our campaign was contagious.

At the same time, we knew we must take on the anti-democratic structure of the referendum process. On July 7, 2023, aligned attorneys filed a federal lawsuit arguing that the law requiring petition gatherers to be Atlanta residents violated the First Amendment.[7] Twenty days later, a federal judge ruled in our favor, restarting the clock to give us more time to gather signatures and allowing anyone to gather signatures.[8] This was a huge win, opening the floodgates for many more people to start knocking on doors and building support.

Creating a Common Line

When we launched the referendum, we were inside a movement ecosystem that had pursued a vast array of tactics. Understanding that many involved in the movement may have been wary of what they perceived as more significant nonprofit involvement and electoral strategy, those involved in the referendum agreed on the following principles of unity, as a way to "show, not tell" how we were thinking about our shared assignments. This was both for the people involved in the referendum itself as well as for our orientation toward the broader movement:

Principles of Unity

- We are united in our shared purpose to Stop Cop City.
- No public shit-talking each other (don't let the enemy divide us). If you have an issue, go to that person directly and get support from others if needed; turn up on the state, not each other.
- Our word is our bond. Do what you say you're going to do or let us know if you cannot.
- Short-term hustle for long-term gain. We want to emerge stronger.
- **No cop city anywhere is the line we are holding.** We don't want to negotiate this facility going to any community.
- We want to have fun and we seriously want to win, so let's do both!
- We need all hands on deck and we want to center local organizing (especially base-building work), while getting national support.
- We will take money as long as it doesn't compromise our politics, strategy, or principles, and we will use that funding to advance the referendum campaign.
- We are directly accountable to each other as individuals, the local Atlanta movement community, and Black and brown and working-class communities that are directly impacted by Cop City.
- Be willing to be transformed in the service of the work.

Our call for direct democracy invited and welcomed many new-comers to the movement who saw a place for themselves in the fight over Cop City for the first time. The petition signers included a broad range of people—from the wealthy Buckhead area to the disinvested West End neighborhood—who in the past hadn't given much thought to Cop City. The more we spoke to people about what it means for the people to decide what gets built with their tax dollars, the more they, whether opposed to Cop City or not, agreed that we should be able to vote on whether the facility gets built.

↓

Black Queer Feminisms was a centerpiece ideological framework for many of us who led this phase of the work, which was not always articulated publicly but demonstrated in our actions. We set out to build a referendum campaign that understood that it wasn't just about Cop City or the election. We understood that all the issues were connected and our task was to ensure we helped to thread the needle for others to see it. We were mindful of how we organized volunteers and who went to what places in the city. When it was time to hire canvassers, we made sure that working-class Black folks had access to the opportunity

As a multiracial coalition, it was critical that we reached *all* parts of Atlanta, especially predominantly Black areas that received less attention in previous iterations of the struggle. We set up field offices on both the West Side and East Side of Atlanta, ensuring that we would reach as many of our people as possible. We did our best to know our audience while holding the tension of what it meant to engage this tactic in a rapidly gentrifying city once known as the Black Mecca. We refused to concede any ground that would make us abandon our abolitionist vision.

Our campaign's diversity was palpable. It was normal to come to one of the campaign offices and see one or some of our children.

Many organizers who were anchoring the work were also juggling young children, so we ensured childcare for internal and external gatherings. Organizations that hadn't worked together in years united for a common cause—spanning electoral, base-building, disability, radical grassroots, faith-based, youth, environmental, racial justice, socialist, migrant justice, student, abolitionist, and queer liberation organizations. These organizations committed staff time, rearranged their work plans, sent members to volunteer, contributed money, set up their own paid canvasses, helped create the financial infrastructure, and shared lessons and tips from previous struggles. Organizations whose bases were located in metro Atlanta sent "ravens" through their deeply connected networks to ensure taxi drivers would sign. National organizations contributed to phone and text banks, endorsed statements, shared their communications staff, sent lunch, amplified our messages, directed funders to us, and let us borrow money when commitments fell through.

We also recognized that a good campaign invites unlikely allies to join. We saw libertarians stand with us, young people who had written off electoral strategies participated in the signature gathering, and even a handful of police officers signed our petition. Although more escalated direct actions continued to occur throughout the summer, there was an informal understanding that referendum-specific events would stay as low-risk as possible. Folks understood the need to build broad-based support, especially with working-class Black people in Atlanta, some of whom had been convinced by the mayor, legacy media, and elites' propaganda that the movement was mostly driven by "outside agitators."

In contrast to the approach of some other formal and nonprofit-driven coalitions, we were clear from the beginning that we would support a diversity of tactics. We held the line when the media tried to demonize one tactic over the other, and, when misguided community members believed the hype, we defended the forest defenders, applauding them for their courage and demanding respect be put on their names. We vocally endorsed the June 2023 Week of Action and joined our comrades at jail vigils when activists were arrested. We denounced, and continue to denounce, the state's heinous repression of Stop Cop City organizers and the Georgia attorney general's use of the RICO case to advance his own political ambitions.

We also remained vigilant in connecting the Stop Cop City struggle to other issues that comrades were organizing around, including the Palestinian freedom struggle, affordable housing, bail reform, jail deaths, closing the city jail, and ongoing police violence. When police murdered Deacon Johnny Hollman, we held a press conference in one of the campaign offices and stood with his family, donated meals, and supported Deacon Hollman's funeral costs.[9] As comrades were indicted under RICO charges and labeled domestic terrorists, we mobilized to support rallies and showed up to court proceedings. Although we were fighting to put Cop City on the ballot, we were clear that the struggle was much larger than any vote.

Fig. 5. Artwork created by the Cop City Vote referendum campaign. (Photo courtesy of Josh Yoder, Look Loud.)

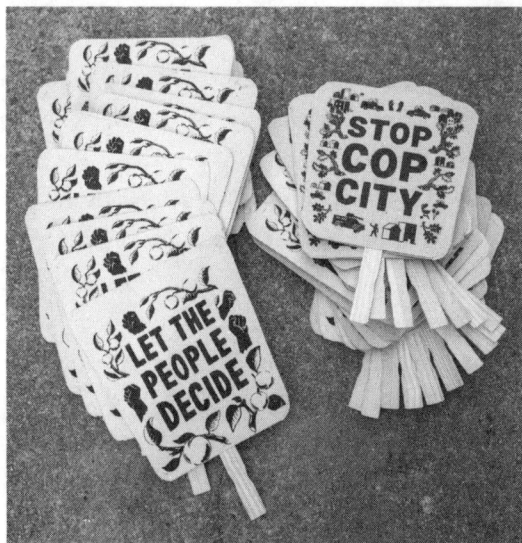

Fig. 6. Signs created by the Cop City Vote referendum campaign. (Photo courtesy of Josh Yoder, Look Loud.)

A People's Victory

The sweet smell of victory was in the air when we turned in our petitions in early September 2023. All in all, we collected over 116,000 signatures—double what we needed to get on the ballot.[10] On that morning, a united front of organizations and individuals gathered at City Hall not just to turn in our many boxes of signatures, but to deliberately make a spectacle and show our numbers. We arranged the delivery as a fire brigade that went through the lobby, up the stairs, and into the municipal clerk's office. We wore the faded T-shirts we'd sported all summer, symbolizing our shared work. Folks brought their #CopCityVote clipboards, demonstrating the weapon we wielded. We chanted and filled the streets and walls of city hall with our excitement, exhaustion, and political will. Those who weren't holding boxes held banners declaring "Let the People Decide"! During the City Council meeting that afternoon, the podium was ignited by the speeches and messages of appreciation that were shared over the mic. Outside of the police and city officials, there was not a single person there who didn't feel like this victory was theirs. The solidarity was beautiful, demonstrating one of the principles that has been consistent across the movement. In that moment, we understood that this campaign was one part of a much larger movement and fight to advance abolition.

The State Hits Back

Despite the feeling of victory, the fight was far from over. The city would fight tooth and nail to prevent the referendum from moving forward—as it had since the beginning of the campaign.

Initially, the city clerk didn't even accept the petition we filed in early June 2023; it wasn't until we filed a lawsuit that we successfully forced the city's hand. The shenanigans didn't stop there. Early in our canvassing days, City Councilmember Dustin Hillis was encouraging constituents to call the police on canvassers if they didn't want us in their neighborhoods.[11] Police frequently kicked petition collectors off public sidewalks. One canvasser was followed and taped—and we ultimately learned that the person following our canvasser was from a group that played a significant role in getting Mayor Dickens elected.

Although we initially won our federal lawsuit to allow anyone to collect referendum signatures, the city appealed the decision, spending millions of dollars in legal fees on a court battle against the referendum that is still ongoing as we write this. Because of this, the city has refused to begin the verification process. As of March 2024, the referendum is in limbo as we wait for a higher court to rule on whether or not it should move forward.[12] Of course, the city is not *forced* to litigate this issue—in fact, the City Council could choose to directly put the issue on the ballot themselves, rather than go through any petition verification process.

Instead, after we turned in our petitions, the city chose a different path altogether. First, the Municipal Clerk's Office published unredacted copies of the petitions online—effectively doxxing Atlanta residents by revealing every petition signer's name, address, and phone number.[13] This not only has a chilling effect for anyone considering initiating (or signing) a future referendum, but is a direct threat and act of state intimidation toward all signers, as Stop Cop City organizers already regularly receive threats and harassment.

Even after we successfully pressured high-level officials including Stacey Abrams, Jon Ossoff, and Raphael Warnock to call for a direct vote on Cop City, and prominent figures like Bernice King (MLK's daughter) did the same, the City Council refused to put the issue on the ballot.[14] After we worked with Marc Elias, a prominent attorney associated with the Democratic Party, to craft legislation that would begin the petition verification process, the City Council refused to pass it (under extreme pressure from the mayor). Instead, in February 2024, the council amended the proposed legislation to include a "signature matching" method to verify signatures—the same type of procedure that Democrats regularly denounce as anti-democratic and ableist.[15] Across the country, Republicans are attempting to gut direct democracy efforts, and in Atlanta, local elected Democrats are doing the same

Onward

Although the referendum fight goes on, we were clear with each other from the beginning that whether or not we won the referendum, our goal was always bigger. In eighty days we mobilized over ninety organizational partners and raised close to $2 million. A total of 1,500 volunteers and five hundred paid canvassers gathered 116,000 signatures while injecting a radical left political vision and analysis into the mainstream. We had thousands of conversations with Atlanta residents about Cop City. We wove together movement forces for deeper collaboration, building new partnerships and alliances. Along with those who continued to work on different fronts, we helped keep the Stop Cop City struggle alive. We were not and are not perfect, though we've learned many lessons along the way.

The impact of our collective efforts will be felt across this city for years to come. No city official has ever received 116,000 votes. Already, organizers are standing up campaign slates to oust city councilmembers and the mayor in preparation for the 2025 election. As Genocide Joe campaigns in the primary election, some organizers have used the relationships and infrastructure we built to run a #LeaveItBlank campaign in Georgia to show our dissent. As we write this, organizations are preparing to converge in late spring of 2024 to build a national campaign against the sixty-nine proposed Cop City sites across the country.[16] So much is possible and so much is needed, but our struggle is protracted and our focus is undeterred. The people will decide the future of this city.

Mary Hooks is a Black, lesbian, feminist, abolitionist, pan-Africanist mother and wife. She is a member of Southerners On New Ground and part of the leadership of the Movement for Black Lives. Her people are migrants of the Great Migration, factory workers, church folks, Black women, hustlers and addicts, dykes, studs, femmes, queens, and all people fighting for the liberation of oppressed people. Hooks has been at the forefront of fights to abolish money bail, defund police, reimagine public safety, and develop new organizers.

Kate Shapiro was raised in and still makes her home in Atlanta with her toddler. Having served in a variety of organizations including Southerners On New Ground, Women's March, and ReFrame, she brings eighteen years of experience in grassroots organizing, campaign development, training, program development, and strategy. She is at her best supporting ordinary people to build teams and schemes that cultivate humor, courage, and vision.

SEVENTEEN

Children Have Always Been at the Center

Rukia Rogers, interviewed by Nolan Huber-Rhoades

The following interview took place in October 2023 with Rukia Rogers, an educator and the founder of the Highlander School, a preschool in East Atlanta Village that is part of the Weelaunee Coalition network. It has been edited for clarity.

Nolan Huber-Rhoades (NHR): As an abolitionist, with all of the talk that we do about imagination, I've always struggled to imagine multigenerational movements that get children involved. Why was involving children important to you? How were you able to get children involved in the Stop Cop City movement?

Rukia Rogers (RR): Children have always been at the center. For example, when we think about the genocide of Indigenous folks, about what's happening in Gaza—to erase their culture, and their memory is to erase the child. The child holds incredible power in their communities. They are the leader; to our ancestors, to their parents, they are our future. So we always want to know what they are thinking. What is their perspective?

We're not thinking of children in economic terms, as workers. We're cultivating a community where they're able to show up for each other and have empathy, which they naturally do. And to act on behalf of each other. I can recall a time when teachers and families were discussing the many ways that our ancestors have come to this country and how our dominant culture tends to celebrate European immigration while demonizing the movement of others. A grandparent shared their story of coming to this country because of the war in Vietnam. Their grandchild brought a picture of their thinking about war, and some found a connection to what they were seeing and hearing on the news. "Yeah, like the kids at the border and Donald Trump doesn't want to let them in." We were surprised by their knowledge of what was happening and immediate response. One child said, "That's not fair. I'm going to tell Donald Trump you can't come to my birthday party." That was the power she had and she was going to exert. We have actually so much to learn from children about how to be informal, and a lot of that is taught out of them in capitalism.

NHR: When I walked into the Highlander School today, I saw all these ribbons tied onto the fence. We're here on Dia de los Muertos, and I noticed that the children had been doing something in solidarity with Palestinian children. What's the activity that the students are participating in today specifically?

RR: We celebrate Dia de los Muertos every year. On the altar we put images of those who've been harmed or killed by the state, like Breonna Taylor or George Floyd. This year we wanted to honor the lives of those children violently killed, buried under rubble, so we invited folks to put a ribbon to represent each child. We've only been able to put about four hundred, though the number is vastly more. We offered flowers, water, and music. Not every child there understood the depths of what's going on, and they shouldn't. But we can never say that a child is too young to participate. We as a community continue to honor people who have been harmed by the state as *part of our* community. We will bear witness. We will teach children that we can have these brave conversations, so that they have the resolve. There are people who say you shouldn't be having these conversations with young children, and we disagree. If there are children in the world that can experience violence, then we can certainly start to have conversations with children, in community, about that. We've often raised children, especially in America, with an inability to experience discomfort, or sadness, and so it was important for us to do that.

NHR: Grief is treated as something to be avoided, something to protect our kids from. But what I'm hearing you say is, actually, it's a part of being human. To be able to learn that in a safe environment is going to do you a lot better for life.

RR: We can really learn from children how to feel all the feels. I often see adults or parents—anytime a child cries or experiences discomfort, they want to immediately stop it. What I often say to parents or caregivers is that for those people in our community who are imperiled, unhoused, we can at least create a culture where children are aware that other people are impacted by their decisions, what our governments do, what our communities are doing. They will have the agency to make different choices.

NHR: You mentioned learning from children and the importance of equitable exchange between generations. What have you learned from children in this movement?

RR: Children have a much more expansive understanding of community. When you ask them who is part of their family, they may describe their mother or their father, but when you ask them, "Who is the garden for?" they say the snakes, the cats, the people who don't have housing—it is for everybody.

I remember one year the children interviewed everyone in the neighborhood—the firefighter, the librarian, the barista—and one of the children stopped us and said we didn't interview the tree. It had never occurred to us to consider the tree as part of our community. Now, every time we plant a tree, we ask, "How should we welcome them?" The kids say, "I would give them my lovey!" You know how children are about their particular lovey?! It was the willingness to give toys, sing songs. Children help us to recognize that the trees are our relatives. There's a deep kinship; if those children had *not* had that kinship with the earth, I don't think cutting down the trees in the Weelaunee Forest would have been such a shock to them.

In order for us to cooperate with these capitalists, we have to disconnect ourselves from nature and see nature as something to be commodified. Because how could you harm your relatives in their way? How could you do this to the land if you felt her as your mother?

Children never throw away anyone. They will fight, they will have an argument. They'll come back, and they'll work it out. Even if someone has really hurt them. If the trees are our relatives, then so are the men and women who are incarcerated in prisons. *We* discard people, *we* throw them away, but if you truly saw people as part of your community, how could you discard them?

NHR: We can actually learn from kids, very practically, how to be abolitionists, right? Highlander is one school in a coalition of multiple schools. Can you talk about that coalition and your role in the movement to stop Cop City?

RR: When we first entered the movement, we started with taking walks in the Weelaunee Forest, led by some of the forest defenders. We'd put down seeds for pollinators, we'd help with the garden. Then we supported the Mvskoke Summit, which included the return of our Mvskoke brothers and sisters from Oklahoma.

The children asked, "Well, why did they leave?" And there was this dance with how much to tell. We started having developmentally appropriate conversations about the displacement of the

Mvskoke people, why they were removed. We showed them a map and explained that they went to Oklahoma. Prepping for the summit, the children created books and gifts for each one of the speakers returning as a kind of welcome home. Our schools talk about them and see them in the past, but they are very much in the present, still and again fighting for land, earth, and water, and we wanted that very present in our curriculum.

As the city's plans for the forest moved forward, we shared with the children that the trees would be cut down. They just couldn't believe it, and they said, "Do the people know? We have to tell them." We asked them how we can communicate it, and the children said, "We can make signs. We can shout it." And so, our first rally in May 2022 came directly from the children, who wanted to shout it in the streets.

We started talking with people from other parts of the movement who had more knowledge and experience with organizing, and it also shifted us from not only thinking about trees but also thinking deeply about the human impact and history of that land, from the displacement of the Mvskoke to the Prison Farm. And so, we helped children connect that to their mural of Breonna Taylor and George Floyd.

At that moment, a lot of forest defenders were experiencing a lot of repression. They had been holding it down for a very long time and felt they could not be visible for their own security and protection. So we made a decision to be the above-facing space for the movement, that part of our role in the movement was to be visible, giving our names, giving interviews, and being visible as parents and educators, because the narrative at that point was that these were wild anarchists from out of town. It was and is important to us that people are not isolated; this is not something that ten or fifteen people should bear.

After the first rally, we got together to formalize who we are, what we want to be, and we decided to continue to be this intergenerational collective of folks and amplify the voices of children and families. We continued to have multiple rallies after that and to hold spaces with food and festivities; that part of our resistance is also joy.

A big turning point for us was when the DeKalb County commissioners closed the park in March 2023. That hurt, because we've not been able to take the children to the park in the same way. So we said okay, let's take the children to the city. We requested a meeting with the mayor—he turned it down—so that became us taking letters from the children to City Hall and speaking to City Council.

For some people within our coalition, that wasn't their ideal strategy. I think it's a hard thing, though, to tell children that no one's going to listen to you, that it doesn't matter. We committed to being with them for the process. We went; educators spoke about the trips to the forest and asked that it be reopened. There were children from the Morgan Oliver School who spoke. Children wrote letters and walked around the hallways passing them out.

NHR: I remember watching at least ten different kids walking around City Hall with a stack of letters, and asking every City Hall employee that they could find, "Have you seen the mayor?" It was a beautiful experience. You would see the employees receive it and be like, "Oh, that's so sweet." Then they would read it, and their expression immediately changed.

RR: We had one negative response from a sheriff who told the child and the teacher, "This is terrible. We do good things for the city." And the teacher was a little nervous about that. This was a person with guns telling the child this was "terrible." But most of the people who received the letters were receptive. The kids felt that if we keep going, if we keep telling people, there will be change. The sad part of an education is that you don't always tell children the end story. Like, "I don't think they're going to listen." They had belief in their own voice, and we believed in being with them for that journey.

The whole community went back to City Hall two more times in the spring of 2023. The children dressed up like trees and read poems and stories. A lot of the City Council were not interested—they had already made their decision.

The coalition has decided at this point not to go back to the city. We felt at this point it was just so disheartening for the children to walk through those spaces and feel ignored, to have the mayor turn down a request to meet with them.

NHR: After the kids had started developing these relationships with the trees at the Cop City site, over eighty acres of trees were cut down. I know that you took at least one child over, just to the entrance. Will you tell us about what happened?

RR: Children throughout the school continue to make gifts for the forest. They wanted to bake a cake and put a turtle on top.[1] They made this beautiful cake and put flowers and everything on it. One child, her mother, and I delivered it just outside. We had gone to the forest many times even before, in between the monthly walks we would take. But this time, as we delivered the cake, the child was very shy, very quiet, pointing towards the barricades. Out loud, she said, "I want to go to the forest." I said, "You can't go," and she said even louder, "I want to go to the forest," to the point of yelling to try to go in. It reminded us of their connection to this space where they had planted trees—pear trees, the fig trees. There was a garden, the rich games they played . . .

NHR: I do find it interesting that the county wanted to close the park. The way that they justified closing it to the public was by saying, well, there will be traps in there that the forest defenders had set and therefore this place is not safe for pets and children.

RR: I believe it was a strategy. We put up a flyer on March 20th inviting children and families to take a walk in the forest with us, and two days before the walk, DeKalb County issued an executive order closing the park specifically because it was unsafe for children. They use the safety of children even to justify incredible things. Like removing books from libraries: Children are quite capable of hearing a story about someone who is transgender and quite capable of navigating lots of brave conversations. But none of us can navigate a world without a sustainable environment, housing, food, and freedom of our own bodies.

Rukia Monique Rogers has worked with young children and their families for over thirty years, including as a preschool and toddler teacher, a studio teacher, and a curriculum coordinator. Rukia holds a bachelor of science in education from Georgia State University, with an endorsement in special education, as well as an associate in early childhood education from Chattahoochee Technical College. In 2013, she founded the Highlander School, a nature-centered preschool program committed to anti-racist and anti-bias work in Atlanta. Rukia believes that education rooted in liberation creates connections between this envisioned world and our daily work and practices as early childhood educators.

Nolan Huber-Rhoades (they/he) is an Emmy Award–winning filmmaker, video journalist, and PhD candidate. Their work combines a passion for storytelling with a commitment to abolitionist futures. Currently, Nolan is the video news producer at Atlanta Community Press Collective, where they orchestrate immersive local news stories with an abolitionist lens. Nolan is co-director of the feature documentary *A City in the Forest*, which delves into the Stop Cop City movement.

EIGHTEEN

Dear Andre Dickens, Save Weelaunee

In spring 2022, children of the Weelaunee Coalition wrote and sent letters to Mayor Andre Dickens after learning about the threat of Cop City to the Weelaunee Forest. They also created art and poetry, including the poem "Save Weelaunee," which was read aloud at an April 2023 City Council meeting.[1]

Letter to Andre Dickens by Emelia B.

Dear Andre Dickens,

My name is Emelia, I am 8 years old, and I go to the Morgan Oliver School. I want to tell you how I feel about tearing down the trees, because the forest gives us vegetables, a home for animals, and shade. Now heres the other part, is as a black man you should know that black people have been traditionally removed from green spaces. Also Muskogee people have been removed from this land too. So make better choices, it's wrong to take away thing that produces air, it's just wrong. So you want to be a hero or a villain? It's up to you.

Sincerely, Emelia

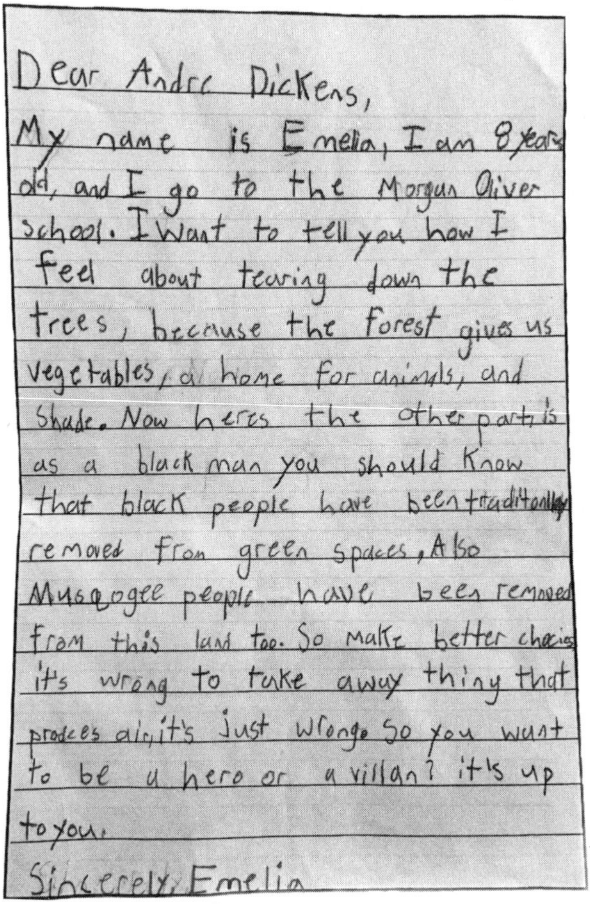

Fig. 7. Letter to Andre Dickens, by Emelia B. (Photo courtesy of Sasha Von Hanna.)

Letter to Andre Dickens by Violet

Dear mayr wat is rong with you! I am so mad. Stop cuting down the trees. Wy are you doing this By Violet.

Fig. 8. Letter to Andre Dickens, by Violet. (Photo courtesy of Sasha Von Hanna.)

Save Weelaunee

By Violet and Mama (Sasha Von Hanna)

There is a magical forest.
It has magic swirling all around.
With plants and mushrooms to learn about
animals, bugs and discoveries abound.

The police don't like this forest.
They want more power.
They want to make us cower.
Said, no more playing here, so we can clear
the trees and pioneer a city of fear.

Friends of the Forest said "No!"
They came in droves.
We gathered, played and planted.
Some friends even made the Forest their home.

This made the police angry.
They attacked the Forest time and time again.
Then a loved one was killed
Manuel "Tortuguita" Paez Teran.

We've occupied, called in, and marched.
Wrote letters and shouted in the streets,
"Don't don't don't cut down the trees."
Mayor Dickens listen to what we really need.

Solidarity and awareness growing.
More friends coming and going
to defend the Atlanta Forest.
No Cop City here or anywhere!
Please Save Weelaunee!

Emelia B. is 11 years old and likes to write stories. She went to the Morgan Oliver School where they helped her become the person she is today. She has a mom, a dad, a little brother, and a bonus parent in her life, all of whom she loves. She loves to eat food and play with her dolls. She is a nice person and loves school. She likes to talk to her friends and laugh. Emily is a person who has her life planned out. She is going to go to Howard University for Engineering, and would also like to become a writer. Emelia hopes her message can inspire you to fight for what's right for all people. Keep this question in mind: do you want to be a hero or a villain?

Violet, they/them, wrote this letter when they were six. Now an eight-year-old self-proclaimed forest defender, Violet lives on unceded Mvskoke Creek land, known as Atlanta, with their parents, two dogs, three snails, and a frog. Violet enjoys swinging, reading, playing with their friends, and thinks there should be more playgrounds for kids, not more cops.

Sasha Von Hanna, she/they, is a multiracial mother and artist, creating, unschooling, and loving on unceded Mvskoke Creek land, six miles from Weelaunee River and Forest. Sasha is a founding member of the Weelaunee Coalition. To see the *Kids of Weelaunee* zine and an illustrated *Save Weelaunee*, go to the Library at TheMissVon.com.

PART 3

ViVA,
ViVA
TORTUGUiTA!

NINETEEN

Little Turtle's War

David Peisner

This piece was originally published by the Bitter Southerner, *two days after the murder of Tortuguita in January 2023. We have left it mostly unedited, to preserve the moment in time that it captures.*

I didn't know Manuel Terán as Manuel Terán. To me, Manuel was Tortuguita. Like pretty much all the forest defenders I met while reporting on the protest movement that has emerged in opposition to the city's plan to build a police training facility in a forest in South Atlanta, Terán went by a forest name in order to maintain anonymity. At one point, Terán—who preferred they/them pronouns but was not particularly concerned when an early draft of my story, "The Forest for the Trees," failed to use "them"—wanted me to refer to them in the story as "[Redacted]," mostly, it seemed, because they thought it was funny.[1]

But "Tortuguita," as Terán explained the first time we met, was not just a cute name chosen at random. Spanish for "Little Turtle," it was a nod to the colonial-era Indigenous military commander of the same name who led Native American forces to one of their most decisive victories against the then-nascent US Army in 1791 near the Wabash River in what is present-day Ohio. Terán was reluctant to publicize this backstory because, as they told me, "That does not make us look like peaceful protesters. We are very peaceful people, I promise."

Terán was shot and killed on the morning of January 18, 2023, in what law enforcement officials described as a firefight during which a Georgia state trooper also sustained a gunshot wound to the abdomen. As of January 19, the trooper is in stable condition. According to Georgia Bureau of Investigation Director Michael Register, Terán, who was 26, opened fire "without warning" at law enforcement officers and was then shot in self-defense.

In the weeks after my initial story was posted in mid-December 2022, the situation in the South River Forest deteriorated markedly. There were massive raids by law enforcement in mid-December that attempted to clear all of the forest defenders off the land in Intrenchment Creek Park and across the creek, on the site where the city intends to build the training facility for police and firefighters. The police reportedly used tear gas, pepper balls, and rubber bullets to help dislodge activists from tree-sits. I visited the forest immediately after these raids, and the encampments had been trashed, structures built by forest defenders had been dismantled, and a community garden had been trampled. Most of the activists had fled the forest, though several were arrested on a host of charges, including, most controversially, domestic terrorism. When I was walking through the forest, I saw a few masked forest defenders who'd surreptitiously returned to the site, but the community they'd built over the previous year was largely in shambles.

In the weeks that followed, construction vehicles tore up the concrete bike and walking path that wove through Intrenchment Creek Park, bulldozed the parking lot, destroyed the gazebo, and pulled down a number of trees. Through all the tumult, there were continued efforts by the activists to return to the forest, and a series of escalating confrontations with law enforcement, up to and including the one that took Terán's life and injured the state trooper.

At the moment, I have no real information about the series of events that morning that led to Terán's death. It is certainly possible that it happened exactly as law enforcement has described it, though it's worth noting that in past killings by police officers—including that of George Floyd—the initial narratives provided by officials have proved to be erroneous. Some may point to the origin of Terán's forest name as evidence of their violent intent, and I suppose that that could be true, but it would not square with the person I got to know over the past six months.

Of the forty or so forest defenders I met and spoke with during my reporting, I probably spent more time talking to Terán than anyone else. I did so not because they were a great source, but because they were great company: curious, engaging, earnest, educated, self-aware, well-read, and very funny. They loved to talk, to connect, to debate, and did so joyfully and passionately, without malice.

Terán had first come to the forest months before we met. "I fell in love with the woods and I also fell in love with the community." The first time we spoke, they admitted that they mostly agreed to talk to me because it was raining and there wasn't much else to do. "I was bored," Terán said with a shrug. We talked about politics, about community building, about books, about music, about the environment, about education, about kids. Terán also spoke passionately and repeatedly about the moral and strategic virtues of nonviolent resistance.

"The right kind of resistance is peaceful, because that's where we win," they told me. "We're not going to beat them at violence. They're very, very good at violence. We're not. We win through nonviolence. That's really the only way we can win. We don't want more people to die. We don't want Atlanta to turn into a war zone."

I've been thinking a lot about Terán's commitment to nonviolence today. Law enforcement and other critics of the forest defenders have continually labeled the movement as "violent," pointing to multiple acts of arson and property destruction as evidence. There were also incidences of throwing rocks, bottles, and—on one occasion—two largely ineffective Molotov cocktails in the direction of police. Forest defenders will point out that their movement is autonomous and decentralized, meaning that no one is giving orders or laying down rules, so there is no collective responsibility for any individual's actions. That may be true on a theoretical basis, but in reality few people outside of the forest defenders and their ardent supporters are making that distinction. That said, until the incident that killed Terán and wounded the trooper, none of the so-called violent acts committed by the forest defenders led to any real injuries that I'm aware of. Some may consider property destruction in and of itself to be violent, but there's been a real blurring of the lines between that looser definition of violence and the one that is aimed at actual people.

Is it possible that Terán was lying to me about their allegiance to peaceful protest? Could they just have been telling me what they thought I wanted to hear or what would look good in print? Of course, that could be true. Is it possible that in the time since we had those conversations—time during which Terán witnessed the increasing destruction of the forest—they'd been radicalized and changed their mind about violence? Sure, that's also a possibility. But I personally saw no evidence of it.

"I'm not an adrenaline junkie," they told me. "I don't crave conflict. I'm out here because I love the forest. I love living in the woods. Being a forest hobo is pretty chill. Some folks probably have flashpoint moments where it's like, 'Oh, yes, the truck is being lit on fire!' But not me. I love it when everything is calm."

Terán struck me as a strategic thinker, and everything they told me about the utility of violence in this scenario remains true to this day. The forest defenders are not going to be successful trying to match the state's capacity for violence. They simply aren't. So if, in fact, the law enforcement narrative is true and Terán shot at police first, I find it troubling on so many levels, but I can only understand it as either a nihilistic act of desperation, or some sort of misguided effort to sacrifice themself on the altar of the cause. We'd spoken about how the optics of a protester's death could be fatally damaging for those who want the police training center built. As I wrote in the original story, "An activist protesting police violence being killed by police is pretty on the nose."

In a lot of ways, the shooting feels like it was the inevitable climax of an escalating confrontation. But it wasn't. This really did not need to happen. There were so many opportunities for de-escalation that weren't taken, so many ways this could have been avoided. During my reporting of this story, I had multiple conversations with people on all sides of this debate about the danger of something like this happening. No one wanted it. Yet here we are. Two people have been shot. One of them is dead. And that's a tragedy.

On some level, Terán knew the risks they were taking and was smart enough to be frightened. "Am I scared of the state?" they said. "Pretty silly not to be. I'm a brown person. I might be killed by the police for existing in certain spaces." To cope with that fear, Terán leaned on a quote from Frank Herbert's Dune: "Fear is the mind-killer." "That's a quote I think about often. I am scared, but you can't let the fear stop you from doing things, from living, from existing, from resisting."

It's hard not to read those words with a dark, fatalistic hue now, but when they were said, the weather was warmer, the mood was lighter, and these deadly serious questions felt largely academic. Now they're not.

So what happens next? There will hopefully be a thorough investigation. More information about what happened down in the forest will come out. But what does this mean for the police training center, for Intrenchment Creek Park, for the larger vision of the South River Forest? In one conversation we had while sitting in the gazebo several months ago, Terán gamed out hypothetical scenarios that feel downright prophetic in retrospect.

"They could come in and completely destroy the place, raze it, arrest everybody that they find, kill anybody who resists arrest—they could do that, and then days later, there would be a shitload of people back here. For every head they cut off, there would be more who would come back to avenge the arrested, to avenge the . . ." Terán stopped before finishing that last thought and started again. "What

I'm saying is, if they do a huge crackdown and completely try to crush the movement, they'll succeed at hurting some people, they'll succeed at destroying some infrastructure, but they're not going to succeed at stopping the movement. That's just going to strengthen the movement. It will draw a lot of attention to the movement. If enough people decide to do this with nonviolent action, you can overwhelm the infrastructure [of the state]. That's something they fear more than violence in the streets. Because violence in the streets, they'll win. They have the guns for it. We don't."

The Native American leader Little Turtle who inspired Terán's pseudonym lived long enough to die of old age at his son-in-law's house. Tortuguita didn't get that chance, and even though I only knew them for a short time, even though I never even knew their real name, that makes me sad. It's a fucking cliché to say that someone died fighting for something they believed in, but Terán certainly did that even if I'd rather it hadn't happened. As an eco-anarchist and a hardcore abolitionist, they knew the scope of the fight they'd taken on.

"The abolitionist mission isn't done until every prison is empty," Terán told me. "When there are no more cops, when the land has been given back, that's when it's over." I must've shaken my head a little at the grandiosity of this statement because Terán immediately broke into a sheepish smile. "I don't expect to live to see that day, necessarily. I mean, hope so. But I smoke."

....

David Peisner is a freelance journalist based in Decatur, Georgia, who writes about pop culture, politics, music, film, technology, and foreign affairs. His work has appeared in the *New York Times*, *Rolling Stone*, *New York Magazine*, *Bloomberg Businessweek*, *Fast Company*, *Atlanta Magazine*, the *Atlanta Journal-Constitution*, and the *Bitter Southerner*. He is the author of *Homey Don't Play That!: The Story of In Living Color and the Black Comedy Revolution*.

TWENTY

Statements by
Tortuguita's Parents

Tortuguita's parents, Belkis Terán and Joel Esteban Paez, delivered the following statements at a press conference in February 2023 after the release of a preliminary autopsy showing that Tortuguita was shot at least thirteen times by Georgia State Troopers.

Belkis Terán

My name is Belkis Terán. I am the mother of Manuel Esteban Paez Terán, for whom we are here. The name of Manuel comes from Emanuel, and means "God with us." Esteban means "victorious." Manuel was born in Maracaibo, Venezuela, on April 23, 1996, therefore Manuel was Venezuelan, Maracucho. Manuel graduated magna cum laude from Florida State University with a bachelor of science, psychology, with an associate's degree in sociology. They began their studies in Panama in an integrated program of two years in Panama and two years in Florida. While in Panama, their participation in the university led them to be an adjunct student of the biology professor, and they taught when the professor asked them to. They also founded and were president of the environmental club that is still operating. They cleaned beaches every week and gave talks to raise awareness about the need to care for beaches and parks. Manuel was very active in recycling, and participated in many activities in the park on weekends with programs for children, adults, and the elderly.

We are horrified by all that has happened to Manuel. I never thought that taking care of a park would be so dangerous. There are many hidden things, and killing a person who was sleeping in a forest does not make sense to me. We are living a horror. It is a social shame that these things happen. For me, this unfortunate event shows the decomposition that this society has. On the other hand, as a family we are also amazed and grateful for so much love, support, and solidarity that we have received.

Manuel worked actively for many years in projects that benefited different communities. During their time as a university student, they developed their organizational capacity for different humanitarian causes. They touched the lives of many people, believers and non-believers, lucky and unlucky, hopeful and hopeless, happy and sad. My complaint is that the university teaches young people to think about the good of others, to dream of a better world, to seek alternatives to old problems, and when they try to put these teachings into practice they are killed, arrested, and treated like criminals. By those who should protect them. Most of these activists are university students.

All Manuel wanted to do was protect a forest, preserve the good of a land for all people, create awareness, and help organize different communities. They had no malice and no intention of committing illegal acts. They were a pacifist and had no intention of resorting to violence as a way of defending themself. Manuel was a defender of the forest. Manuel had a heart full of love for people, animals, and the trees. Manuel had a great interest in helping the disenfranchised, the voiceless. Manuel cared and loved groups of people who are rejected for being different.

All human beings were important to them. They were worthy of love, consideration, and solidarity. Manuel tried to solve and mitigate people's pain by meeting that person's needs. Manuel worked with social networks to create awareness campaigns asking for financial support for others, and always made sure that the donations would reach those who needed them. Manuel worked day and night for the good of others. They were very respectful, with good manners, very intellectual, critical, they read a lot, but Manuel's main concern was the forest. Manuel suffered a lot when a tree was cut down. They were very sorry when there was destruction in the forest.

When they planned an activity in the forest, Manuel felt peace, Manuel felt love, Manuel felt the presence of God. They were happy in the forest. We are asking as a family that those who loved Manuel and those who feel touched by their example plant a tree and take care of it. Plant a tree in memory of Manuel.

Joel Esteban Paez

I want to begin with the biblical greeting: Grace and Peace from Lord Almighty, Creator of the Universe and His Son Jesus Christ my Lord.

It's not easy to be in front of you today after physically losing a child and special human being, Manuel Paez Terán. We are heartbroken by the dark circumstances under which their life was taken from us.

I pray for the full recovery of the officer we were told was shot on the same dark morning. I pray for all individuals unjustly accused of "terrorism" who, like my child, want to preserve and protect just a piece of the forest perfectly created by God.

Since Manuel was a child, I remember their natural ability to make friends in just a few minutes. Manuel also was a young person who worried about others, especially those who were indigent, homeless, and in need of care. Manuel was the one who would stop in the middle of the street to give a hundred dollars to a needy person, take care of the homeless, help rebuild the homes destroyed during

Florida storms, and build gardens. They fondly loved their mother and siblings. Manuel was so worried for the whole of humanity.

From my point of view, they needed to get a "formal" job, settle down, have a family . . . have a life. They were always respectful of my point of view, and I respected theirs. At times we would agree to disagree. Manuel was always honest with their ideals.

A couple of years ago, while talking about what I thought their future should be I told them, "Manuel you cannot worry about the whole world! No puedes abarcar todo el mundo!" You need to concentrate on one thing at a time! You are not Greta Thunberg!"

I was so wrong! Manuel was able to reach the whole world! Manuel was the first environmentalist that has given their life for their ideals in United States of America. Manuel was able to accomplish so much, they were able to do so many things in their short life guided by their ideals, love, passion, and determination.

The Bible says in Romans, Chapter 8, that the creation is suffering of childbirth pain, the creation is anxious for the redemption of the Lord. Manuel was suffering the same distress as the creation. They cried when a tree was torn down. Manuel was happy looking at how a recent planted tree was little by little growing, like a parent happy to see how their children are growing.

We are certain that Manuel will live forever with all of us, and all those around the world that are meeting them since January 18. Manuel left us a legacy. I will repeat what Manuel's mother suggested: If you care about their legacy, in any part of the USA or the world that you are listening to this message, PLEASE plant a tree in memory of Manuel Esteban Paez Terán.

I end now by saying to my child in heaven: Manuel, I SEE YOU!

TWENTY-ONE

In Their Own Words

The following are excerpts from a journal allegedly belonging to Tortuguita, published here with permission from Tortuguita's family. Even after killing Tortuguita, the state is still trying to criminalize them and the movement they cared about: In November 2023, the state sought to enter the journal into evidence to support its theory that the Defend the Atlanta Forest movement is a criminal enterprise.[1] The journal contains poetry, ideas for memes, personal reflections, meeting notes, illustrations, draft speeches, to-do lists, brainstorms for zines, plans for fruit, vegetable, flower, and medicinal gardens, and more. We have tried to faithfully transcribe the words as written. More tributes are available at https://stopcop.city/memories-of-tort.

Untitled Entry (no date)

Water pressure affects water but it does not change it. Water becomes more forceful under pressure, it can crush and cut. You don't know how water presses down until you have been under it, the deeper you go the greater the pressure. It weighs down with quantity. The individual drops of water do not weigh much, billions of drops crush shit. Water as a person is calm and goes with the pressure, it becomes stronger but it does not change. Water fills its container, it can expand and contract. Be a body of water, not a molecule. What a body of water is . . .

Why ACAB (no date)

All cops are bastards because they enforce unjust laws by choice. Individual LEOs [law enforcement officers] may be upstanding and fair people at heart, but their compliance with the judicial system makes them bastards. By definition, bastardization means that someone or something has made another thing impure or corrupt. ACAB because they are not meant to protect people, they protect property and property owning entities. Police officers do not prevent crime, they show up afterwards and sometimes dole out punishment. Strong communities prevent crime. Access to opportunities prevents crime. People who are connected to their communities prevent crime. Simply put, cops terrorize marginalized groups to protect the interests of the rich. They only care about property. We cannot allow them to subjugate us! The system is corrupt.

Ideas for Praxis (no date)

- Painting over signs that say things we don't agree with
- Getting people involved in planning decentralized protests around town
- Wheatpasting on [government] buildings w/ propaganda
- Tagging overpasses & bridges w/ propaganda
- Literature drops & canvassing [apartment] complexes
- Performance art in public spaces
- Pop up traffic blocks w/ propaganda
- Destruction of city property & [property] vandalism
- Sabotaging police equipment & vehicles
- Kettling the cops & setting traps w/ paint
- Strategic nonviolence
- Recon: keep tabs on police activity
- Evade arrest by any means necessary

- Do not engage in alternative praxis alone
- Move swiftly, leave no trail
- Always act in bloc
- Have money for bail and emergency expenses
- Neutralize threats promptly
- Only kill fascists if they try to kill you!
- Escalate only to the level you are [prepared] for
- Radicalize everyone
- Shoot racists

Revolution, 5/12/21

If you want revolution plant a garden
feed your friends and strangers too
grow your power to resist
before any shots are fired, show love
fight fire with water
violence is only part of the answer
being a revolutionary takes a toll
we must pay our tolls so that we can build
build a better society for our descendants
fight the police and their power
chip away at the monolith
abolish the prison in your mind
kill the cop in your heart
remember that you were once a fool
teach everyone what you can
be gentle in your resistance
be tenacious as hell
revolt, resist, rebuild
renew your faith in a better world
be free

be loving and humble
and chip away at the power they built
the first holes to its foundation will
Serve as space for high explosives
chip away then blow it up
We must fight
with love and compassion
and immortal resolve
peace will come with justice and freedom

A Poem under a Tree, 5/10/21

I feel such joy sitting here
doing nothing other than existing
enjoying my time
time goes away and never returns
I sit smiling like an idiot at the bees
they are so precious and must be protected
I love bees, they remind me of all that is possible
We can go camping and forget the obligations and debts and coer-
cion that subjugates us into hating our lives and wanting to be
maybe dead or just done with all this
the beauty of a lover's touch should be free and so should everything else one needs to live
The gentle reminder that everything dies and returns to cosmic
dust, makes me think about how precious each moment is, each
atom of eternity. The vastness of it all amazes me, comforts me
and leaves me grateful for the awesome greatness of our universe of earth.
Earth, without art would be nothing of interest
For me the little things make life worth living
Chop wood water plants rest and repeat

Chop wood, carry water
So it goes

Living Revolutionarily, 6/8/21

for me it's dropping out of the workforce, living in the informal economy and mutual aid hotspots. It's treating people with kindness and respect but not taking any shit. It is refusing to have a boss and being a boss. It is decolonizing your mind and bedroom, and not in a racial way, but in a structural one. If we want to dismantle the patriarchy, we must start at home. To kill power we must be willing to let it die. Power meaning domination—not the ability to do things or whatever power is in physics. The control one person has over another—that needs to go away. Influence will not go away, but power—especially coercive power—must. But we must also live to fight another day, revolution is a slow process until it's not. Take care of yourself and others first—then fight.

On Loving Freely, 8/3/21

My love flows from me like a waterfall
It falls and hits the rocks with force
It froths and splashes and gets everywhere
My love is beautiful and free
It is older than me
Younger than the universe
I do not know where it came from or where it will go tomorrow
All i know is that it is free
It exists in the space between moments and atoms and the lips of my
        lovers and it is intense and lights up my skies
It drips from my brow effortlessly

Swallows my fears and pains and rage
It begs for peace and places to stay
I give it all that I can, tired and worn out moments make it stronger
I love it and do not fear for it to go far away from my present moment
Time does not hurt
Love does not die
What is hate to love's power?

Class War, 8/20/21

What do you call it when the sick can't get the medicine they need
    without becoming slaves?
Class war
What do you call it when the rent is due?
Class war
What do you call it when the few have bunkers and the many have
    only debt?
Class war
When the bosses steal with impunity?
Class war
When extrajudicial killings abound?
Class war
When there's food going to waste while people starve?
Class war
When suicide over imaginary currency is tempting
Class war
When they make us sick to sell us drugs
Class war
When you must sell your blood to live?
Class war
When they own us all?
Class war

When all hope seems lost?
Class war
We must kill them before they win.

On Praxis, 2/1/21

I regret nothing done in good praxis
I am not worried about consequences

If The Cops Kill Me, 12/18/2021

If the cops kill me I want you to riot
Burn down their stations and set their cars alight
Know that I went out fighting and wish we all could just have peace
and be free
I want nothing but a better world, for the environmental crisis to be
mitigated.
To protect the water, to free the oppressed, the palestinians of the
world—and feed everyone.
We cannot have peace until this empire falls.
Even then, peace takes work and freedom is a constant struggle. If
the cops kill me I want you to riot, to kill as many of them as
you can.
They are terrorists, all they do is keep us subjugated. They serve and
protect capital, Not people
The cops are evil and do not protect people—they are slavers. I
think they should all quit their jobs or die. I would love to live a
long and peaceful life but I do not fear violence.
All their propaganda and bribery and intimidation can't save them
from moral outrage. I am not a violent person but I will not tolerate evil. Cops are known to be rapists and domestic abusers

and even if a cop is neither it's still weird to want to be a police officer like gross wtf.

Being Ready to Die, 12/26/2021

It is radical and reckless and not very smart to be ready to die at any moment. It takes a lot of practice to have your shit together and you don't need to have your shit together to be ready to die at any moment—for a cause, or not. I have lived a life that I don't regret. I have had so much fun and been oh so lucky. Blessed, and unstressed for a lot of it. The stress is, or has been, kinda good for my development—at least for making me a little more ready to do whatever I need to do. To be ready to die is to affirm having a good life and no attachment. I do not know when I will die and that does not bother me. fuck the police and the government and all those damn fools that uphold these systems that fuck us all over and destroy the planet. Gotta get those gains so you can knock the fucking cops out if they try to grab you. Burn down the prisons and kill all the prison guards and their backers and owners and stockholders.

Forest Antifa! 12/15/2022

Editor's note: This is the last entry in the journal, written after the December 2022 raid of the forest. It was roughly one month before police murdered Tortuguita.

Yesterday the fash [fascists] destroyed our camp, the day before that they kidnapped 5-6 comrades, and a very good dog. Those bastards. The state which calls us terrorists is fascist. They call us terrorists for trying to defend the forest, for sitting in trees to prevent them from being felled. Our beautiful camp was smashed by a bobcat. My friends jailed. The garden razed. The cafe obliterated. Ryan Millsap still wants to steal the public park. Who knows what comes next. I know the struggle is not over—fuck the naysayers—fuck all those who believe that the state will triumph. Our resistance cannot be stopped. Momma didn't raise a coward—fear will not stop me. Fear cannot be allowed to stop us. There are more of us than them. We are poor but our strength lies in solidarity—something they know nothing about or maybe they do, when one of their buddies beats their spouse. When they rape and rob and terrorize targeted communities. Fuck 12, I hope every judge, KKKop, and bootlicker dies painfully and is remembered as scum. Death to all who stand in the way of liberation for all oppressed people.

PART 4

REPRESSION

TWENTY-TWO

How Georgia Indicted a Movement

Zohra Ahmed and Elizabeth Taxel

On September 5, 2023, Georgia indicted a social movement, formally charging sixty-one people associated with the Stop Cop City movement under Georgia's Racketeer Influenced and Corrupt Organizations (RICO) statute. RICO gives the state vast power to prosecute large groups of individuals by alleging they form a criminal enterprise, no matter how loosely associated they may be, and even if no one violated any other law. The Georgia attorney general's indictment, in its scope and explicitness, is astonishingly honest in its ambitions to crush Georgia's left.

Despite the air of repression, on the day after the indictment was announced, five organizers and clergy members chained themselves to construction equipment at the Cop City site. In the name of a "people's injunction," they handed out bright orange notices, ordering the workers to stop building Cop City. Police arrested the protesters, who now face criminal charges.[1] The activists' determination, courage, and wit are hallmarks of the movement to stop Cop City and defend the Atlanta forest—but the campaign faces a vicious criminal punishment system.

When Georgia's Republican attorney general, Chris Carr, announced the indictment, Atlanta's Democratic leadership, the majority of whom support the construction of Cop City, remained silent. Both the prosecutions and the training facility have bipartisan support in a state that is otherwise deeply divided. And it's not just Cop City. Rather than engage in meaningful efforts to confront the violence endemic to US policing, Georgia's political leadership sees mass criminalization and a fortified police force as the best solutions for many of the challenges facing the city and state.

In the last few years, Georgia's legislature has increased the sentences for a range of criminal offenses—from gang-related charges to drag racing. The progress Atlanta made in cash-bail reform has not only been reversed, but has been replaced by mandatory cash bail for a growing list of offenses, including petty misdemeanors.[2] In 2017, Georgia passed a domestic terrorism statute, which lists "damage to critical infrastructure" as an act of terror. The attorney general first used it against forty-two Stop Cop City protesters in 2022.[3] In 2023, Georgia's domestic terrorism statute was broadened even further, expanding the definition of "critical infrastructure" to include property damage to "any vital public service."[4] To further cement its support for Cop City, the legislature also amended Georgia's tax code in 2022 to provide massive tax incentives for both individuals and corporations who donate to police foundations.[5]

Meanwhile, anticipating Carr's charges and city officials' indifference, community activists announced their own indictment in the form of "The People's RICO"—a sharp, if dark, parody of the coordinated effort by Democrats, Republicans, law enforcement, City Council, prosecutors, and private equity to ensure the construction of Cop City. The People's RICO concludes, "After an extensive investigation, we've determined that there is an active criminal enterprise with clear intentions to extort and conspire to destroy our treasured South River Forest."[6]

With the RICO indictment, the Stop Cop City movement and its members face a struggle for their lives. The accused could face up to two decades in prison. The legal complexity inherent to RICO prosecutions will likely take years to unfold in the Fulton County court system, which is already in crisis: In the local jail, a record number of people died in 2023.[7] Protesters are facing two layers of repression: these extraordinary charges and the quotidian deadly machinations of criminal court.

An Attack on Solidarity

The indictment is an escalation in the criminal process, but it is also an escalation politically, presenting a sweeping condemnation of mutual aid, bail funds, anarchism, community care, and basic acts of protest. In its trainings, the Prosecuting Attorneys' Council of Georgia encourages Georgia prosecutors to capitalize on the breadth of RICO's charges and the tactical advantages that they convey.[8] Given the statute's broad scope, prosecutors often turn to RICO to pursue convictions in otherwise weak cases. RICO indictments often begin with a lengthy introduction that tells the story behind the criminal enterprise the prosecutor claims to have discovered. These openings tend to invite exaggerations and generalizations. Even so, Carr's 109-page indictment is unlike any we have seen.

In its attempt to characterize the Defend the Atlanta Forest as a criminal enterprise, the indictment describes common human practices, but from the vantage of someone who cannot understand why anyone would help anyone else. To the attorney general, writing a letter to someone who is incarcerated and coming together to offer material support when the government fails to help are markers of criminality. The indictment homes in on "mutual aid" as "a term popularized by anarchists to describe individuals who exchange goods and services to assist other individuals in society without government intervention." By declaring mutual aid criminal, the state embarrasses even the most paranoid among us.

The attorney general tries to diminish the efforts of one group of defendants, the staff of the Atlanta Solidarity Fund (ASF), who formed a community bail fund to pay the bonds of individuals arrested for protest-related activity. While framing ASF staff as criminal masterminds behind a non-existent criminal enterprise, the indictment perversely suggests that bailing out protesters—not overzealous prosecutors and punitive judges—contributes to mass incarceration by neglecting to bail out all indigent defendants.

In its rewriting of history, the indictment also dates the inception of the "Defend the Atlanta Forest Movement" to the "high-profile" killing of George Floyd in May 2020—nearly a year before Cop City was even publicly announced. Alleging that a criminal enterprise was born out of the 2020 racial justice protests makes clear the state's political motivations: The attorney general is charging an entire movement and accusing Black Lives Matter of being a criminal conspiracy.

Georgia's RICO law requires that a person actually do something—sometimes referred to as the "overt act" requirement—to be convicted under RICO. Much of what the prosecution argues are the "overt acts" that further a "RICO conspiracy" are banal. Eighty-eight of the 225 acts involve small money transfers, 45 reference anonymous blog posts and information sharing, and 12 concern "trespassing" on the campgrounds in the Weelaunee Forest. Buying camping tarps and signing one's name as "ACAB" are the kinds of acts that hold together the prosecutor's charges. Several people are accused of being part of a group, or a "mob" that was "designed to overwhelm the police" at a widely attended musical festival. The attorney general apparently believes that mere presence is enough to show membership in a criminal conspiracy, as long as the person is progressive.

The indictment is a document of profound alienation from community, neighborhood, and friendship. It describes ordinary forms of political community, like offering emotional support to a fellow activist, as seditious, conspiratorial acts that threaten the state. This is a prosecution designed to crush an empowered and self-reliant left in Georgia, which has become too powerful to tolerate.

On the one hand, all of this points to the weaknesses of the attorney general's case. With little evidence of a criminal venture, the attorney general could not produce a coherent criminal indictment. Only one page of the document charges specific people with specific crimes like property destruction. The remainder of the indictment lists more familiar but no less disturbing criminal charges, such as the fifteen counts of money laundering against members of the nonprofit ASF. Each count represents relatively petty money transfers, such as an $11.91 transfer from the 501(c)(3) to an individual for glue. These are allegations that even a DeKalb County magistrate judge described as "not impressive" and "lacking in meat" at the bail fund members' first appearance hearing.[9]

But while the case is flimsy, the indictment and ongoing prosecutions set a dangerous precedent. Attorney General Carr makes no attempt to distinguish protected political speech from unprotected property damage, despite clear legislative intent to exclude "isolated incidents of misdemeanor conduct or acts of civil disobedience" from RICO.[10] Even groups whose members may engage in unlawful activity are entitled to First Amendment protection. But constitutional relief may arrive too late.

Take the protesters charged in April 2023 with felony intimidation of an officer in Bartow County, Georgia, for distributing flyers naming the police officer who killed Manuel "Tortuguita" Terán. If the First Amendment doesn't protect the flyering of publicly available information, it doesn't cover anything. Despite clear Georgia Supreme Court precedent that unquestionably invalidates these protesters' charges, they were each jailed in solitary confinement and initially denied bond. One protester spent three months in jail, because the judge took into account the allegation that she received a reimbursement from the Atlanta Solidarity Fund for art supplies.[11] In the indictment, flyer distribution is listed as an overt racketeering act. Although constitutional challenges will undoubtedly follow, substantial harm has already been done.

This indictment comes out of secret proceedings—the grand jury. In Georgia, there is no court reporter recording the testimony and evidence that the state presents. Without a transcript, it is impossible to discover prosecutorial misconduct. And when evidence of prosecutorial conduct is found, courts consistently shield prosecutors from accountability for violating the law and their ethical responsibilities. When accountability exists, the Georgia legislature has reserved it for prosecutors who dare to offer modest critiques of mass incarceration, not ones like Carr.[12]

A Vast, Fraying Net

These RICO charges widen an already vast net for criminal liability, because Carr has pursued the most capacious theory of liability under RICO: conspiracy. Rather than requiring the state to prove that a person committed every element of a specific crime beyond a reasonable doubt, the state merely has to show that there is an agreement between at least two people to commit a crime and that one of the persons has done something, anything, to advance this agreement. The agreement can be tacit—proven by indirect or circumstantial evidence. The law only requires one person to take a concrete step (an overt act) to fulfill that agreement. The other person can do nothing and be held criminally responsible for acts committed by other people, so long as the state convinces the jury that this person is part of the group that had an agreement to carry out some sort of criminal scheme.

Carr conspicuously chose to file his sprawling RICO indictment in Fulton County—a county plagued with criminal case backlogs, a failing indigent defense system, and a notorious jail. In his 2023 State of the Judiciary, Georgia Supreme Court Justice Michael Boggs cited Fulton County as having one of the largest criminal case backlogs in the country, with more than eighteen thousand open felony cases.[13] Despite receiving $5.5 million in CARES Act funding to address a backlog previously attributed to COVID, Fani Willis—the Fulton

County DA who indicted Donald Trump and his cronies for trying to overturn the 2020 presidential election—channels much of her resources into high-profile, complex RICO indictments such as the case against Young Stoner Life (YSL) Records.[14] She first rose to notoriety for using the same statute to prosecute mostly Black women educators in the so-called Atlanta Public Schools cheating scandal.[15] She boasts about prosecuting "more RICO indictments in the last 18–30 months than the city has seen in decades."[16] Now, Carr's RICO prosecutions will overwhelm an already overwhelmed system.

This tangle of sixty-one defendants, some with multiple charges, will harm thousands of others hauled into criminal court in Fulton County who face more ordinary but no less consequential charges. In Judge Kimberly Adams's courtroom, where the Stop Cop City cases are being heard, incarcerated individuals are waiting anywhere from 20 to 130 days for a bond hearing. At the time of Carr's indictment, one person waiting for a bond hearing had been detained pretrial for 762 days.[17] Each of the twenty Fulton County superior court judges is estimated to preside over fourteen hundred cases per year. When one case consumes the time and resources of an entire courtroom, thousands of individuals experience oppressive case delays. The attorney general's decision to include sixty-one people in a single indictment will potentially break an already stretched thin public-defense system.

Carr's choice to charge RICO in a sloppy and specious indictment will result in complicated, expensive, logistically challenging, time-consuming litigation. The protesters will experience a persistent truth about criminal courts: The process is the punishment. Despite an array of defense motions attacking the substance and constitutionality of the indictment Carr filed last November, as of March 2024, no hearings on any of these motions have been scheduled. The ongoing YSL trial offers a preview of the roadblocks ahead. The parties spent ten months picking a jury. The trial is expected to last over a year.[18] One court-appointed lawyer moved to withdraw from representation because the state pays too little for such a time-consuming, complex case.[19] Few jurors will be able to survive on the $25 per day stipend the court offers, raising the risk of defections or truncated deliberations.

Even as this case drags on, Atlanta and Georgia police are pursuing new charges. As acts of sabotage against Cop City machinery and contractors continue, the Atlanta Police Department announced its purchase of 450 billboards across the country advertising a $200,000 reward for information leading to arrests of alleged arsonists.[20] In February 2024, police conducted a SWAT raid of residential homes in East Atlanta, charging one individual with arson. As of this writing, it is unclear whether Carr will add new arrestees to the RICO indictment.[21]

As the state continues to escalate its repression, Stop Cop City protesters face a hostile legal terrain and institutions that are collapsing under their own oppressive weight. But this new front of repression also creates opportunities for creative resistance. These cases offer the chance for deepening solidarity between protesters as they navigate their prosecutions, but perhaps more importantly with other criminalized Atlantans. Highlighting the connections between these political trials and more run-of-the-mill prosecutions against Atlanta's low-income communities can help underscore the case against Cop City, and more generally against policing, prosecution, and incarceration. This is precisely the kind of solidarity that terrifies the attorney general and Atlanta's political leadership.

A version of this piece was originally published in The Nation *in September 2023.*

Zohra Ahmed is a law professor and former public defender.

Elizabeth Taxel is an assistant clinical law professor at the University of Georgia and directs the school's Criminal Defense Practicum. She was previously a public defender in DeKalb County, Georgia.

TWENTY-THREE

Thirty-One Days in DeKalb County Hell

Priscilla Grim

"One day closer to home." Those words were etched on the wall above the bunk bed in cell 212 at the DeKalb County Jail. They were the first thing I saw when I woke up between 3 and 5 a.m. for the first food delivery of the day. They were also the last thing I saw around 10 p.m. as I meditated on all who had laid in the bunk before me. I would eventually force myself to sleep by covering my face with a blanket to shield my eyes from the omnipresent lights.

I was taken to jail after being arrested—in an arrest that felt more like a kidnapping—at a music festival in the Weelaunee Forest in March 2023 and charged with bogus domestic terrorism charges. Later that year, I would be indicted on RICO charges along with sixty others. Each of us now faces political prosecutions by the State of Georgia, not because of anything we did but because of the state's incessant drive to build Cop City.

I had come to Atlanta in March 2023 to camp among the swaying pines of the Weelaunee Forest in solidarity with the people of Atlanta. I answered the call to help Stop Cop City. If two days of public testimony to the Atlanta City Council overwhelmingly rejecting the Cop City proposal did not stop the project, perhaps my joining the camp would show those in power that a different future is desired by all. I came to Atlanta because, as a New Yorker, I did not want the NYPD to have a policing playground in which they would be indoctrinated even further to see the people of NYC as enemy combatants. I came to Atlanta because of the calls demanding that neighboring Black communities be heard in their rejection of the proposed Cop City—and their desire to rename Intrenchment Creek Park to honor Indigenous nations and illuminate the manipulation of city processes by corporate interests. I came to Atlanta because the police assassinated Tortuguita, a forest defender, and tried to cover it up by posting photos online of a standard police-issued handgun "found" on the site.

I came to Atlanta because it's where I was born. I grew up between there and Murfreesboro, Tennessee, in the 1980s. Both sets of my grandparents were from Atlanta. My father's family settled in Avondale Estates in the 1940s, and my grandfather Grim was a lecturer in the School of Mechanical Engineering at Georgia Tech in the '60s and '70s. My mother's parents moved to a house on Diamond Head Circle in Decatur in the '70s, following my mother to her new home and fleeing the unrest of New York City. It was their second new home after they had both left Puerto Rico to escape colonialist violence at the hands of the United States.

My abuelito would insist that my brothers and I wake up at 7 a.m. to climb into his car filled with our towels, snacks, and toys for trips to the now-closed beach at Stone Mountain. Being Puerto Rican, he would always find a beach or beach-type place wherever he landed. While at DeKalb County Jail, I would watch the sunrise over the mountain in the mornings from my narrow cell window and remember Abuelito's smile and hugs. I would remember our trips to the International Food Market and nights of never-ending domino games, even as my thoughts were disrupted by the loud banging of metal doors slammed shut or of people screaming from their cells, desperate for anyone to notice their pain.

Lashawn Thompson, the man revealed to have been eaten alive by insects in Fulton County Jail in September 2022, is not the only one who suffered from torture at the hands of jailers in the Atlanta area.[1] In 2023, at least ten people died in Fulton County Jail, with five deaths in August alone.[2] In July, Noni Battiste-Kosoko, a teenager, was found dead in the Atlanta City Detention Center.[3] Thirty-one days in DeKalb County Jail gave me eyewitness testimony of the torture at the hands of jailers in the Atlanta area. While in my podcage in the women's section of the jail, 4 Southeast, I saw six people locked into cells 24/7 because of their mental health classification, one of whom attempted suicide during my time there. Another did not have running water in her cell, so others used bags they saved from food deliveries, filling them with water and sliding them under her door to stop her from drinking her urine to survive. Another woman found herself on permanent lockdown after she started running around the common area naked. After days of screaming to be let out, she knotted a bed sheet and tried to hang herself. Others watched her through the transparent glass of the door. When our podcage comrades yelled at the guards to come to help her, the guards laughed and slowly strolled over. After they took her to medical, a sergeant arrived and told us that the entire podcage was on lockdown. We were collectively warned not to cause "further trouble."

Instead of our jailers, who chose to lock in and isolate a woman in her cell as "mental health care," it was we who were blamed for her suicide attempt. Half of the people in the podcage witnessed this suicide attempt, and instead of grief counseling, we were locked into cells—most of which had broken toilets and no running water—for four hours following the incident.

When I first arrived at the jail, I only wanted to take a shower and lie down to sleep. My first cellmate, Raja, was, like many in jail, without a home and incarcerated because of complications that happen when you have no home. She had only a few days to go on her nine-day sentence for alleged trespassing, which she was charged with after not waiting to leave a hospital before she was well. She tried to help me acclimate to jail life. I paid attention and attempted to remember all the tips for cleaning and maintaining the cell. The painted cinder block walls reminded me of public school buildings and state university dorm rooms. I wondered if the people who built those structures and these cells were the same.

Screams often erupted from the lower level of the cell rooms.

"She's a 'Twenty-Two,'" Raja told me, explaining that people with extreme mental health challenges are classified as such and locked into their cells 24/7.

"How do they receive medicines or therapy?" I naively asked. Raja shrugged. New screams from the lower level of the podcage reverberated off the walls to inform us that lunch "sacks" of bologna sandwiches had arrived. She remarked that the food arrived early, likely because of the other activists and me. I learned she was right. It was only a short time before we were back to the normal shifts of receiving food just twice a day, every twelve to fourteen hours, depending on the moods and temperaments of the guards on shift.

"The entire block is moving differently 'cuz of y'all," she drawled. Later, the last of my cellmates, Dulce, confessed that when she saw a group of youngish white women arrive in the podcage, she thought that we were all sex workers—but our appearance confused her because we did not seem to be the usual type. One of the women we were in the holding cell with during processing, Divinity, told the others about our domestic terrorism charges. One by one, we started to make friends as we shivered in the podcage, which was kept under 60 degrees at all times.

I was especially sensitive to these temperatures because I am perimenopausal and tend to have a very high body temperature. My time in jail is the first time in five years that I have been actively cold for an extended period of time. I keep my Brooklyn bedroom around 60 degrees all year round to avoid hot flashes. The podcage was much colder, and I shivered to sleep for a week before receiving thermal underwear that I had to purchase through the commissary. Extra blankets were forbidden, so we had to organize our podcage mates to submit grievances about the cold climate, which we did through the jail's third party–monitored grievance system. Even still, I saw guards engage in the sadistic ceremony of violently taking and throwing out more than a few extra blankets.

Friends shared their struggles. The struggles I heard about and experienced convinced me that the State of Georgia does not run county jails—it runs concentration camps that it calls county jails. The last local seat of responsibility for these county jails seems to be the elected "Chief Executive Officer" of the state's counties. All of our grievances are connected to the strange and cruel corporate structures found in the elected offices of the United States of America.

Our new comrades had no idea that the rate of local incarceration was lower in other major cities or that serving two days to a week in jail because of a traffic violation is unheard of in places like NYC. The other activists and I spoke about the movement to abolish jails, prisons, and police. We talked about other alternatives both in development and in dreams of replacing this system. We had a lot of time to talk about many things, as we were rarely taken into the outdoor recreation area—an area we could see from the podcage.

In my thirty-one days in DeKalb County Jail, I and the others in our caged community only received three hours total of sunlight and fresh air in the outdoor recreation area. The "inmate handbook," available in a digital kiosk on the wall, stated that we were entitled to five hours a week. Dulce had been incarcerated without a formal charge for over fifteen months. She stated she could count on her hands the hours of sunlight she experienced in jail. During her time there, she was held for seven months in a windowless room in medical solitary confinement because she was pregnant when arrested, could not pay her bond, and had such high blood pressure that the jailers were afraid she would have a stroke, killing both her and her baby in their cage.

During the second week we were caged, our comrade Myla woke with an excruciating toothache. She tried to convince one of us to help her pull it out of her mouth. On further discussion, we all decided it would be better to file as many grievances as possible, see who had Tylenol to share, talk to the guards, and file a medical request. She had to wait three days before the jail's dental team saw her. They put her on Tylenol with Codeine and gave her an appointment with Grady Hospital to pull her tooth. It was supposed to happen in four to six weeks, but when I spoke to Myla weeks later, she still had not had her tooth treated, nor had she been scheduled for treatment. She was still on Tylenol with Codeine, still brushing her teeth constantly to slow the inevitable compacted infection and protect herself from it turning lethally septic.

After I was released from DeKalb, I called frequently to try to locate Myla's public defender and get an order from the court to bring Myla to the hospital for her tooth to be pulled. After a month and a half, all my calls were sent directly to voicemail. It did not matter what time of day I called. I ran out of money to give her for phone calls. She finally got out in November. I am now working on reconnecting with her. I don't know what happened with her tooth.

A new jail will not fix the problems of Atlanta's jails.[4] The people of Atlanta know that a new jail is not the solution because so many have spent time in the Fulton and DeKalb county jails. How will a new building solve the problems of jailers who see detained people as insects? How will a new building solve the problems of people with mental health issues caused by a life of economic crisis? How will a new jail solve the problem of tens of thousands of people being caged for the most minor of infractions?

In 2008, the city of Cincinnati closed down a city jail, the Queensgate Correctional Facility. What happened? A massive drop in arrests and violent crime. Officers with fewer jail beds to fill no longer used arrests as a default response to calls. Misdemeanor arrests dropped by over 30 percent, and felony arrests dropped by over 40 percent. Today, lives have been saved, the community is safer, and crime rates have continued to drop.[5] The jail building has now been renovated to hold small businesses and artist studios.

The only way forward is to close down the jails of Atlanta, stop Cop City, and begin treating the people of Atlanta as if they are members of the beloved community. From NYC to Atlanta, we know that caring for each other—not cruelty, cages, or cop cities—will keep us collectively safe.

A version of this piece was originally published in Scalawag Magazine *in May 2023.*

Priscilla Grim (she/her) is a Brooklyn-based Nuyorican, mom, comrade, and activist. She has written for *Scalawag*, the Atlanta Community Press Collective, *The Indypendent*, and others. She is proudest of her work with the Occupy Wall Street social media teams, the *Occupied Wall Street Journal*, and the *We Are The 99 Percent* Tumblr blog. She enjoys gazing at graffiti, scribbling in notebooks, and dancing with headphones on beaches, in parks, or anywhere with trees and sunshine.

TWENTY-FOUR

Defending the Movement

Lessons in Anti-repression

Marlon Kautz

Early on May 31, 2023, SWAT police surrounded our home. With ballistic shields and assault rifles ready, they woke us by breaking down the front door with a battering ram. At first, I was confused about the purpose of their visit, but when we heard police planning to throw flash-bang grenades into our living room, when they pointed their guns at us, I realized they had arrived prepared to attack and kill us. This was a shock, but not a surprise. Similarly militarized police had been executing raids against activists in the Weelaunee Forest since the previous winter, destroying their belongings, pointing rifles at them, and threatening to shoot. Indeed, they had already murdered a protester. In years past, other homes in my neighborhood had been raided by SWAT: kids' bedrooms flooded with tear gas, Black people in pajamas and handcuffs sitting on the curbs outside. It's what police are trained to do, what they're equipped to do, and in fact what they do regularly. This time it happened to us. It happened to us because of Cop City.

I'm a founding organizer of the Atlanta Solidarity Fund, which responds to the criminalization of political protest by providing bail and legal support to activists who are targeted in raids just like this. Ironically, it was because we aid Cop City protesters who are attacked by the state that I and two fellow organizers found ourselves attacked. We were hauled away in cuffs while our house was ransacked by state investigators. That day, we experienced firsthand how far the police were willing to go to make Cop City happen.

Cop City is not possible in a truly free society. People simply don't want it. Given meaningful control over the priorities of their own society, people reject Cop City and every project like it. The powerful interests behind such a project can only advance it by interfering with public participation in governance, and such interference requires repression. This is a major obstacle for the movement against Cop City, and one which any future movement must prepare for if it intends to challenge the powerful and win.

Repression

Repression is, of course, not the only force preventing people from governing their own society. The most important checks against popular governance are deeply systemic: segregation, economic inequality, patriarchy and white supremacy, the prison-industrial complex. These are the means by which a power elite prevents challenges to injustice from even emerging. A truly free and just society will never exist until these systems are undone. That work is ongoing, and the deeply entrenched nature of these systems means it may take generations before they are finally resolved.

But what about those moments when social movements do emerge? When people together manage to overcome the weight of systemic oppression—even if just temporarily—find common cause, and claim some power? In these periods, ruling institutions risk losing their dominance, and even systemic oppression is not enough to insulate them. They must resort to a more direct intervention, and this is where political repression comes in.

Even before Cop City, Atlanta was no stranger to repression. I've been here long enough to witness countless examples over the years: In 2011, police sought to decisively end the Occupy movement in

Atlanta by making arrests at every protest until people stopped marching. Protesters were targeted for offenses as minor as littering or stepping off the sidewalk. In 2018, police repeatedly attacked demonstrators camped in front of the city jail who were calling for an end to ICE detention there. In 2020, during protests against racist police violence, the city government went so far as to declare a citywide curfew to quell protests. The curfew authorized police to arrest anyone outdoors after 9 p.m. on sight, and was selectively used to arrest Black youth and people who appeared critical of the police. Repression has been a consistent reaction to protest of all kinds.

The movement against Cop City has seen several waves of criminalization. In September 2021, protesters were arrested while holding signs outside a city councilperson's house. Weeks later, a protester was arrested for writing "No Cop City" in chalk on a public sidewalk. These early arrests were a message: Even legal activity that opposes Cop City will make you a police target. Rather than subduing the movement, though, it created more outrage and motivated more people to get involved. Authorities in turn stepped it up: Starting in January 2022, police made repeated arrests at the public park near the Cop City site on allegations of trespassing. By that May, state police had attacked a neighborhood march, mass arresting dozens of protesters, journalists, and bystanders.

When even an increase in arrests didn't quell protests, the authorities escalated by introducing "terrorism" as a talking point and legal strategy. Protesters in December 2022 were arrested indiscriminately and charged with domestic terrorism, a felony carrying a prison sentence of up to thirty-five years. Even though these activists were being held in jail and threatened with life-destroying sentences, protest against Cop City didn't stop, and in fact increased. In January 2023, militarized city and state police raided the forest and killed Tortuguita, accusing them of trying to attack police. Once again, police abuse led to a surge of support and awareness about the movement.

Ultimately, we found ourselves targets of the very abuses we protect others from. As the movement against Cop City grew to include hundreds, then thousands, then (according to opinion polls) half the population of Atlanta, Georgia authorities made a desperate attempt to isolate activists from the legal support we provide: They charged us, three Atlanta Solidarity Fund organizers, with running a fraudulent charity, money laundering, and violating the Georgia RICO Act along with fifty-eight other people. As I write this, we are facing decades in prison if convicted on these baseless charges. In early 2024, the Georgia legislature passed a bill that is designed to outlaw bail funds in the State of Georgia altogether.[1] While even these acts of astonishingly blatant overreach haven't stopped activists from continuing to organize against Cop City, they have made clear that repression is the main force that holds back movements when they're on the verge of success.

Responding to Repression

Despite the veneer of law enforcement, repression is not confined to the rules and boundaries of the legal system. It represents all the direct interventions powerful institutions can take against a social movement to try to break its power. We have seen police try to break the movement against Cop City through illegal mass arrests. We have seen authorities tell lies about activists both in the media and under oath. They have raided homes under false pretenses, manipulated courts to keep innocent activists jailed for months. They have murdered. Many of these acts are, on paper, illegal. They are knowingly directed against innocent people. This shows that for organizers, obeying the law is not a reliable strategy for avoiding repression.

In fact, we have learned that avoiding repression is a fruitless goal in general. Over the past fifteen years, every grassroots movement that has seriously challenged the political establishment has been met with repression. The only movements that have avoided it have been those that failed to get off the ground, or that compromised their organizing to avoid threatening powerful interests. Put another way: A plan to avoid repression is a plan to lose. Movements that intend to win must plan from the beginning to *withstand* repression.

The Atlanta Solidarity Fund begins from this idea. Tired of seeing activists scramble to collect bail money every time police decided to make an arrest, we started a rolling bail fund. This wasn't a new idea, but it's a good one. Money donated into the fund can be used to pay bail immediately, providing direct support to people facing repression. The bail money is eventually returned to the fund, ensuring that funds will also be on hand the next time a protester needs to be bailed out. Planning for the next need before it emerges allows organizers to step out of a cycle of crisis response. Every arrest of an activist no longer requires organizers to stop what they were doing and problem-solve. Movements are thus able to maintain momentum.

Once we realized the impact that a simple intervention around bail could have, we started to notice other ways repression was used to kill the momentum of movements. Most of them are based in creating fear and uncertainty among protesters. For example, most people aren't aware that they can get support if they're arrested at a protest, which makes it intimidating for people to protest even if they aren't targeted. So, we created a hotline that anyone could call to report an arrest, and organized volunteers to widely share flyers with the phone number at events. This allowed people to feel more confidence in exercising their rights, and less uncertain about what might happen if they're arrested.

We noticed that even after getting out of jail, protesters were still burdened with navigating a hostile court system, and afraid of the long-term effects of conviction on bogus charges. So we worked to ensure that protesters have access to attorneys and the resources to fight their charges in court. We noticed that protesters face all sorts of other disruptions to their lives: Being arrested can disrupt someone's employment; court dates come with childcare challenges and transportation expenses; the carceral system strains mental health. We developed programs to address all of these harms. For example, a protester who is traumatized from being violently arrested can get access to therapy through our wellness assistance program. This need might seem minor compared to the crisis of incarceration, but a holistic anti-repression approach calls attention to impacts of the carceral system that would otherwise remain invisible, and shows by example the depth of social solidarity.

We also recognized that although much political repression is anti-social and illegal, the perpetrators generally face no consequence for their actions. Police who brutalize protesters generally go on to receive praise and raises. Prosecutors who target protesters receive promotions. Politicians who condemn protesters in the media receive campaign contributions. We identified cases where protesters' rights have been most clearly violated and helped them bring lawsuits against the officers and departments responsible, winning settlements and policy changes. We started using our platform as a civil liberties organization to highlight misconduct in the media, and to call out lies when police spokespeople try to demonize activists.

Our work is grounded in the specific needs that we see in Atlanta political movements, but we have a relatively long operating history and have seen many different instances of repression over the years. Drawing from that experience, we can offer some advice to those in other contexts who are motivated to prepare for repression, whether fighting a Cop City in their town or waging another struggle.

Lessons in Anti-repression

First: Accept that effective movements will be criminalized— regardless of the tactics used, the tone of the rhetoric, the identity or respectability of the participants. This may seem counterintuitive, because when a movement is young and relatively non-threatening to power, it may experience little to no repression. Additionally, the authorities often try to divide movements internally by directing repression against certain participants but not others. These factors can create an impression that if organizers steer away from confronting power or distance themselves from confrontational participants, it's possible to avoid criminalization. But as long as a movement's power grows, so too will the scope of who is criminalized. Recognizing this makes it possible to frame repression appropriately: There are no "good" or "bad" protesters. Those who are arrested and accused of crimes are not bad actors to be denounced or put at a distance; they are victims of an inevitable process of criminalization. If this process isn't called out up front, it will be used to isolate more and more participants as the movement spreads.

Second: Build the infrastructure that can sustain a movement through repression. Start with the immediate, and then extend the time and scope as far as you can. If a protester gets arrested at a march tomorrow, who will respond and what resources will they need? What if ten organizers are charged with felonies and denied bail for a month? What if every movement-adjacent space in town is raided and shut down? When you take seriously the possibility—even likelihood—that these things will happen in the future, it becomes possible to prepare for them. By preparing, and showing your community that you're prepared, you rob the authorities of some of their power of intimidation.

Finally: Go beyond the goal of resilience—of merely surviving the state's attacks. A system is "anti-fragile" when it reacts to damage by becoming stronger rather than weaker. Many natural systems work this way, and by learning from them we can go beyond a vision of anti-repression as simply harm reduction, as cleaning up the damage caused by an all-powerful oppressive force. We find a great example of anti-fragility in Hong Kong: In 2019, police began picking off pro-independence protesters as they were headed to or from demonstrations. The protesters' response was to start riding the subway together in large numbers, addressing the threat while also expanding their demonstrations into a new space. When police shut down the subway, supporters created a volunteer rideshare service to transport protesters, bringing thousands of new people into the movement as drivers. It is true that the authorities are constantly discovering new ways to attack social movements, but each attack also brings new lessons, opportunities for us to revise and expand our own practices.

Particularly when movements are powerful and effective, the authorities are more willing to take drastic new action, cutting off resources and suppressing tactics that were previously taken for granted. When each new move by the authorities brings a new crisis, it is tempting to fall into an attitude of hopeless tenacity, fighting in a doomed war against an invincible adversary. Drastic attacks may seem to come from a place of power, but when the state deploys new forms of repression against activists, it actually makes itself vulnerable. It's revealing capabilities that it already possessed but had preferred to keep concealed.

Why do the authorities prefer to conceal their repressive capabilities? There are two reasons: First, new repressive tactics are unpopular and offensive to a public that isn't used to them. By using them, authorities risk scandal and rebellion. The use of RICO charges against activists, for example, has triggered national attention and questioning of the legitimacy of the RICO statute itself. The use of military-style raids against eco-activists has prompted international outrage and investigation of Georgia law enforcement. Second, revealing the repression playbook gives anti-repression organizers an opportunity to respond, learn, develop countermeasures, and prepare for the next time. By approaching each new attack as an engine for future growth, we preserve our curiosity and creativity in the face of the state's brutality.

As long as the police state exists, repression is inevitable, but succumbing to it is not. The state is deeply invested in convincing us that whenever it cracks down on rebellion, that's the end of the story. By building infrastructure that anticipates the crackdown, meaningfully protects people from its harms, and grows to be ever more prepared for next time, we can help our communities escape fear and move with hope and determination toward a different world.

Marlon Kautz is a cofounder of the Atlanta Solidarity Fund, Copwatch of East Atlanta, and Food4Life. His organizing work focuses on building infrastructure for popular struggle, with an emphasis on technology, mutual aid, and abolition. Marlon has lived in Atlanta since 2009.

PART 5

NO COP WORLD

TWENTY-FIVE

You Can't Reform a War Away

On Creative Aggression

Craig Gilmore and Ruth Wilson Gilmore

For Barbara Harlow

Craig and Ruthie talked for several hours over a few days about some key themes they have noticed in work around the world. The conversation has been edited for clarity.

Organized Abandonment, Organized Violence

Ruth Wilson Gilmore (RWG): We've talked a lot about how the crisis *of* neoliberalism has produced a variety of outcomes: on the one hand, a rise in fascism and, on the other, enhanced institutional power of the forces of organized violence (especially, although not exclusively, in the United States) to get the resources—money and materials—they demand to do more of what they do.

Craig Gilmore (CG): You and I have often used the work of Toni Negri and Stuart Hall from the seventies, which predicted the increased use of state violence, and policing in particular, as one of the crucial infrastructures of what at that point was not yet called neoliberalism. And it seems to me that one of the things we're seeing now in the crisis since 2008 is that the role of state force—of policing and prisons and borders—is coming increasingly under attack, is in danger of losing legitimacy. Certainly in the US, the coincidence of the 2008 housing crisis, the Obama bailout of the banks while throwing mortgage holders under the bus, and the rise of Black Lives Matter in Ferguson seemed to me to be a single moment, out of which the last twelve or thirteen years have come. And understanding how those things have come together seems essential for understanding what's happening in Atlanta around Cop City and the broader and similar movements around the world.

RWG: I think you have your finger on something urgently important, which is that the rise in the institutional power of the forces of organized violence has not been smooth. It encounters not only resistance but really concerted opposition. That's what we're seeing today in Atlanta with Cop City, and elsewhere. Structural adjustment and austerity have played into the hands of the forces of organized violence. The administrators of those forces have pretty consistently made the argument that they *should* be funded because even if all the welfare institutions of the state are dismantled or privatized, policing and prisons, they say, will be necessary to contain the upheavals that austerity and structural adjustment produce. That insistence on absorbing more resources into repression persists in the context of more and more organized opposition to it.

CG: There's no question that it persists. We've seen surprise and dismay by some people at the level of state repression in Atlanta. The levels of both direct violence and the use of law to incapacitate the movement are certainly not unprecedented in US history, and there are very similar things going on around the world. Nevertheless, it surprised a lot of people in the US to see those levels happening—in the US in 2022–2023 in Atlanta. I can't help but think that the powers that be, the police and their backers in Atlanta, saw what happened around the world in 2020 and have doubled down on this tried-and-true method of getting more funding, promising minor reforms, promising better policing while in fact growing the surveillance and policing state. And I think that a lot of the powers that be in Atlanta and across the US are surprised that it's not working very well.

RWG: Yes. The fact that the plan to enhance and augment policing is not smoothly displacing crises can be traced to many causes. I'll talk about two. One is the "narrative"—the official story about why Atlanta needs Cop City, or why Chicago needs more police, or why the police-state socialists argue for more police. They all tell us that an augmented police presence in urban and rural United States—and beyond—will produce conditions of stability. According to this scheme, police-enabled stability will enable the people most vulnerable to police violence to have access to jobs, move freely around in public transportation, live in apartments, get health care, and so forth. In this policy narrative, policing is the precondition for all other social benefits. It's not surprising to me that in many of the major cities of the United States—though not only there—the people who advocate more police, more police training, more police budget, and so forth are themselves Black or other people of color, and or are themselves women and so on. In other words, many of today's advocates are demographically similar to people who our movements have, rightly, persistently presented as those most likely to suffer from the violence of policing. So we're at a peculiar crossroads, the sort that Greg Meyerson and Michael Roberto described some decades ago as "multicultural fascism." That's one thread.

And the other thread is that, especially in the wake of the 2020 COVID-induced economic meltdown, cities are trying to figure out how to revive their revenue streams in order to pay for policing or whatever else. So, one of the things Cop City proponents present to

Atlantans—and their county and the world—is that the facility will become a training center where police from anywhere will gather to learn "racially sensitive" policing, or whatever they're calling it now. In other words, Cop City will sell training. But, of course, Atlanta's not the only city that is thinking of this sort of economic remedy. I'm reminded of how, thirty or forty years ago, hard-strapped cities pursued sporting arenas, or convention centers, or casinos, or detention centers, or prisons, or jails or other capacities to bring in revenue from outside. They frequently took on debt to do so, convinced by investment bankers the revenue scheme could not fail. Many of them failed! Now, as then, many cities are planning to sell identical services to each other.

CG: One of the things we saw as a result of the 2008 crisis was capital looking for fresh outlets in which it could wait out the crisis and eventually grow. Both urban housing and rural farmland became places where capital invested with the expectation that it would at the very least maintain value and probably go up in value and thus could be turned into profit on an acceptable timeline. And we're seeing this kind of capitalist investment across the United States. We're seeing it with land grabs around the world. The cities that now have Black far-right mayors or police chiefs or both tend to be cities with a huge percentage of their remaining affordable housing in precarious situations. Policing in those cities is clearly a move to protect capital coming in, taking over housing, and flipping it for investors—at least as much for investors as for high-income renters. So, we see in San Francisco and Atlanta and Chicago and New York major policing efforts coming out of the attempt to protect these investments. Those cities have always had substantial rentier capitalist sectors, but to the extent that those sectors have become bigger and more powerful since 2008, we're seeing more police necessary to bring about the gentrification—whether gentry actually move into the housing or not—of neighborhoods.

RWG: We also have to recognize how this kind of capital activity isn't actually a new thing. Nobody's arguing that this started in 2008 or in 1988, but rather it's a regular feature of capitalist crises. The challenge for people who control capital is to ensure that, as you put it earlier, at some point they'll be able to turn the capital they sink into real estate or into land into a usable profit. Thus, policing is in part to control the participation of ordinary people in the use of that land, whether we're talking about housing or agriculture or parks or anything related to land use, land grabbing, and in general the effective control of land.

CG: Additionally, there's the question of who gets to decide how the decisions are made around land use, which we're seeing boldly played out in Atlanta, but not exclusively there. Again, in other places in the US and around the world, the question isn't simply that the powers that be have made the wrong decision or a bad decision or a prejudiced decision with regard to how land might be used. But rather, they're making the decision very forcibly to shut certain people out of the land *and* the process, and in places like Atlanta where people are trying to force their way into the decision-making process, they're being met with increased police force.

RWG: One of the things that you've been thinking about a lot is the prevalence of assassinations as part of organized violence. In every direction we look, state and non-state actors murder people in order to disrupt social movement. Could you talk a little bit about that?

CG: People in the US were shocked at the police killing of Tortuguita in Atlanta. And, I think, more shocked when the official autopsy and police reports came out and it was shown how many times they were shot, etcetera. And I think that the horror around that execution is justified, but the surprise might have been a little naive, because we see that deadly force has a long history of being used in the US, has a long history of being used elsewhere, and it's not exactly fallen out of fashion. It's not like we haven't seen someone killed by the police since Fred Hampton was killed, for example. Recently, we can point to the killing of Portland activist Michael Reinoehl and the relative lack of outrage in the liberal media about that execution. We might start by reviewing some of the people who have been killed, as you say, sometimes by police and military, and sometimes by assassins who seem not to be directly in the employ of the state at all (although they often have some connection to the state or to individuals in the state or to political parties that rule). So, for example, we could talk about Marielle Franco's killing in Brazil. We could talk about Berta Cáceres's killing. We could talk about the assassinations in Durban and elsewhere in South Africa of activists who are leading success-ful attempts to build residences on land in urban areas that, regard-less of who owns it, isn't currently being used for any other purpose. And we could look back on some of the histories of political assassi-nation: Steve Biko, Ken Saro-Wiwa, Rosa Luxemburg, members of the MOVE organization in Philadelphia, Panthers across the United States, Bay Area Earth First! activists Judi Bari and Darryl Cherney's car being bombed. So, what did these assassinations do? In many cases, they remove leadership—however horizontal we might imag-ine we want our political organizations to be, there are in fact key members whose removal leaves a huge hole that can't be easily filled. The assassinations also intimidate other people in the movement. The assassinations take up time as people in the movement, people who worked with the assassinated people, struggle to deal with their own rage and their own grief, and they work to help each other work through that rage and grief. And for better or worse, this often takes away from the organizing that they were doing collectively. Although it ought to be emphasized that in many cases—we're seeing this in Gaza now, it has a long history in South Africa—the funerals of the martyrs often become points of organization and mobilization, helping to publicize the atrocities done by the opposition, and to either recruit more people to the cause or deepen and radicalize the positions of people who were already organized. And I guess the last thing I want to raise, which is something that you've written about before and that we will discuss shortly when we talk about the politics of analysis, is how the assassinations themselves, the executions themselves, and the criminalization we are about to discuss are used by law enforcement, the police, and their allies to further marginalize and discredit not just the people who've been killed and their movements, but more broadly the purpose of the movements they were part of in the first place. And so, if the police kill someone, they must be a "criminal," or if the army executes someone, they must be a "terrorist." The assassination, rather than reflecting badly on those who commit it, is manipulated to destroy the reputation of the organizers and activists among those people who are not yet committed to one side or another. This includes then people who might be mobilized to support our work in a wide and growing variety of ways—by seeing in abolition a clarifying political view of and support for their own already existing activities.

Austerity

CG: We've got a crisis that affects the majority of people in very serious ways, and many people are not seeing a path out of it. The old center-right and the old center-left both seem bankrupt when it comes to offering a vision that—whether it actually will lift people into a comfortable and secure life—declares it will do so. I think that we're seeing in a number of the movements we will touch on in this conversation people who are trying to organize themselves differently, organize relations among themselves differently, in order to provide safety and security for themselves, for their community, for their families, and so on. And it's one of the places I think where what we might call a grassroots need—a very broadly based grassroots need—has met up with twenty years of abolitionist organizing and political education around questions of, What is security, what is safety, what is safety for you and your people? Increasingly, people are rejecting the claim that safety means more police. But more, people are showing that safety means housing, that it means food, that it means looking for ways to organize and reproduce themselves outside a capitalist economy that continues to squeeze them even further. So, as capitalists seem to think they can get away with pushing even more austerity, people are increasingly fed up with the austerity of the last several decades, certainly since 2008.

RWG: That's exactly right, and what's happening, if I'm understanding the point you made, is that people are organizing themselves from the ground up in a variety of ways to deal with the ongoing crises that austerity imposes on them and their households and communities. At the same time, the churn of people and places that austerity produces provides the forces of organized violence an agenda to maintain that churn at the edges, to police it at the edges, to criminalize it at the edges, to come down with the iron fist over and over again. Every edge is also the middle of something or somebody. And it seems important to emphasize one more thing: Although we are having this discussion because of a book about Cop City and resistance to it, we recognize not only that this is a problem people are facing all over the world, but also that it is not only an urban problem; it is rural as well.

CG: Yeah, I'm reminded of a meeting we had last summer with a group of mostly middle-aged, mostly women from Catalonia, most of whom were not from Barcelona. They were from smaller cities and towns. And they have been organizing to provide basic goods and services to migrants and refugees in Catalonia without having had a particular political agenda for the most part. My understanding was that most of the women came into this work as simple, self-organized efforts. And the work that they did brought them to the understanding that, in order to provide the means by which migrants and refugees could live comfortably in Catalonia, the organizers had to take up a more political stance. They didn't come from a political position to the question of borders and refugees; they came from the needs of refugees to a much more expansive and left and abolitionist political position. And I think we have seen across the United States—and we're seeing it in other places in the world—situations in which the provision of very basic needs, or the inability or difficulty of providing very basic needs for people, is politicizing a number of people, and not all of them are moving towards fascism. Some of them are moving in exactly the opposite direction.

RWG: Mm-hmm, and I'd like to underscore here that when we say "providing basic needs," it might sound like what we're talking about is, say, a food pantry with a few cans or bags, or some type of charity. And while we're not *not* talking about that, our conversation with the women in Catalonia made crystal clear that we're talking about people having access to whatever they need to maintain a dignified, healthy life. We had a whole discussion about access to health care for migrants who lack specific paperwork. So that's another example. When we talk about women organizing themselves—"to serve the people," as the Black Panther Party for Self-Defense used to say—they came to the work from a whole lot of starting positions, including organizing as long-distance migrants in Catalonia who simultaneously organize as colonized peoples of Peru. It seemed in the context of our discussion that a lot of the work was the sort of collective self-help that becomes political. Why does it become political? Because people keep noticing the systematic nature of the problems they're having such a hard time solving, and they notice as well the systematic nature of what makes their achievement hard. To speak of papers, then, is to speak of systems: If you don't have certain papers, you can't have health care, or if you don't have certain papers, your child is more likely to be taken from you by the police, etcetera. These contradictions become very apparent to people who are organizing about things that "bite into their existence," as Stuart Hall put it.

We see organized violence expanding its remit in relation to these struggles. That remit shows us very clearly the rise of criminalization as an everyday feature of governance. We'll get back to this later. But now let's continue talking about the far right and liberal anti-fascism.

CG: One thing that the 2008 crisis and relentless spread of austerity has produced is dramatic growth in the far right. In recent years we've noticed a revival of the idea that enhanced policing is a bulwark against it. And again, it's not just Trump and the paramilitaries in the United States—it's all around the world. We're seeing an international far-right movement take power in a lot of places. Could we talk a little bit about how "liberal anti-fascists" seem oblivious to the notion that putting more money into police is in fact *supporting* the growth of fascism in Atlanta and in the United States? I mean, it's as though they know nothing of the current state of relations between the non-state far right and law enforcement in the United States, Germany, and elsewhere. As if they know nothing about the history, say, of the Klan and sheriffs' departments in the United States. As if they know nothing about what's going on in Germany today, where the far right has taken over many police forces and are using police databases to target people on the left. This is happening all over, yet those who profess to be anti-fascists maintain that more police, and the allegedly better and more humane policing that Cop City purports to provide, will fight fascists.

RWG: Well, the logic underlying enhanced policing is to use fascism to fight fascism—and both the liberals and the police-state socialists who support expanded policing ignore the practical fact that ever-aggrandizing institutions of organized violence—that develop relatively autonomous political power—work against social goods. They do so because structurally, the forces of organized violence absorb surplus—the social wage—that should be allocated for general well-being. And then they define—through influence on parties, media, and directly gaining political office—what general social well-being should consist of, for whom, and to what end. This, then, with calm brutality excludes those who have been criminalized by a moving line of legality and shifting definitions of what counts as crime. Rather than harm being reduced, it's compounded and extended.

State Lawfare and Criminalization

CG: It seems worthwhile at this point to talk about state lawfare, criminalization, and violence. One of the things that has marked the reaction to Stop Cop City has been increased and very visible use of both direct violence on protesters—the killing of one person in the forest by the police—and a number of techniques of criminalization and state lawfare which, while not in themselves new or unique, have come together in a new way, recently in US history, in Atlanta to fight the Stop Cop City movement. Although many people in the US, especially many younger activists in this country, might be surprised to see this collection of state repressive techniques in action, individually and collectively, there's a long history in the US and elsewhere of using these techniques together to stop threats to property, to the current regime, to any number of things. For example, the South African apartheid regime, while it was prosecuting members of the African National Congress (including Nelson Mandela) in the Treason Trial, killed sixty-nine grassroots protesters in Sharpeville. Those two forms of state violence often go together, and thinking about the ways that they have been used separately and together in other places might give us a clearer idea of what's being done in Atlanta, and how we might fight it even better. I thought one way we might start, for our readers for whom ideas of "criminalization" and "state lawfare" are new terms, Ruthie, is for you to give short definitions or descriptions of what they are.

RWG: Okay, I'm going to start with "state lawfare" and then move to "criminalization." "Lawfare," and the "state lawfare" variant, has a relatively recent history. In the 1980s, colonial and imperial powers—especially Israel and the United States—condemned the international use of legal challenges and courts as weapons of the weak, with those powers coining the term "lawfare" to designate such activity as, indeed, part of war writ large. We see this with crystal clarity in South Africa's mostly successful petition to the International Court of Justice charging genocide in Gaza. In 2013 Lisa Hajjar coined "state lawfare" to analyze how colonial and imperial powers explain away drone killings and missile killings of thousands of people in Palestine and around the world. Governments write and interpret laws that excuse such killing by elaborately defining targeted persons or places as outside the protection of nation-state or international law, or by defining the killers as outside the jurisdiction of any court. Some people have brought the notion of state lawfare into analyzing domestic forces of organized violence. Domestic state lawfare didn't follow after its international version but rather developed simultaneously. When considering state lawfare, we look at how institutions craft laws to advance repression, on the one hand, and to impede ordinary resistance and opposition, on the other.

This leads us to "criminalization," which is a little more straightforward, I think, than state lawfare, but obviously related to it. Over the past half century in the United States, and over different periods in other places, governments have expanded the scope and detail of laws forbidding certain kinds of activity. Practices that on one day are not criminal *become* criminal because people write laws to change the interpretation of specific behaviors. Criminalization has come to mean, for many of us, the kind of extensive and intensive dragnet of laws that not only prohibit and therefore punish, sometimes with death, certain kinds of activity, but also that change individuals' and communities' relationships with each other and with the state because more and more people come to wear a "criminal" jacket for part or all of their lives. Criminalization means that people cannot go certain places, cannot do many things. It shapes the possibilities of all aspects of ordinary everyday life.

CG: If I'm understanding you, there is some overlap in what is state lawfare and what is criminalization. But not all state lawfare is criminalization. For example, changing laws that allow evictions to happen more easily or changing laws that allow land to be seized more easily doesn't necessarily criminalize the people who are being evicted. And so, it appears not all criminalization is state lawfare. Some criminalization might be undertaken without a clear and direct political goal, which state lawfare always has. State lawfare has an opponent who's being targeted. That's why it's "-fare." That's the "warfare" in lawfare—the opponent. We're seeing things like that happening all around the world, against all sorts of opponents, particularly in the forms of new laws and regulations that target organizers who are threats to what the state or what capital is trying to do, or new or more intensive enforcement of laws and regulations that were already on the books. So, for example, the RICO laws that have been brought against the Atlanta organizers are not new laws. But I think it's surprised a lot of people to see racketeering charges being brought against people who are organizing a bail fund.

RWG: Right. State lawfare does have designated opponents, though they might be defined after the fact. But, I just have to remark that people who were surprised by RICO's usage in Atlanta have not had the opportunity to pay attention to history. That use of racketeering laws is in itself not new.

CG: Right. Dan Berger's written a really good short essay that gives people who don't know that history a great overview of how it's been used against left organizers.

RWG: Exactly. One of the points that you made when we were preparing for this conversation was "lack of confidence in the order of things is part of the order of things." So much of both state lawfare and criminalization lands well with many different kinds of people who lack confidence in the order of things. This lack of confidence sets the conditions for the reproduction and aggrandizement of the forces of organized violence, of capital concentration, and so on. The kinds of criminalizing processes brought to bear on this particular cadre of resisters and organizers, as you were saying, raises many questions—all of which present organizing opportunities—about land use, land seizure, land theft, and so forth (see Laura Harjo or Clyde Woods).

CG: Let's talk a little bit about why not just in Atlanta, but why in South Africa, in France, in the UK, perhaps in Brazil, we're seeing the need, or the perceived need, at least—the actionable need—to increase or innovate these repressive apparatuses. We see increasing resistance to the austerity of neoliberalism, and anti-austerity actions, whether they be people marching in the street or blockading roads as the *gilets jaunes* have done in France, or occupations by the *gilets noirs* in France, whether it's people seizing land to live on or grow food on, whether it's people blocking buses and airplanes to prevent deportations. (Vanessa Thompson's work in this area is exemplary.) We're seeing not only more of that kind of activity, but, likewise, a number of different states—conservative or liberal—freaking out and bringing new forms of repression to bear, including freshly criminalizing behaviors or adding punishment to behaviors that were already crimes, as you pointed out with regard to the history of criminalization in the US. Blocking a road was already against the law, but when you block a road to prevent a detention flight, it's suddenly a more serious offense. And so, it's not as though it's just behavior that's newly criminalized, but rather that the political context in which that behavior takes place is itself criminalized.

RWG: You've raised a number of important points here. The last point, about criminalizing politics, clarifies something we must emphasize. What has been happening in the world, in Atlanta, in South Africa, in the UK, in Brazil, in Indonesia, has not been going in a single direction. It's not as though the global forces of capitalism are merely mowing down everybody that's in their way.

CG: Right.

RWG: Or that the forces of the capitalist state are merely holding up or lifting up the forces of capitalism so capitalists can get what they want. It's not that straightforward. There are always contradictions and there are therefore always dialectical relationships that matter: It's our task to exploit them. So if, in the case of so many places today, states are expanding criminalization, and intensifying punishment for crimes that were already on the books, the question is, why is that? On the one hand, people take action to refuse the shriveled future that austerity offers them. Yet, at the same time, many institutions of the state have either become absorbed by the forces of organized violence or are imitating the forces of organized violence. Policing, military, prisons, and so forth—institutions that have, relatively speaking, tended to do better than welfare institutions of the state— have grown and expanded their remit by gathering resources, getting money, getting equipment. They have also become, ideologically and practically, models for success. Welfare agencies, struggling for adequate resources, present themselves to the political class as policing forces, while at the same time, police absorb welfare functions of the state and present themselves as social workers or health care workers or mental health care workers or tutors.

CG: I thought you were going in a different direction there. Most of the state repression that we observe around the world has come out of the traditional state repressive arms: It's come out of the police, the border patrol, the courts, the prisons, etcetera. So while it's spreading, as you were saying, into other state agencies and non-state agencies, I think for the most part those less traditional repressive apparatuses have played a lesser role—I think. For example, police in the USA killed more people in 2023 than any other year on record, with Albuquerque again the deadliest place. But also, I'm thinking about the ways that in South Africa, for example, the crisis for the state caused by massive occupation of empty land in which people build housing for themselves, or the occupation of empty buildings which people take over for housing, has generated an entirely new arm of law enforcement that does, simply, evictions. There's an eviction police that is separate from the criminal police, and is separate from the border police, and is separate from these other police forces. And in the US, in the UK, in France—certainly going back at least as far as the anti-Communist squads of the middle of the twentieth century and the SWAT teams that started fifty-five years ago—we're seeing more and more specialist squads, or the growth of already existing specialist squads to deal with demonstrations and to deal with evictions, agencies that have specific roles which are hard to define other than "political policing." The laws they're enforcing are criminalization in the most stark sense of the term.

The Politics of Analysis: Toward Creative Aggression

RWG: The ideological and behavioral effect of assassinations is to push away people who otherwise might be at least curious about the movement. It also, I think, frightens people who have been active. Fear dissolves confidence to pursue struggles for many reasons: because they're afraid to die; because they're afraid people they care about will be hurt or killed; because they were surprised to learn that what they believed was necessary for the well-being of the people is bloodily distorted, by those in power, into an enemy of the people. I've been saying a long time that people who use violence to produce and maintain power represent those they kill and fight against as perpetual enemies who must always be fought and can never be conquered. More than thirty years ago, in the context of the 1992 LA Uprising, Mothers Reclaiming Our Children continued organizing to relieve the dreadful weight of criminalization and imprisonment that had fallen on their adult and juvenile loved ones. One day, a Black cop said to one of the Black mothers, "Your loved one would have a better outcome to their case if you stopped running around with communists." A profound crisis flared throughout the organization, as the women worried over such a perfect example of exactly what I mean by "perpetual enemy." In this case, whether or not many of the people in Mothers ROC had been or continued to be members of communist formations, the very suggestion that police violence was really about political economy and class struggle under racial capitalism caused people to stop and ask themselves whether they were doing the right thing. Eventually, a lot of the women embraced enemy status, though from entirely different starting points than party membership. And we find in terrorism and racketeering charges similar patterns that indicate the political and social power of assigning certain categories to people's efforts. In this context, people who have been organizing can feel compelled to wonder if they should continue, or whether it would make more sense to take a less committed and more liberal and reformist path. Here is where lack of confidence in the order of things can result in dramatic swings in how people think they can do politics.

CG: But I'm seeing—and I'm encouraged by this—at least as many people who, in part because they're fed up with austerity, or austerity has made them desperate to a point that they weren't a few years ago, now have far less faith in the patient petition that liberalism offers as the only way forward. You know: Ask and organize quietly, and ask again and organize quietly, and continue meekly wishing and asking for what it is you need to survive day by day. And I'm also seeing—and again, this is in the US, in Brazil, in France, in Portugal, in South Africa, I'm seeing it all around the world—leadership helping people who are more desperate and who are less patient see other ways to move forward politically. That is, helping people to more clearly define their problem, more clearly define what needs to change, and more clearly help them come up with things that they can do in the short run toward those long-term goals. And certainly, we're seeing that in Atlanta. Further, the protests of 2020 made it clear that twenty years of abolitionist political education and organizing in the US had created a broad base of people across the country who had the tools to step into community meetings and make arguments that brought people who had not previously known anything about abolition to abolitionist points of view, whether those positions were called abolitionist or not.

RWG: I think that the direction you're taking our conversation today is really essential, because it is very easy, as we did at the beginning of our conversation, to focus on the broadening repressive effects of certain actions, of certain murders, of certain expressions of the right to rule realized through murder and other forms of violence. The purpose of political analysis is not and cannot be only to more clearly and effectively describe harm. It must also be to show where contradictions enable people to combine their energy to do something else in the world. And certainly the fact that, as I think you said, more and more people around the world, uncowed by criminalization, are moving to make possible their own well-being by building houses or occupying land to start farms, or occupying empty houses to provide themselves not just with shelter, but with a living community, is all really important for us to focus on now. A direct way to say what's happening is this: People are engaged in creative aggression. Having plenty of motive, they are finding means. They are aggressively making something. And that is true whether what they're trying to make are the conditions of possibility to interrupt Cop City, to maintain a park space, and to make vital the possibilities for social reproduction in Atlanta. Or in Brazil, the Landless Workers' Movement (MST), facing both state and non-state violence, occupy land to make a community and grow food for themselves and others in a healthy and environmentally sustainable way, as we learn from Maria Luísa Mendonça. Anybody and everybody engaged in creative aggression uses whatever weapons are available—which sometimes can be things like constitutional provisions, using lawfare to fight—to support that creative aggression reworking social reality to make abolition geography.

War

CG: Let me follow up. When people hear you say "creative aggression," I'm not sure they take "aggression" as literally as I do. But one of the arguments we want to make in this conversation, I believe, is that state lawfare, criminalization, and execution are three tools in the same tool kit. It's not as though there's state lawfare and criminalization, on the one hand, and then occasionally there's a trigger-happy racist policeman who kills somebody, on the other. In the US and elsewhere in the world, execution or assassination goes hand in hand with what are thought of as less violent means of repression. I know that you did a panel on Ori Burton's new book recently, in which you were very taken with the way he recovered the notion of war as a literal state of being from the Black revolutionaries whom he interviewed and whose works he read. I wonder if you could talk a little bit about aggression: Say a little bit more about war and how perhaps more of our comrades need to take a little more seriously the fact that we will be shot at.

RWG: Sure. First of all, Ori Burton's book *Tip of the Spear* is a fantastic study of what Burton calls the "Long Attica Revolt," and he uses "long" to show that there's so much precedent for what eventually erupted in Attica, and that it didn't end then, but has continued into the present. The war he zeros in on is not only a war involving a small group of Black people with a radical idea of what emancipation should be. Rather, the entire history of US Black people who descended from slaves is fundamentally a history of war. Slavery comes from war. It's part of the various extensive and intensive wars that have characterized all of modernity. Burton helps us see how and to what extent battles in these lengthy wars erupt: what pushes them into crisis and then what happens. It's not a metaphor. Mass incarceration and criminalization are class war. Therefore, I intend "creative aggression" to bring a very bright focus on the fact that the struggle for emancipation, the struggle to change social reality is profound, and it's revolutionary. As Burton's prison protagonists learned and warned, this crisis cannot be resolved through merely expanding the social reality a little bit at the edges to let a few more people participate in the world as it currently is.

CG: Which is to say you can't reform a war away.

RWG: You can't reform a war away. Thank you for getting right to the point. This is why we talk. [*Laughter.*] You can't reform a war away. And the second thing I want to say is that the ongoing relations of war that have persisted into the present are relations that crystallize, over and over again, in the context of organized abandonment *and* the organized violence that enables organized abandonment to happen, to be maintained, and to be reproduced. And the third thing is this: War makes many travelers. Here I'm thinking not only of the many people involuntarily displaced from one place to another through imperial and civil and resource wars, including colonialism and enslavement, as well as climate refugees. But also the people who, having been displaced over many years and sometimes many generations, struggle in the context of the current social reality to create freedom, which is always a problem of how to make place and be at home, as Christina Heatherton explains in her book and Shellyne Rodriguez composes in her drawings.

CG: You make me think of other work that's been important to us: the way that Nick Estes and the Red Nation framed the Dakota Access Pipeline fight as part of a 500-plus-year colonial war. That is to say, this was simply the latest battle in an ongoing war. Burton and Estes here seem to be two reference points for thinking about the struggle we're in as a war and the necessity of asking—as you often say to people—"Are you prepared for what you're going to do the day after we win?" And, if I could rephrase it in the current context, it might be the day after we win a battle but have not won the war. They are going to be reorganizing to come back after us; are we thinking about what they're going to do and how we're going to be ready for it, or what our next step is going to be?

Land and the Politics of Use

CG: One of the things that's often remarked upon in the Stop Cop City fight is the way that it has brought organizers who are working on the preservation of the forest—so climate change and ecology, broadly—together with people who are working on police and prisons, in a single fight. And what we want to talk about now are the connections between and precedents for that sort of work, why it's important, and where it might go. Let me start, speaking of pipelines, with a quick story. In the work that you and I started doing in California in the nineties, among our key inspirations and models was the work of the Madres del Este de Los Angeles, who in the 1980s stopped both a prison and a pipeline, as well as an incinerator, from going into East Los Angeles. Their work showed us how to connect, at a very basic grassroots level, questions of criminal justice, policing, and prisons with environmental justice. In large part it inspired the conference that we organized with Rose Braz and others, Joining Forces, in 2001, at which Juana Gutiérrez, the founder of the Madres, was our keynote speaker. Ruthie, I wonder if you want to talk a little bit about the ways you've seen struggles over land use and control coming together with struggles around policing in different parts of the world.

RWG: Yeah, sure. Let me be bold: Everything we struggle over comes down to land use. What processes shift land from a repository for capital storage to the beautiful and fragile means to sustain life? Who can pause where and under what circumstances? Who is kept away and how? The story that you just told about the Madres is a story about land use, about people in an urban area becoming political activists, as Mary Pardo shows. What propelled them into action at the outset was shock about a land-use decision that would have put a prison in their midst. They were motivated by care for children, and that energy expanded their struggles, as you pointed out, over many overlapping and interlocking social challenges, including ones we might recognize more straightforwardly as environmental challenges. If we think about land use, lots of things come into focus. We see that, on the one hand, for the first time in human history, slightly more than half of all people on the planet live in urban areas. They live in megacities like Jakarta or Accra or México or Manila, or they live in other sorts of urbanized areas. And many of the people who have moved to cities of all sizes have moved for a number of reasons. As we talked about earlier, war makes many travelers. Many people have been pushed out of where they live because of imperial, civil, and regional conflicts. Also, given the broad monetization of human activity, people move to where they can work, either to remain there or to send remittances home. The necessity to work for money means people move to where the markets might be for their products or their labor. Most workers work in the informal sector. So we see in urban areas, in places as far apart as Durban, South Africa, and Jakarta, Indonesia, and elsewhere, self-built communities as the necessary remedy for the fact that the urban world does not have enough affordable housing. In 2022 in Egypt, nearly 80 percent of new housing added to the stock was built by the informal sector. And as people struggle over whether or not land in urban areas should be available for housing, they're clearly also struggling over control of the land. They're struggling over the fact that governments and firms have funded extensive and intensive policing to prevent people from building houses and inhabiting abandoned buildings. So that's one example. But we must also look at rural areas. While it is true that slightly more than half of the planet's eight billion people live in urban areas, that means that slightly under half do not. And while not all rural dwellers are involved in producing food, most of our food comes from rural parts of the world, 70 percent grown by small producers, as Maria Luísa Mendonça and others have shown. In Brazil, the MST, the rural Landless Workers' Movement, has been organizing for forty years to remedy the landlessness of rural workers through land occupations in order to transform land that had been owned either by the state or by private owners but had not been fulfilling its constitutionally mandated social purpose. The MST cadre, each site comprising at least ten households, occupy the land and fight against violent state and non-state actors to remain. They bring the social purpose of land to life by building villages with schools and other institutions, and planting the land to grow healthy food for themselves, for their communities, and also for places where people are hungry—including Venezuela, for example, and other places experiencing US-led blockades.

CG: In two of the examples you've just mentioned—South Africans who are building housing in and on the peripheries of already existing cities, and Brazilians who are seizing rural land in order to grow food for their own use and to sell to support themselves—in both cases, part of what's made those movements as successful as they have been has been clauses in the respective constitutions of South Africa and Brazil. You mentioned the constitutional provision in Brazil. As you know, there's a huge debate in the last few years among abolitionists about what position we should take towards the state. And this isn't the place to lay that out. But I think it might be useful to talk a little bit about how organizers in South Africa and organizers in Brazil approach their constitutions not as a guarantee, but as a tool that might be useful. They see that there are these things in the Constitution, in the current law, in the way the laws are enforced—whether they're written that way exactly or not—that define the terrain on which they're struggling. And that sort of engagement with the state is not the same as trying to achieve state power, but it's acknowledging that the state is an internally contradictory player. It also acknowledges that the state *as* a player is different from place to place, it's different over time in the same place, and that we as organizers need to be cognizant of what it is we're up against, and what in that big and complicated thing called "the state" we can use against other parts of the state, and capital, and landowners, et cetera, et cetera, et cetera.

RWG: People use the weapons they can lay their hands on to fight, and they use the tools they can lay their hands on to build things. Using a weapon or a tool is not the same thing as yielding one's entire political vision to those who developed or originally owned the weapon or the tool. You've heard me say a jillion times over the years that the most radical part of Audre Lorde's often repeated statement, "the master's tools will never dismantle the master's house," is the apostrophe in "master's"—that it's the effective control of the tool rather than its object-ness that matters.

CG: And that effective control can be temporary.

RWG: It can be temporary, yeah. And using something, as we have seen with land, becomes a kind of provisional communist ownership, which is to say community effective control.

CG: Let me go back to something you said to maybe clarify something and talk a little bit about what's going on in France. You mentioned how the exodus from rural places continues because, as you said, there are jobs, or at least the hope of jobs, in urban centers. But the flip side of that—the decreasing ability of people to support themselves in rural places—is not natural. It is a result of changing relations of production across North, South, developed, underdeveloped, overdeveloped parts of the world. The rural world is changing very quickly, and people are not simply leaving rural places in hopes of a better life in urban places. I think it's not too strong to say that they're being driven out of rural places in order for those who control those rural places—in many cases, new owners—to develop them in new ways. And our comrade in South Africa, Yvonne Phyllis, has written a lovely pamphlet about how the people who end up in some of these self-built communities in Cape Town and in Durban have been driven out of the Eastern Cape. There's a movement currently going on in France, Les Soulèvements de la Terre, which has been organizing against rural development, and particularly rural development of water basins that steal water—or take water legally, as the case may be—to put it into giant storage basins so it can be used by the new corporate owners of rural land. Les Soulèvements have been doing direct action—destroying machinery, destroying pipes, destroying the basins—and they've also taken up other projects like highways that are going to go through forests, etcetera. They are a group organizing primarily but not exclusively in rural France, and have generated support among large numbers of villagers and small-town residents who, they rightly point out, are often ignored by left urban organizers in cities. To contrast what's going on in France now with what's going on in Germany, we see the inability of the German left to organize among independent farmers and ranchers has left them open to being swept into the country's far-right movement. Meanwhile, the French government officially dissolved the organization of Les Soulèvements last year—although it's not an organization per se—which means that, after the dissolution, anyone who continues to work as part of Les Soulèvements is open to a three-year prison term and a 45,000 euro fine. Nevertheless, for example, in March of last year, thirty thousand people turned out to attack one of the water-catchment basin-building sites. They were met by the forces of organized violence: Five thousand grenades were fired at them, two people were in comas as a result of the military action the government took, and so on. Ruthie, what I'd like to hear you talk about a little bit is why do the stakes seem to be rising for both sides?

RWG: Why do the stakes seem to be rising for both sides? I think that the answer to the question has a number of dimensions to it. As you rightly pointed out, accumulation of humans living in urban areas is not a result of nature. People are pushed out of rural areas for a number of reasons that are more and less violent. Some are quite clearly examples of war and terrorism, as we've discussed. Other cases exemplify quiet violence, the inability to go through the normal processes of social reproduction. It comes to the same thing: Changing land use compels people to move (and this is true for urban dwellers as well). So that's one aspect: People in many parts of the world—very vividly in France—are aware that they will not be able to stay where they are if the kinds of changes being wrought to those places are allowed to proceed. Meanwhile, there are those who are trying to force those changes—whether they are large-scale landowners who want to convert cropland to biofuels, or people who want to site Bitcoin mines that use enormous amounts of energy and water, other kinds of mines, and other revised land uses that will drive out ordinary people, landed or landless. This increases the stakes. Now there's a bad analysis of this general phenomenon that whines, "Oh, the planet has reached its carrying capacity. This is why everybody's fighting." And that's just bullshit. The planet has ample land available to grow food, to host housing, and so forth. The problem is the control of that land. So there's that problem—the allocation of the control of the land, which is very material. But mentioning the "too many people" nonsense reminds us we must be aware of the symbolic layer, including the commonsense assumptions people bring to problems to evaluate what is happening and why. Here I'm echoing the thinking of Stuart Hall. The symbolic and ideological problems scream for attention not only when some people contend that the problem is overpopulation. But also, for example, a certain dominant view of how to remedy climate change also distorts understanding, in a classically imperial way, when it reasons that croplands must be converted to biofuels to further the development of green capitalism and assuage the consciences of Global North drivers. This crisis in "the global misallocation of symbolic and material resources," as Hall put it, underlies both causes of conflicts and the various ways people understand them. (Here I'll remind readers the discussion of lawfare versus state lawfare shows how a single type of struggle produces properly antagonistic analytical categories.) And those conflicts give us some insight into how and why fascism is growing in popularity. Fascism purports not only to prevent certain kinds of changes in communities, but also to stabilize and improve forms of life that people are afraid to lose. On the other hand, on the left side, the antagonism also means that more and more people understand the necessity of engaging in creative aggression, which is something far in excess of protests—although protests are important—or other kinds of demonstrations, or oral or written condemnations of the order of things. People are actually taking it on themselves to rearrange the order of things, to seize, to hold—temporarily in the case of occupation in the forest in Atlanta, and longer term when it comes to other emancipatory occupations.

CG: One of the things I wonder about is the extent to which the various arenas of struggle that we've talked about in this conversation are themselves new. Or, to riff on Césaire, what we're seeing is people in France paying attention to what's going on in rural France because it's what France was doing in the colonies for centuries and could in that context be ignored, glorified, whatever. But now that it's happening to someone who certain French urban dwellers identify as their great-grandmother who used to live in rural France, suddenly it's a problem. I might suggest that, while the violence over who gets to live on land and what they get to do on it, who gets to profit off land and who doesn't, might not be new, one of the things that is new is the forms of resistance to that. And I think one of the things that your comments have made me think about is that questions of how we can reproduce ourselves, how we can maintain ourselves with some modest comfort and dignity—questions of reproduction— and questions of repression are unavoidably linked in more and more of the world. Organizers, I think, are doing ever more thinking about that conjunction of organizing around the points of reproduction and organizing around the points of repression as a single arena of struggle rather than separate arenas of struggle.

Political Vision, Theorizing from the Ground Up

RWG: I was just reading a piece by Tithi Bhattacharya—who is a social reproduction theorist—and she, trying to save social reproduction theory from liberals who water it down, insists that though it describes the challenges associated with social reproduction in many parts of the world, *abolition* provides the *political* vision to see what should be done. And I find that a really exciting way of bringing things together.

CG: Well, if I understood what you just said, it reminds me of the people who invited you to South Africa two years ago, people who were involved in occupation on land in order to build housing, and occupation of pre-existing buildings for housing. They wanted to talk to you as someone who's involved in police and prison abolition. They wanted to talk to you not as someone who knows how to occupy land, but rather as someone who understands something complementary—they've come to the understanding that their occupations of land can't exist without significant organizing around and against policing and prisons, and perhaps bordering as well. So that's the same sort of thing Bhattacharya is talking about.

RWG: Yeah, exactly.

CG: That's happening both, if I may, at the levels of left intellectual production, and also happening from the grassroots as a problem that's not on the distant horizon. It's a problem knocking on the door every day.

....

Our deep thanks to Patrick DeDauw for stellar transcription and editing.

Craig Gilmore has been organizing against police & prisons since late in the twentieth century. He was among the organizers of the California Prison Moratorium Project and coedited *Prison Focus*. He & Ruthie have rambling conversations over breakfast most mornings.

Ruth Wilson Gilmore is a professor at the City University of New York Graduate Center. Cofounder of many grassroots organizations including California Prison Moratorium Project, Critical Resistance, and the Central California Environmental Justice Network, her publications include *Abolition Geography: Essays Towards Liberation* (Verso, 2022) and *Golden Gulag: Prisons, Surplus, Crisis, and Opposition in Globalizing California* (UC Press, 2007). *Change Everything: Racial Capitalism and the Case for Abolition* is forthcoming from Haymarket.

Resources

Berger, Dan. "RICO and Stop Cop City: The Long War Against the Left." *LPE Project*, September 11, 2023.

Bhattacharya, Tithi. "Social Reproduction Theory as Diagnostic, Abolition as Politics: Reimagining Anticapitalism." Forthcoming in Special Issue of *Labor: Studies in Working-Class History*.

Burton, Orisanmi. *Tip of the Spear: Black Radicalism, Prison Repression, and the Long Attica Revolt*. University of California Press, 2023.

Estes, Nick. *Our History Is the Future: Standing Rock Versus the Dakota Access Pipeline, and the Long Tradition of Indigenous Resistance*. Verso Books, 2019.

Hall, Stuart. *Selected Writings on Race and Difference*. Duke University Press, 2021.

Hall, Stuart, Chas Critcher, Tony Jefferson, John Clarke, and Brian Roberts. *Policing the Crisis: Mugging, the State, and Law and Order*. Red Globe Press, 2013.

Harjo, Laura. *Spiral to the Stars: Mvskoke Tools of Futurity*. University of Arizona Press, 2019.

Harlow, Barbara. *After Lives: Legacies of Revolutionary Writing*. Verso Books, 1996.

Heatherton, Christina. *Arise! Global Radicalism in the Age of the Mexican Revolution*. University of California Press, 2022.

Mendonça, Maria Luisa. *The Political Economy of Agribusiness: A Critical Development Perspective*. Fernwood Publishing, 2023.

Meyerson, Gregory, and Michael Joseph Roberto. "It Could Happen Here." *Monthly Review Commentary*, October 2006.

Pardo, Mary. *Mexican American Women Activists: Identity and Resistance in Two Los Angeles Communities*. Temple University Press, 1998.

Phyllis, Yvonne. *This Land Is the Land of Our Ancestors*. TriContinental, June 6, 2022.

Rodriguez, Shellyne. https://www.shellynerodriguez.com.

Thompson, Vanessa Eileen. "Surplus People of the World, Unite! On Borders, Policing, and Abolition." Chap. 3 in *Border Abolition Now*. Edited by Sara Riva et al. Pluto Press, 2024.

Woods, Clyde. *Development Arrested: Race, Power, and the Blues in the Mississippi Delta*. Verso Books, 1998.

Zikode, S'bu, and Richard Pithouse. "South Africa's Enduring Unfreedom." *Boston Review*, April 24, 2024.

TWENTY-SIX

From No Cop Academy to Stop Cop City

Benji Hart

The battle to #StopCopCity in the Weelaunee Forest is a crucial one for marginalized communities around the globe to support. The campaign is supported by a broad, politically diverse coalition, drawing concrete connections between environmental justice and police and prison abolition. It also understands the militarized compound as a threat not just to lives of those in the Black neighborhood its construction disrupts, but Black and brown communities the world over who will face the repressive tactics of the armed bodies who will be trained at the facility, rallying solidarity across state and national borders.

But as terrifying a project as Cop City undeniably is, it is crucial to recognize that it is not the first compound of its type, nor is it slated to be the last. As parallel projects crop up around the US, and indeed around the world, our communities must not only practice solidarity with those resisting the construction of Cop City in Atlanta, but learn from the successes of the campaign, and prepare for similar battles in our own backyards.

Many #StopCopCity organizers did this themselves, studying the tactics of previous struggles, including the one around a recently opened police academy in Garfield Park, Chicago—and the youth-led #NoCopAcademy campaign that fought its construction over six years ago.[1]

After closing half of Chicago's free mental health clinics and forty-nine public schools in almost exclusively Black neighborhoods between 2012 and 2013, then mayor Rahm Emanuel announced in July 2017 that the Chicago Police Department (CPD)—which already received 40 percent of the city's annual budget—would receive a new $95 million investment in the form of a state-of-the-art training facility.

Like Cop City in Atlanta, the sprawling campus would include a mock city block in which to practice raids and other militarized maneuvers, in addition to a swimming pool, food court, and shooting range. In the wake of the 2014 CPD murder of 17-year-old Laquan McDonald, the US Department of Justice issued a report recommending an upgrade in "CPD's physical training facilities." In response, the city claimed the new academy would help improve community relations with police following the Black Lives Matter uprisings that took place after video of McDonald's killing was released to the public.

That's not the only similarity. Cop City is slated to be built on the same site as the former prison farm where Atlanta once consigned incarcerated people to labor. The police academy in Chicago is located in a predominantly poor, Black community with a long history of disinvestment and carceral violence. Both compounds were forced onto residents by Democratic mayors—including women mayors of color—despite being unpopular and vocally opposed by the public.[2]

The construction of both compounds has been materially supported by some of the most craven organizations not just in the carceral sector, but in the destruction of the environment as well. Behemoth multinational firm AECOM won the contract to build Cop Academy in Chicago, despite a long history of defrauding taxpayers and building unsafe facilities.[3] Meanwhile, Norfolk Southern, the company responsible for the 2023 toxic train crash in East Palestine, Ohio, is one of the funders of Cop City.[4]

But it's not just the occupation of communities of color by corporate interests that unites these projects. They are also bound by the growing grassroots resistance they have sparked, and the diverse range of tactics they've both employed and invented to resist their respective targets.

#NoCopAcademy centered the voices of those most impacted by our city's cuts to education and hyper-spending on mass incarceration—Black and brown young people. Youth from the South and West Sides, many of them Austin and West Garfield Park residents, hosted weekly meetings, wrote public statements, held press conferences, led train takeovers, attended trainings and workshops, and organized die-ins—all with the purpose of determining their own messaging and distilling their own values. Dozens of teenagers developed into experienced organizers over the course of the year-and-a-half-long struggle, and were the backbone and unapologetic voice of the campaign. These youth are well trained, fired up, and poised to take on new battles in their respective corners of Chicago.

The multiracial and multigenerational coalition brought together organizations that are often siloed in Chicago organizing. Communities that rarely interact—and even have been historically at odds—not only recognized the danger of the academy's imminent construction, but the need to connect their struggles to resist it. Muslim youth disrupted Rahm Emanuel's iftar dinner, Black leaders joined Organized Communities Against Deportations to head the #ChingaLaMigra march in the Loop, and the queer Asian organization Invisible 2 Invincible brought a #NoCopAcademy contingent to the Lunar New Year Parade. Young people from the South and West Sides marched in Uptown against 46th Ward alderman James Cappleman, chair of the zoning committee, uniting in the fight against school closings across Black neighborhoods. On the day of the budget committee's final vote on the academy, members of Raise Your Hand IL and the Chicago Teachers Union linked arms with Black and brown youth to block elevators at City Hall, while West Siders from Black Workers Matter spoke out against the misuse of Tax Increment Finance funds meant for their communities.

One hundred and five organizations from across the city stood together to state their support for the defunding of police and the increased funding of social services. Most didn't merely offer symbolic endorsements, but drew on their membership to throw down and speak up on behalf of the demands of youth organizers. This alone was a massive shift, and a monumental political achievement.

#NoCopAcademy also developed new tactics to fight Chicago's political machine. Organizers canvassed five hundred Garfield Park residents, then released a report demonstrating the lack of support for the academy and outlining the kinds of investments wanted in the neighborhood. When Black youth were barred from comment at public hearings, they sued the city and won a settlement, forcing 34th Ward alderman Carrie Austin, chair of the budget committee, to hold public comment at the next committee vote. They petitioned for government documents and researched the flow of private money into aldermanic pockets. They led workshops for organizers and communities, educating many for the first time on the contours of local politics.

After a rare defer-and-publish maneuver delayed a vote on partial funding for the Cop Academy, Rahm Emanuel taunted organizers, telling the *Sun-Times*, "Between today and Friday . . . there's not gonna be a vote change."[5] By the end of the campaign, twelve different aldermen—a stunning 24 percent of City Council—abstained, deferred, or flat-out voted against at least one of the proposals for the academy, and both candidates in the mayoral runoff opposed aspects of the project. #NoCopAcademy studied the machine and shook it thoroughly without playing by its rules.

Chicago organizers who have led the national conversation on abolishing police and prisons can attest that the message of abolition has long been deemed too radical for mainstream political discussions—even those facilitated by the left. A deep-seated belief in the indispensability of carceral institutions, and concerns about what would replace them, have regularly drowned out the voices of communities with clear answers to these quandaries.

By jumping on the construction of the academy and highlighting the city's hypocritical claims of being "broke" when it closed half its mental health clinics and forty-nine public schools only years prior, #NoCopAcademy provided a concrete example of the abolitionist politic in action, asking: Why can't Chicago find money to heal and educate our communities, yet can always find money to police and incarcerate them? What if we reversed the spending flow, divesting from the failed institution of policing, and investing in the support systems that can prevent crime and violence in the first place?

With every fresh life stolen and each new act of violence caught on camera, defenders of the carceral state profess that these debacles necessitate further investments to "train" police out of their aggression and racism. Tragedies like the 2023 fatal beating of Tyre Nichols and the 2022 Uvalde school shooting were immediately used to justify massive expansions of policing in their respective jurisdictions. The establishment strategically claims these deaths in the name of fortifying the prison-industrial complex, while everyday people can rightfully point to them as proof of its myriad failures.

Simultaneously, as the climate warms, as storms and disasters worsen, as infrastructure crumbles, and as more and more people are left jobless and houseless, the true reason the political class pumps ever more resources into militarization is being revealed: It's not to protect against some supposed "crime wave" the corporate media constantly fearmongers about, but instead to police the very collapse of capitalism itself.

Keeping poor and working people at bay while their communities are dismantled, their lands are poisoned, and their lives deemed insignificant can only be achieved through brute force. We are witnessing the robber barons barricade themselves in, sealed away from the catastrophes they created, with the same resources they stole from the people on the other side of the wall.

Solidarity across states and borders is necessary as new campaigns take up the fight against the proposed militarization of their communities at the expense of their most basic resources. Where #NoCopAcademy made clear the reasons we must collectively resist these projects, #StopCopCity is building off that momentum—and still has a chance to win. The time is now for us to unilaterally shut down projects like Cop City, to reclaim those dollars for poor and working people, for health care, for housing, and for combating climate change. The time is now to follow the lead of both #NoCopAcademy and #StopCopCity, to stop believing the corporate lie that the police and prison system will protect us from the conditions it has been key in fostering. The time has come to redefine public safety as everyone on our planet having access to the resources required to thrive, and to demand those resources be redistributed through the defunding and abolishing of police, prisons, and militarization across the board.

No cop city in Atlanta, in Chicago, in Palestine, or anywhere else.

Parts of this piece were originally published in the Chicago Reader *in April 2019 and* In These Times *in February 2023.*

Benji Hart is an interdisciplinary artist, author, and educator whose work centers Black radicalism, queer liberation, and prison abolition. Their words have appeared in numerous anthologies, and been published at *Time*, *Teen Vogue*, and *The Advocate*. They have led popular education and arts-based workshops for organizations internationally, and presented at the Barnard Center for Research on Women, the American Repertory Theater, and the National Museum of African American History and Culture.

TWENTY-SEVEN

Cop Cities
in a Militarized World

Azadeh Shahshahani

Just eleven days after Georgia state troopers murdered Tortuguita in January 2023, two water defenders from Guapinol, Honduras, Aly Domínguez and Jairo Bonilla, were assassinated by unidentified gunmen.[1] The two were cofounders of a group responsible for leading an occupation of the Los Pinares mine to protest against exploitative mining operations that would pollute their water source, the Guapinol River. The Honduran government has refused to investigate the matter further, instead blaming the murders on a robbery attempt.

Between December 2022 and February 2023, at least seven land defenders and community members across the Bajo Aguán region—a fertile and heavily militarized region in northern Honduras—were killed, including campesino leader Hipólito Rivas of the Gregorio Chavez Cooperative; his son Jose Omar Cruz Tome, president of the Los Laureles cooperative; and his father-in-law, Andy Martinez Murillo.[2] For decades, communities in the Bajo Aguán and international solidarity organizations have denounced the collaboration between private security firms working for palm oil and mining corporations and military and police-backed paramilitary forces heavily supported by the United States to violently repress organized opposition to the land theft and environmental destruction upon which the industries depend.

Meanwhile, in northern El Salvador, just a week before the deadly raid in the Weelaunee Forest, state police were engaged in a raid of their own. Residents of the rural community of Santa Marta awoke in the middle of the night to sirens and floodlights as police arrested Antonio Pacheco, the executive director of the Association of Economic and Social Development of Santa Marta, who helped lead El Salvador's powerful anti-mining movement.[3] Four other community leaders—Miguel Ángel Gámez, Alejandro Laínez García, Pedro Antonio Rivas Laínez, and Saúl Agustín Rivas Ortega—were also arrested. The scene was all too familiar to a community that suffered a horrific massacre and brutal state violence during El Salvador's US-backed war against leftist revolutionary forces in the 1980s.

So while the Georgia State Patrol's murder of Tortuguita marked the first known instance of state forces killing an environmental protester in the United States, the killing of land defenders is heartbreakingly common in South and Central America. Latin America has long been the deadliest region for human rights and environmental defenders. In its 2022 analysis, Frontline Defenders noted that four out of the five countries contributing to 80 percent of the murders of human rights defenders worldwide that year were in Latin America. Other reports show that 75 percent of all killings of environmental activists worldwide have occurred there, and that it is particularly deadly for Indigenous environmental activists.[4] These statistics reveal what land defenders across the world have long known: State violence against environmental protesters is not confined to the United States.

But if not exclusively contained within its borders, the United States certainly has had an active role in its spread. It has a long history in Latin America of promoting economic policies to benefit corporations engaged in extractive and otherwise exploitative industries, while simultaneously training, arming, and supporting the state and paramilitary forces that brutally repress those who resist such policies. In short, the US brand of policing—the kind that would be taught and exported from Cop City—exists to protect capital and property. The crackdown against those fighting it, in Atlanta and in Honduras, El Salvador, and across the world, offers a frightening glimpse into a potential future: one of increasing state violence against communities everywhere who struggle to defend water, land, and ecosystems from corporate greed.

This new reality for US environmental activists is one that organized popular movements in Central America, where the police and military have received extensive US training for decades, know all too well.

As in Atlanta, accusations of terrorism have been used to dehumanize the state's enemies. In El Salvador's case, environmental activists and community leaders have been labeled as gang members. The charges have also been deployed to justify and glamorize state violence, with government photographs of masses of handcuffed prisoners circulated to simultaneously invoke fear and normalize degradation. The government calls its new prison, claimed to be one of the largest in the world, the "Terrorist Confinement Center."[5] Against this backdrop, El Salvador's Bukele regime has arrested not only anti-mining activists, but also union leaders, youth organizers, and political opponents.

The attorney general's operation against the Santa Marta Five, as the jailed anti-mining protesters have come to be known, occurred amid a campaign of massive arrests launched in March 2022, when the government of Nayib Bukele suspended key constitutional rights under the pretext of combating gang violence.[6] Legislators from Bukele's party have continuously—and illegally—reapproved a thirty-day emergency measure known as a "state of exception" for the past twenty-six months, beginning in March 2022.[7] The Salvadoran government's steamrolling of due process has become a nightmare for working-class families whose communities have been militarized, with over seventy-one thousand people arrested, many without warrants, evidence, or investigation. By July 2023, Salvadoran human rights organizations had documented over 6,400 human rights violations, mainly arbitrary arrests, and the deaths of at least 153 people in prison, whether from torture, beatings, or lack of access to medical care. None had been found guilty of a crime.[8]

These policies are the culmination of two decades of US-backed repressive policing. As scholars Leisy Abrego and Steven Osuna outline, right-wing governments first implemented an "iron fist" anti-gang plan in El Salvador "modeled on U.S. zero-tolerance policies and broken windows policing" in 2003.[9] Like the counterinsurgency campaigns of the 1980s, the US policing and security strategies exported over the past thirty years have armed governments throughout Central and South America with tools to repress impoverished communities, including those organizing to defend land and water.

In 2006, the far-right Nationalist Republican Alliance (Alianza Republicana Nacionalista, or ARENA) administration passed an anti-terrorism law modeled closely on the USA Patriot Act. Grassroots organizers in El Salvador loudly opposed the law for its sweeping nature, warning it would open the door to political persecution. Among the first people to be charged under the new statutes were fourteen community activists from the community of Suchitoto who were protesting water privatization. Accompanied by successful international solidarity efforts, they were freed in 2007 and charges were dropped.[10]

The training of security forces in South and Central America is a pillar of US geopolitical strategy in the region: It ensures that those in power remain friendly to US business interests. The infamous School of the Americas, first based in Panama and later relocated to Fort Moore, Georgia (and subsequently rebranded to the "Western Hemisphere Institute for Security Cooperation" after being accused of training its graduates in torture and assassination techniques), hosts South and Central American military officers and offers courses from "tactical training to advanced theory on the application of military doctrine." Among the school's graduates in El Salvador are Col. Domingo Monterrosa, who led the infamous Atlacatl Battalion that massacred hundreds in El Mozote in 1981, and Roberto D'Aubuisson, who planned the 1980 assassination of Salvadoran archbishop Óscar Romero, an outspoken critic of the military government.[11] The institute remains operational and reports "graduating 1,200–1,900 military, police, and civilian students from across the Hemisphere annually."[12]

In the mid-2000s, the United States expanded its focus more specifically to policing. In 2005, as part of an effort to shore up confidence for US investors in the newly passed Dominican Republic–Central America Free Trade Agreement (DR-CAFTA), the Bush administration opened a new branch of the Clinton-era international police training school, the International Law Enforcement Academy (ILEA), in San Salvador.[13] The United States frames this work as police "professionalization"—a suspect term, considering the fact that the US remains the high-income country with by far the highest rate of police killings in the world. What's been called the "School of the Americas for Police" has graduated thousands of police officers throughout Central and South America who receive training from the FBI, DEA, and other agencies based in the United States, including state and local police forces. These trainings used to include courses led by the Atlanta Police Department through its partnership with the State Department.[14]

In 2007, the Bush administration launched the Mérida Initiative, said to focus on border surveillance and assisting Mexican and other Central American governments in the War on Drugs. Experts argued early on that it would merely strengthen organized crime networks and were soon proven right.[15] The Central America Regional Security Initiative soon followed, which purported to "stop the flow of narcotics, arms, weapons, and bulk cash generated by illicit drug sales" and "[strengthen] and [integrate] security efforts from the U.S. Southwest border to Panama."[16]

By 2017, the Inter-American Commission on Human Rights was hearing cases regarding rising numbers of extrajudicial killings at the hands of Salvadoran police, and by 2018, the United Nations special rapporteur on extrajudicial, summary, and arbitrary executions reported "a pattern of behavior amongst security personnel, amounting to extrajudicial executions and excessive use of force," citing "elements of the legal framework, such as the 2006 Counter-terrorism Law," as key contributors to these violations.[17]

A central component of US police reform efforts in Central America has been to create, develop, and train elite police units to specialize in the fight against organized crime—often to deadly ends.[18] Investigators connected El Salvador's Specialized Reaction Forces, a joint police and military unit backed by significant US funding, to the murder of forty-three suspected gang members in the first half of 2017 alone. Though officially disbanded, many of its members transitioned to a new US-backed unit, the Jaguars.[19] In neighboring Honduras, the United States heavily invested in the creation of the TIGRES (Intelligence Troops and Special Security Response Groups).[20] Launched in 2012, TIGRES officers have, on multiple occasions, been implicated in drug trafficking, corruption, and state repression of protesters.[21]

In recent years, some of the most notorious US-trained security forces around the world have become the trainers, often with funding from various US agencies. Colombian soldiers now offer trainings in Honduras through the United States Southern Command (SOUTHCOM). The Atlanta police, too, have received training from Colombia, as well as from Israel and elsewhere, through a program subsidized by the US Department of Justice.[22] Activists have argued that, if built, Cop City might host similar trainings for international forces.

Through US-funded training and capacity-building programs, many of the most dangerous elements of policing practices now circulate internationally. Since the founding of US-backed police schools in El Salvador, the country's incarceration rate per capita surpassed that of the United States; it is now the highest in the world.[23]

When Salvadoran president Nayib Bukele appeared on Tucker Carlson's show on Fox News in September 2022 to celebrate his crackdown, Carlson exhorted the mayors of Baltimore; Gary, Indiana; and New York City—cities traditionally led by Democratic administrations—to reach out to Bukele for his guidance.[24] Amid ongoing protests against Cop City, Governor Brian Kemp welcomed Salvadoran ambassador Milena Mayorga to Georgia in March of 2023.[25] That same month, Mayorga would go on to invite Atlanta mayor Andre Dickens to visit El Salvador on an upcoming delegation.[26] As Georgia and the Salvadoran government forge stronger diplomatic ties, the US export of "expertise" to police and military in Central America is no longer a straight line but has instead come full circle.

※

Fifteen years ago, the directors of ILEA were remarkably clear when discussing their goals for opening a new police training academy in El Salvador: to make Latin America "safe for foreign investment" by "providing regional security and economic stability and combating crime." Such comments were recently echoed by Laura Richardson, head of SOUTHCOM for Latin America, when she framed the importance of US military operations in Latin America in terms of the region's "rich resources and rare earth elements," like lithium and oil.[27]

It's no coincidence that corporations from Wells Fargo to Axon, the manufacturers of Tasers, have been major donors to the Atlanta Police Foundation and to police foundations across the country. For decades, liberal governance prioritizing maximal corporate profits has protected the ever-increasing acquisition and exploitation of natural resources, which in turn excludes local communities from the means to sustain themselves. This exclusion is further intensified by the ongoing climate crisis, with ecosystems that have hung in a stable-yet-delicate balance for millennia now being devastated by rising temperatures and turbulent weather conditions.

The resulting environmental blight forces communities to relocate to new hubs that already struggle with diminishing resources at the hands of corporate takeover and their own forms of catastrophic climate change. Corporate donors, like the police they fund, foresee that this zero-sum struggle for natural resources will incite grassroots uprisings for equitable popular control over the land and resources currently in their possession. The funding of Cop City and the network of state-legitimized violence nationwide and in the Global South, hence, serves the purpose of ensuring their property remains in corporate hands for indefinite exploitation in the face of a desperate population.

But there is some room for hope. Just as forest defenders in Atlanta have significantly stalled the project and reduced its scale, land and water defenders in El Salvador have successfully prevented mining operations.[28] In 2017, the country became the first in the world to ban metal mining, due in large part to the communities who worked relentlessly for nearly two decades to organize against it, despite threats and harassment. Other communities and movements throughout the region are following suit, refusing to give in to coercive and violent US-backed military and paramilitary forces. In a 2015 case in Honduras, the Inter-American Commission on Human Rights found that the state violated the human rights of the Indigenous Garifuna communities by expanding urban developments into the community's land. This decision marked a victory for the recognition of Garifuna land rights, though the Honduran government has yet to implement any measures in accordance with the decision.[29]

Environmental movements have also been able to fight back against the criminalization of land and water defenders. After an international outcry, the charges against eight water defenders from Guapinol, arrested in 2019 for opposing the Los Pinares mining project, were dropped in 2022.[30] And on September 5, 2023, the five Santa Marta water defenders arrested in January of that year were moved from prison to house arrest following an international campaign, though the struggle to drop all the charges against them continues.[31]

That the United States' investment in controlling territories, resources, and entire populations through policing now mirrors the tactics that it helped usher into existence in Central America is cause for concern. But it is also an indicator that the movements against them in both the United States and Central America are capable of posing significant threats to the racialized order that such investment seeks to uphold through shared tactics such as legal attacks and terrorist labeling. Despite the risks, organized communities in Central America are not backing down. Nor are the organizers in Atlanta. Together, they are envisioning urgently needed alternatives to both environmental destruction and militarization.

A version of this piece was originally published in Boston Review *in September 2023.*

Azadeh Shahshahani, legal and advocacy director with Project South, advances a practice of movement lawyering, focused on confronting state repression and dismantling systems of surveillance, incarceration, and deportation. Azadeh has organized for two decades to protect and defend migrants and Black and Muslim communities from systemic Islamophobia, xenophobia, and anti-Black racism. She also provides support to social justice movements in the Global South, from Brazil to Palestine. Azadeh is a past president of the National Lawyers Guild.

TWENTY-EIGHT

Atlanta's Attack on Protesters Should Be a Warning to Us All

Angela Y. Davis and Barbara Ransby

The ongoing attack on the network of environmental and abolitionist activists in Atlanta should make all people concerned with the right to protest, the future of the environment, and the rise of militarized police forces take notice. There we see an all-out assault on two movements—the environmental justice movement and the movement against policing and prisons—that have seen growing popular support and influence in recent years.

The struggle in Atlanta is a part of a bigger story. With corporations like Amazon, Wells Fargo, and Delta backing the Atlanta Police Foundation's development of this project, the direct link between the police state and encroaching environmental degradation becomes obvious. Moreover, Black and working-class people are losing their lives to both at a record pace.[1] And when brave community members and their supporters have stepped forward to defend the forest and object to a training ground designed to further perfect the use of state violence, they themselves have been systematically targeted.

As egregious as they might seem, the police attacks on activists in Atlanta do not constitute a new trend. We know that at least 1,700 environmental activists have been murdered around the world in the past decade.[2] Corporate hitmen and state violence are used to bludgeon anything that gets in the way of profit and power. Atlanta's business elite and political class have pulled from this playbook and have worked to misrepresent the movement as the work of "outside agitators." It's ironic to hear classic segregationist rhetoric from those who claim to uphold the legacy of Martin Luther King Jr. The same lines were used against the Freedom Riders and voter rights volunteers, after all, when they traveled to the South to participate in the Black Freedom Movement in the 1960s.

Black student protesters, a coalition of movement organizations, and Black communities that are opposed to Cop City are being outright ignored by a Black establishment. Even when students and faculty from historically Black colleges and universities like Morehouse and Spelman joined the outcry against Cop City, Mayor Andre Dickens didn't stop pushing for this facility. When the decision to sign off on domestic terrorism warrants came before Fatima El-Amin, a Black judge, she signed them.[3] And Atlanta's Black police officers have never broken ranks with their white counterparts. This is not a simple matter that political representation will sort out for us; it is a question that must be answered by abolitionist praxis, which means both creating alternatives to police and prisons to achieve harm reduction, and continuing the ongoing work of building a more just society.

In our view, the money that it takes to build police training facilities would be better spent advancing deteriorating infrastructure. Atlanta has the highest income inequality in the nation, and more police won't fix that.[4] Resources for health care, housing, and education could change the politically preordained circumstances that create such oppressive conditions.

The call to stop Cop City is much bigger than just one facility. It is also connected to the years-long fight against the West Side Cop Academy in Chicago and against Urban Shield in Oakland. It is also directly linked to the uprisings in Ferguson and Baltimore and the massive response to the public execution of George Floyd. Because the forest where the City of Atlanta wants to construct the training facility consists of land that was taken from Mvskoke Creek people, resisting Cop City is directly linked to Indigenous struggles against the Keystone XL Pipeline and other extractive infrastructure. Neither corporate nor government elites want another precedent of conscientious activists interrupting an unethical, profit-driven project, which is why they are waging war against the "Stop Cop City" movement.

The movement for the abolition of police and prisons and the urgent and growing movement for environmental justice are two key pillars of a collective vision for a more hopeful, egalitarian future. The targeting of organizers in Atlanta seeks to send a dangerous and chilling message to the larger national and global movements. We must oppose this effort and support and defend the Atlanta organizers now being attacked, harassed, and persecuted for daring to speak truth to power and organize for a more just future.

A version of this piece was originally published in Truthout *in June 2023.*

Angela Y. Davis is Professor Emerita of History of Consciousness and Feminist Studies at UC Santa Cruz. An activist, writer, and lecturer, her work focuses on prisons, police, abolition, and the related intersections of race, gender, and class. She is the author of many books, from *Angela Davis: An Autobiography* to *Freedom Is a Constant Struggle.*

Dr. Barbara Ransby is a widely acclaimed historian of the Black Freedom Movement, award-winning author, and longtime activist. She is the John D. MacArthur Chair and Distinguished Professor in the Departments of Black Studies, Gender and Women's Studies, and History at the University of Illinois at Chicago. Ransby is the author of multiple books, including the award-winning *Ella Baker and the Black Freedom Movement: A Radical Democratic Vision* and *Making All Black Lives Matter: Reimagining Freedom in the Twenty-First Century.*

TWENTY-NINE

Please Keep Playing

A Letter to My Son, Remix

Ariana Brazier

Remix,

I've been mentally and emotionally exhausted these last few weeks for some familiar and new reasons that I can only explain by addressing you directly.

A few weeks ago, I took you across the street to the vacant baseball field to play soccer. When I kicked the ball in one direction, you would grin at me mischievously and wait for me to take off sprinting behind the ball before you mimicked me. We raced to the ball before taking turns on the next kick. You cracked me up because as you would run behind the ball, you were careful to avoid the taller weed patches in this field overgrown by weeds and overrun with ant beds. I was so proud of us for making this time for each other and so grateful for the struggle that led us to our little East Point home.

But the moment could not exist in this blissful bubble, as it became apparent to me how quickly this and future moments could be snatched from us. As we were playing, I noticed an East Point police car with two officers drive past and take an extended pause at the stop sign just outside the field's gates, directly in front of our home. Annoyed and on alert, I invited you to keep playing with me. When the car circled the block, I became anxious. And when the cop car circled a third time, I fearfully picked you up, gathered our items, and walked home. I closed the blinds, locked the doors, set the alarm, and began our daily bedtime routine with all the generational paranoia of a Black mother raising her Black son in a militarized police state.

The fears and questions continue to proliferate as I scroll through Twitter and note another Black person harassed or murdered by police (Breonna Taylor, Atatiana Jefferson, Aura Rosser, Botham Jean, Janisha Fonville, and Michelle Cusseaux, in addition to the growing number of Georgians fatally shot by police—more than a third of whom the state killed in their own home).[1]

There is no material defense against or legal recourse for these attacks. As I rock you to sleep and tuck you in each night, I wonder with heavy guilt if you should be sleeping with me in my bed. I imagine my body as a defense between you and them. I wonder if they would notice the fullness of our lives if they barged in through the living room—the Little Tykes basketball hoop, the tiny trampoline, the miniature kitchen set, the dining table caked with yogurt and cluttered with documents. I wonder if I've paid all my bills, filed all my paperwork, updated my registration. I wonder if I unintentionally pissed off any more cops today (the week following our park date, I informed a police officer that we do not speak to cops, and he began yelling at me about his humanity). I think of anything else that might increase the distance between you and the police.

I ruminate on the police murder of Korryn Gaines, a 23-year-old mother of two young children who was murdered in front of her 5-year-old son in a police shootout at her home. The reason for the intrusion: a warrant and failure to appear in court on charges related to a traffic stop. The knowledge that this could be me—us—never leaves me, especially now as I obsessively follow minute-by-minute updates on #StopCopCity efforts. Our little home, that vacant field, and our favorite playgrounds are all located in the most heavily surveilled city in the country, Atlanta, Georgia. Our private moments of joy, like that day on the field, are encircled by police officers, cameras, and technology.

Acknowledging all of this continually forces me to contend

with the limitations to the types of safety I can physically provide you, specifically as the sole individual charged with protecting your well-being. With this said, committing to the work of abolition as a process and outcome, even more, the endeavor to integrate abolition as a premier ethic of our daily living, is the only means of guaranteeing safety for you—for all of us. To achieve abolition, we must revise and co-construct a definition of safety. In doing so, we must access and foreground collective health, wellness, and imagination through ongoing mutual aid: collective problem-solving that humanizes the process of change.

You, at only twenty-three months, are an integral participant in this work. We are building a grassroots network of relationships replete with resources, skills, and language. You should never have to call the police. You should never even feel the urge to consider the police, because there are at least five other people you can call to meet your needs responsibly with care and recognition.

Remix, as a child, your only obligation to this work is to take up space shamelessly through the Black joy and play inherent to your body and spirit. Through play, centered within and informed by your kinship network, you are learning and practicing self-definition. Play is teaching you mutual aid—how to meet someone's needs, as well as allowing others to meet yours; how to resource your community, struggle collectively, build and exchange power, and co-construct safety. We can look to your recent playground experiences as quintessential examples:

During one recent visit, you allowed another toddler to walk you across the shaky bridge you feared. Once across, you two became partners—she assisted you with ascending the rock-climbing wall and chain-link ladder. She insisted that she be your support, and you responded graciously.

On another occasion, you wanted to play with the big kids. In this climbable, spinning spherical orb on the playground were younger kids, and pushing the orb were bigger kids—but nestled within the center, holding tightly to the pole, were the toddlers. Everyone had a protective role and played their part to generate a collective Black joy.

In and through your play, you are linking Blackness to safety. Your work is as much a threat to Cop City and militarized police efforts as the adults crowding the streets and raising their voices in City Council meetings to #StopCopCity and prioritize and invest in an authentic form of safety that rests in the people. Cop City can never be built. It is a prevalent threat to our individual and collective livelihoods. The #StopCopCity efforts are teaching us how to lean into and grow in the fullness of our lives; how we proliferate solutions and resources.

These are collective efforts. These are your people. Remembering this and reflecting on the lessons in your joyous play are how I catch my breath each night.

I love you, and I thank you, in and across every universe.

Mama <3

A version of this piece was originally published in Scalawag Magazine *in May 2023.*

Ariana Denise Brazier, PhD, is a Black queer feminist and smiley sad mom-girl. She is a play-driven community organizer and educator who is motivated to raise a joyous, free Black child. She documents how Black child play is a grassroots method of community-based storytelling, teaching, and organizing. She is the president of the nonprofit ATL Parent Like A Boss, Inc. (Parent LAB), whose mission is to enhance generational literacies through play in underserved Black communities.

No Cop City, No Cop World

Cop City Is Everywhere

Just as Atlanta's Cop City followed Chicago's Cop Academy, proposals for militarized police training centers are proliferating across the country. At the time of this writing, proposals include a $43 million project in San Pablo, California; a $70 million facility in Reno, Nevada; $79 and $152 million facilities in El Paso and Dallas, Texas; a $330 million compound in Baltimore, Maryland; an $85 million facility in Gilbert, Arizona; a $415 million mega-center in Nashville, Tennessee; $120 million and $300 million centers in Newark and Trenton, New Jersey; $300 and $120 million facilities in Hershey and Pittsburgh, Pennsylvania; a $73 million facility in Lenexa, Kansas; a $108 million building in Brockton, Massachusetts; a $49 million center in Rice, Minnesota; and a $43 million facility in Lacey, Washington. This is just a selection of over sixty such proposals on the table.[1]

Beyond specific proposals for police "training" centers, cop *cities*—where policing dominates local public expenditure—are everywhere. Municipalities across the country are increasing their policing budgets, building new jails, and installing new surveillance infrastructure, aided by private capital infused through local police foundations. At the same time, local governments are closing libraries and hospitals, shuttering what's left of public housing, cutting and privatizing basic services, and deepening the spiral of organized abandonment. The dynamics fueling Cop City in Atlanta—environmental extraction and devastation, hypergentrification and displacement, and mass policing and surveillance as forms of social control—are driving the consolidation of police and capitalist power in both rural and urban areas across the country.

In eastern Kentucky, we are seeing the same dynamics of carceral expansion and environmental devastation as federal and local officials revive a plan to build what would be the most expensive federal prison in US history on a mountaintop removal site—a mountain blown to pieces with thousands of pounds of explosives to facilitate the removal of coal at devastating environmental costs. The result? Just as the Atlanta Police Foundation (APF) seeks to transform the Weelaunee Forest into Cop City, "mountaintop removal has created the conditions . . . for mountains to become prisons, once and would-be miners to become guards, and heavy rains to become floods," writes geographer Judah Schept.[2]

In a three-hundred-mile stretch of land from West Virginia to North Carolina, fracking companies collaborating with government backers are working to construct the Mountain Valley Pipeline, a pipeline that would transport two billion cubic feet of fracked methane per day between the two states. For residents, notes journalist Katie Myers, it would mean "razed trees, disturbed landscapes, water running brown from the tap, and, in the end, a frightening risk of leaks and explosions." For corporations, the pipeline would spell massive profits and, consequently, an expansion of their power to bend governments to their will.[3]

In Michigan, the National Guard has been pushing to more than double the size of its military training base by expanding onto an additional 162,000 acres of land for "training activities in modern cyber, air, and space warfare"—a plan fiercely opposed by environmental, Indigenous, and other activists. As of this writing, the proposed acreage has been reduced to 52,000 acres in a "compromise" deal still opposed by activists.[4]

Each of these projects is just a glimpse into the world that the Cop City architects desire: mountains obliterated and replaced with prisons; forests razed and replaced with cop cities; miles of land and water uprooted and polluted, replaced with pipelines and trampled by soldiers.

This vision for a world defined by extraction, exploitation, and domination maintained through the violence of policing and militarism is a fundamentally global one of Western hegemony. As sociologist Stuart Schrader has written, the US is the global policeman, both exporting and importing techniques of police repression and violence. Some of the US's policing is highly visible: The US regularly launches operations from its over eight hundred military bases around the world, engages in joint operations and missions, and exports massive amounts of arms. But as Schrader explains, it is security assistance, offered in the form of training and technology for local police and military forces around the world—and particularly in Africa, Asia, and Latin America—that "puts the *police* in *global policeman*."[5]

Combating "terrorism" is frequently the connective tissue between domestic and international policing. Rather than being a reference to any particular conduct, the "terrorist" label is often a stand-in for those who challenge the oppressive power of the state. Atlanta forest defenders are called terrorists. Students on college campuses and protesters who occupy bridges in New York to protest genocide are called terrorists. Palestinian freedom fighters and children are called terrorists. Environmental activists in El Salvador are called terrorists. The Department of Defense's Africa Command (AFRICOM) facilitates "partnerships" with military forces of various countries in Africa to conduct "counterterrorism" efforts—and just as importantly, to secure the US's economic interests on the continent. Scratch the terrorist label, and you will find an immense network of state violence that produced it.

The same public-private partnerships working locally and globally to facilitate extraction and exploitation are also tightening laws against protest to provide a pretext for a police-military crackdown. For example, a slew of states have passed critical infrastructure laws in recent years to intensify penalties for protests near oil, gas, electric, and other infrastructure deemed critical.[6] In 2024, the Georgia legislature passed a bill that adds protest-related offenses to the list of crimes that are ineligible forcash bail, and outlaws bail funds like the Atlanta Solidarity Fund, criminalizing organizations that post bail for more than three people in one year.[7] In other words, the state is passing laws to ban attacks against state and corporate infrastructure while directly attacking movement infrastructure.

Through prosecutions and arrests, legal and extralegal executions, attacks on mutual-aid infrastructure, anti-democratic legal maneuvers, and sheer military power, the forces of capital and the state are committed to victory by any means necessary. But so is the resistance.

Resistance Is Everywhere

The Stop Cop City movement is just one of many current struggles against environmental extraction, carceral expansion, and capitalist consolidation. As Craig Gilmore and Ruth Wilson Gilmore remind us, we are at war, and you can't reform a war away. And across the world, people are fighting to win.

We cannot overstate the importance of militant direct action and acts of sabotage to ongoing liberation struggles, whether in battles against pipelines, cop cities, jail construction, or imperialist violence. By directly, physically disrupting extractive and oppressive machinery, we challenge the state's right to govern.

One day in late January, we learned of two new attacks on the machinery of empire and Western capital, occurring within hours of each other. The first was a Houthi missile strike on an oil tanker, part of a series of attacks on Western ships in the Red Sea over Israel's genocidal war against Palestinians.[8] The second was the burning of four pieces of construction equipment at the Cop City site, an act of sabotage by anonymous activists that was just the latest in a years-long string of hundreds of similar actions against companies associated with Cop City.[9]

Just a couple days later, we learned of another pair of actions: In Atlanta, two activists used pipes to lock themselves to a Midtown construction site of Cop City contractor Brasfield & Gorrie.[10] On the same day, over four hundred miles away, an Appalachian mother used pipes to lock herself to a Mountain Valley Pipeline drill, halting construction for the day—one of many actions in the ongoing legal battles and militant protests that continue to stall the project.[11] Both actions were flanked by supporters who rallied nearby.

Since the intensification of the Israeli genocide of Palestinians in October 2023, massive crowds have protested across the world, while groups like Palestine Action have engaged in militant direct action against genocide contractors—blocking entrances, breaking windows, occupying buildings, and more. And just as similar tactics have forced contractors to pull out of Cop City, Palestine Action's efforts led to transportation company Kuehne+Nagel's announcement in February 2024 that it cut ties with Elbit Systems, Israel's main weapons supplier.[12]

Through struggle, the Stop Cop City movement has peeled off contractors, delayed construction of the project, raised the cost of the project, and forced the reduction of its total acreage. Activists have continually unearthed the city's backroom dealings with APF and exposed its corporate power structure, highlighting the deadly harmony between Atlanta's Democratic leadership, Georgia's Republican officials, and multinational corporations. The movement has revealed time and again that the ruling class, regardless of any individual's race, party, or politics, supports Cop City.

The Stop Cop City movement has also illustrated the power of a true diversity of tactics, strategies, and formations to fight back against local and global capital and white supremacy. We need deep, intentional base building and the cultivation of community leadership—not celebrity status. We need students and faculty organizing on and off campuses and revitalizing the tradition of student organizing. We need families and neighbors and children like those in the Weelaunee Coalition organizing each other. We need play and joy. We need to mobilize faith communities and recognize places of worship as sites of organizing. We need lawyers suing to defend forests under environmental protection statutes while forest defenders physically defend the very same land. We need mutual-aid networks and bail funds to support and defend criminalized protesters, while advocates at the Capitol and City Hall fight against laws that would further criminalize dissent. We need Hail Mary moves like the referendum campaign to keep the fight alive and channel nonprofit money into door-knocking efforts that reach tens of thousands of residents. We need weeks of action with large mobilizations and sustained organizing in between. We need movement elders who offer their insights and guidance. We need demands for land back, and for non-Indigenous organizers to be in right relationship with those whose land was stolen from them. We need self-determination for oppressed communities. We need people chaining themselves to destructive equipment and burning the machinery that would build police infrastructure. We need to make connections across place—from Atlanta to Palestine to Congo to Brazil to Haiti to Yemen to India and beyond—and to make connections across struggles. We need the courage and community to truly embrace a broad range of tactics, and the humility to shift course as the terrain of struggle changes.

For Tortuguita, for Palestine, for the forest defenders and the land defenders, for all struggling for liberation locally and globally, we must continue to fight and to say: *No Cop City, No Cop World!*

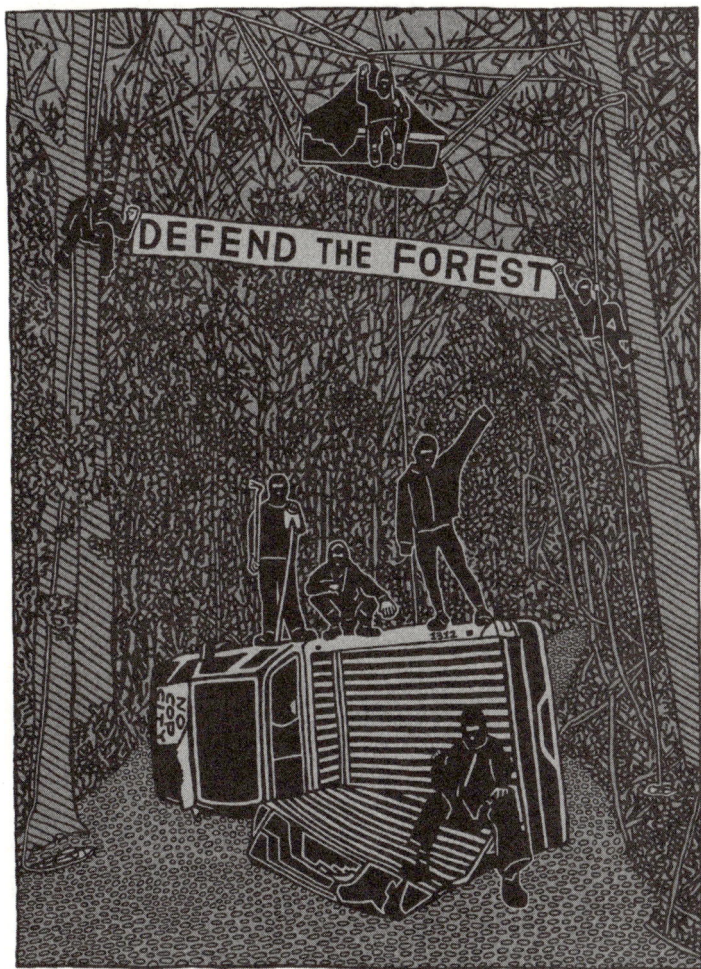

Fig. 9. Defend the Forest artwork. (Courtesy of Breakaway via CrimeThinc.)

Acknowledgments

We knew from our earliest discussions about a possible Stop Cop City book that any such project would need to be as collaborative and expansive as the movement itself. While no book could fully capture the boldness, creativity, imagination, radicalism, and diversity of the Stop Cop City struggle, we are grateful to every contributor who helped paint a picture of this decentralized movement. Most of all, we are grateful to the hundreds and thousands who have taken action to stop Cop City, whether in Atlanta or across the world. There is no Stop Cop City movement without the many who have shaped it through their solidarity, action, care, and dedication.

We are particularly indebted to the many grassroots and independent media formations and journalists who have tirelessly exposed the lies told by Atlanta's ruling class. Much of what was documented in this book would not be possible without the fantastic movement journalists at the *Atlanta Community Press Collective, Mainline, The Intercept, The Guardian, Truthout, Scalawag,* and elsewhere. We are also grateful to the outlets that granted permission to re-publish pieces, including *Boston Review, Hammer and Hope,* the *Chicago Reader, In These Times, The Nation, Scalawag,* and *Bitter Southerner.*

We are also grateful to the entire Haymarket Books team, including our wonderful editors, Katy O'Donnell and Anthony Arnove, who understood our vision and helped bring it to life; Jameka Williams, who shepherded the book through production; and Naomi Murakawa, who suggested titling the book *No Cop City, No Cop World.*

Kamau: I would like to thank Edget Betru for being my life partner and the strongest person I have ever known. Love to my children

Maya and Kaleb for being beautiful little people. Creating Community Movement Builders was the best organizing decision I have ever made. Thank you to everyone who has taken a stance against Cop City in Atlanta and across the globe. It is through your strength and courage that movements for the people are born.

Mariah: This journey would not be possible without my son, Aesop, who everyday reminds me of the stakes of this struggle and propels me forward. As well, I thank all those whose care for us has been a lifeline during this project and this movement: my best friend Paul, my mama, Mattie, and aunt Kat, and our family at the Highlander School. I am also full of gratitude for my steadiest spring of revolutionary optimism: my labor movement family. I extend thanks to Laurel and Ben especially for their mentorship and grace.

Micah: There are no words to adequately express my appreciation for my family, friends, comrades, and mentors, to whom I owe everything. I am endlessly grateful to my Atlanta family and organizing community, to the many who supported me through my first year of law school while creating this book, to those who taught me how to think, write, and edit, and to those who have shaped my understanding of this world and instilled my commitment to collectively transforming it. Naming names would inevitably lead to inadvertent omissions, but you all know who you are. Thank you, from the bottom of my heart.

Notes

Introduction

1. Mike Jordan, "The US Activists Holed Up in Treehouses to Block $90m 'Cop City,'" *The Guardian*, June 16, 2022, https://www.theguardian.com/environment/2022/jun/16/us-activists-protest-atlanta-cop-city-training-forest; Alexa Liacko and Diana Zito, "Why the 'Cop City' Police Training Center Sparked National Controversy," *Scripps News*, June 4, 2023, https://scrippsnews.com/stories/why-the-cop-city-police-training-center-sparked-national-controversy/.
2. Micah Herskind, "Cop City and the Prison Industrial Complex in Atlanta," *Mainline*, February 7, 2022, https://www.mainlinezine.com/cop-city-and-the-prison-industrial-complex-in-atlanta/.
3. Timothy Pratt, "'The Birds Stopped Singing': Inside the Battle for Atlanta's South River Forest," *Atlanta Magazine*, January 20, 2023, https://www.atlantamagazine.com/great-reads/the-birds-stopped-singing-inside-the-battle-for-atlantas-south-river-forest/.
4. Center for Biological Diversity, "Center for Biological Diversity Calls for Protection of Atlanta Forest, Independent Probe of Activist Killing," press release, February 23, 2023, https://biologicaldiversity.org/w/news/press-releases/center-for-biological-diversity-calls-for-protection-of-atlanta-forest-independent-probe-of-activist-killing-2023-02-23/.
5. Alex Edwards, "A Walk Through Weelaunee Forest," *The Xylom*, March 29, 2023, https://www.thexylom.com/post/perspective-a-walk-through-weelaunee-forest.
6. Pratt, "'The Birds Stopped Singing.'"
7. Herskind, "Cop City and the Prison Industrial Complex in Atlanta."
8. Tia Brown, "Meet the Major Corporations and Cultural Institutions Helping Build Cop City in Atlanta," LittleSis, November 15, 2022, https://news.littlesis.org/2022/11/15/meet-the-major-corporations-and-cultural-institutions-helping-build-cop-city-in-atlanta/.

9. Jessenia Class, "Corporations Are Keeping Cop City Alive." *The [F]law,* May 13, 2023, https://theflaw.org/articles/corporations-are-keeping-cop-city-alive/.

10. Herskind, "Cop City and the Prison Industrial Complex in Atlanta."

11. Jonathan Raymond, "Cop City Atlanta Appeal to DeKalb County Building Permit," 11Alive, February 7, 2023, https://www.11alive.com/article/news/local/appeal-filed-land-disturbance-permit-atlanta-public-safety-training-center-cop-city/85-db3a4ba8-15c3-4bdd-ac90-c9f9eb9f4b13.

12. Southern Center for Human Rights, "Protecting Dissent: SCHR Launches First Amendment Lawyer Bridge," July 17, 2023, https://www.schr.org/protecting-dissent-schr-launches-first-amendment-lawyer-bridge/.

13. Madeline Thigpen, "The Atlanta Professors and Students Protesting Cop City," *Capital B Atlanta,* April 27, 2023, https://atlanta.capitalbnews.org/cop-city-professors-students/.

14. Dean Hesse, "Clergy Call on City of Atlanta to Stop 'Cop City' Construction," *Decaturish,* March 7, 2023, https://decaturish.com/2023/03/photos-clergy-call-on-city-of-atlanta-to-stop-cop-city-construction/; Cody Bloomfield, "Stop Cop City Activists Plan Mass Return to Weelaunee Forest," *Truthout,* November 5, 2023.

15. Riley Bunch and Brian Eason, "City Council Passes Funding Legislation for Training Center," *Atlanta Journal-Constitution,* June 6, 2023.

16. Willy Blackmore, "The Area Around Cop City Is Flooding," *Word in Black,* January 12, 2024, https://wordinblack.com/2024/01/the-area-around-cop-city-is-flooding.

17. Candice Bernd, "Inside Forest Defenders' Blockade of Atlanta's 'Cop City' Training Compound," *Truthout,* February 23, 2022, https://truthout.org/articles/inside-forest-defenders-blockade-of-atlantas-cop-city-training-compound/.

Chapter 1: Why Cop City? Why Here? Why Now?

1. Ruth Wilson Gilmore and Craig Gilmore, "Beyond Bratton," in *Policing the Planet: Why the Policing Crisis Led to Black Lives Matter,* ed. Jordan T. Camp and Christina Heatherton (Brooklyn: Verso Books, 2016), 198.

2. Micah Herskind and Tiffany Roberts, "The Failure of Police Reform," *New York Magazine,* January 31, 2022, https://nymag.com/intelligencer/2022/01/atlanta-police-reform-failure.html.

3. Dan Immergluck, "Atlanta's BeltLine: How an Urban Park Can Drive Green Gentrification," *Governing Magazine,* January 29, 2023, https://www.governing.com/community/atlantas-beltline-how-an-urban-park-can-drive-green-gentrification.

4. Brian Eason and John Perry, "Across Metro Atlanta, Large Companies Are Buying Up Single-Family Houses," *Atlanta Journal-Constitution*, February 9, 2023, https://www.ajc.com/american-dream/investor-owned-houses-atlanta/.

5. Kristen Bahlers, "Atlanta Is the Best Place to Live in the U.S.," *Money*, September 29, 2022, https://money.com/atlanta-georgia-best-places-to-live-2022/; Melissa D. Tracey, "10 Housing Markets Expected to Lead the Nation in 2023," *Realtor Magazine*, December 13, 2022, https://www.nar.realtor/magazine/real-estate-news/10-housing-markets-expected-to-lead-the-nation-in-2023.

6. Dylan Jackson, "Atlanta Has the Highest Income Inequality in the Nation, Census Data Shows," *Atlanta Journal-Constitution*, November 28, 2022, https://www.ajc.com/news/investigations/atlanta-has-the-highest-income-inequality-in-the-nation-census-data-shows/YJRZ6A4UGBFWTMYICTG2BCOUPU/; Thomas Wheatley, "Atlanta's Surveillance Network Keeps Growing," *Atlanta Magazine*, November 11, 2021, https://www.atlantamagazine.com/news-culture-articles/atlantas-surveillance-network-keeps-growing-and-growing-and/.

7. Dan Immergluck, *Red Hot City: Housing, Race, and Exclusion in Twenty-First-Century Atlanta* (Oakland: University of California Press), 7.

8. Maurice J. Hobson, *The Legend of the Black Mecca: Politics and Class in the Making of Modern Atlanta* (Chapel Hill: University of North Carolina Press, 2017), 170.

9. Seth Gustafson, "Displacement and the Racial State in Olympic Atlanta, 1990–1996" *Southeastern Geographer* 53, no. 3 (Summer 2013): 198–213,

10. Bill Littlefield, "The Olympic Juggernaut: Displacing the Poor from Atlanta to Rio," WBUR, August 5, 2016, https://www.wbur.org/onlygame/2016/08/05/autodromo-rio-atlanta-olympics.

11. Littlefield, "The Olympic Juggernaut."

12. Dan Immergluck and Tharunya Balan, "Sustainable for Whom? Green Urban Development, Environmental Gentrification, and the Atlanta Beltline," *Urban Geography* 39, no. 4 (2018): 546–62.

13. Immergluck, "Atlanta's BeltLine."

14. Neil deMause, "Why Are Georgia Taxpayers Paying $700m for a New NFL Stadium?," *The Guardian*, September 29, 2017, https://www.theguardian.com/sport/2017/sep/29/why-are-georgia-taxpayers-paying-700m-for-a-new-nfl-stadium.

15. Scott Trubey, Leon Stafford, and Chris Vivlamore, "Philips Arena to Get $192.5 Million Facelift," *Atlanta Journal-Constitution*, November 1, 2016, https://www.ajc.com/news/local-govt--politics/philips-arena-get-192-million-facelift/p0pmAXHuT9TXdTwYq9USwO/.

16. Collin Kelley, "Report: $17 Million in Tax Breaks Approved for Summer-hill, Midtown Projects," *Rough Draft Atlanta*, September 22, 2017, https://roughdraftatlanta.com/2017/09/22/report-17-million-tax-breaks-ap-proved-summerhill-midtown-projects/; Scott Trubey, "Protesters Camp Out at Turner Field," *Atlanta Journal-Constitution*, April 3, 2017, https://www.ajc.com/news/local/group-takes-tents-protest-georgia-state-plans-for-turner-field/nuzsKO2bppa7vYHXAvHYcP/.

17. Maggie Lee, "Critics Rallying to 'Redlight the Gulch'; Call It a Bad Deal for Atlanta," *Saporta Report*, October 5, 2018, https://saportareport.com/critics-rallying-to-redlight-the-gulch-call-it-a-bad-deal-for-atlanta/sec-tions/reports/maggie/.

18. Immergluck, *Red Hot City*, 92.

19. Heather Buckner, "Is Atlanta Losing Out on Millions of Dollars in Rev-enue Each Year in Property Taxes?," *Atlanta Magazine*, January 6, 2023, https://www.atlantamagazine.com/news-culture-articles/is-atlanta-los-ing-out-on-millions-of-dollars-in-revenue-each-year-in-property-taxes/.

20. Chauncey Alcorn, "Mayor Andre Dickens Responds to Housing Backlash," *Capital B Atlanta*, May 13, 2022, https://atlanta.capitalbnews.org/politi-cal-reporters-notebook-dickens-housing-trust-fund/.

21. Micah Herskind, "The Fight to Stop Cop City Has Decades-Old Roots," *Prism Reports*, March 2, 2023, https://prismreports.org/2023/03/02/fight-stop-cop-city/.

22. ATLBudget – The People's Guide to the City of Atlanta's Budget, https://atlbudget.org/.

23. Wheatley, "Atlanta's Surveillance Network Keeps Growing"; Elizabeth Weill-Greenberg, "Half of Atlanta's Fulton County Jail Has Not Been Charged with Crime," The Appeal, October 12, 2022, https://theappeal.org/fulton-county-jail-aclu-study/.

24. John Ruch, "How Occupy Atlanta Changed City Politics 10 Years Later," *Saporta Report*, October 4, 2021, https://saportareport.com/how-occu-py-atlanta-changed-city-politics-10-years-later/columnists/johnruch/; Herskind and Roberts, "The Failure of Police Reform."

25. Che Johnson-Long, "Starving the Beast: Practical Abolition in Atlanta," *National Lawyers Guild Review* 77, no. 2 (Summer 2022): 57–80.

26. Stephen Deere, "Atlanta City Council Votes Down Withholding Police Funding," *Atlanta Journal-Constitution*, June 20, 2020, https://www.ajc.com/news/local-govt--politics/atlanta-city-council-votes-down-withhold-ing-police-funding/dkVvkxqu62JTekBIYqzPON/.

27. Zachary Hansen, "170 Officers Called Out Sick Following Charges in Rayshard Brooks Case," *Atlanta Journal-Con-stitution*, June 26, 2020, https://www.ajc.com/news/

crime--law/170-atlanta-police-officers-called-out-sick-during-blue-flu-pro-
tests-records-show/RIDIMWuApAM0Ytmdiwx01H/.

28. Christian Boone, "APD Morale at All-Time Low Following Tumultuous
    Two Weeks," *Atlanta Journal-Constitution*, June 18, 2020, https://www.
    ajc.com/news/crime--law/apd-morale-all-time-low-following-tumultu-
    ous-two-weeks/7MHgPuuCPbkhUXYnuQyZ8O/; Kylie Murdock and
    Nathan Kasai, "The Crime of the Crime Narrative," *Third Way*, September 13,
    2021, https://www.thirdway.org/memo/the-crime-of-the-crime-narrative.

29. Maria Saporta, "Atlanta Committee for Progress to Help Fight Crime
    in the City," *Saporta Report*, April 1, 2021, https://saportareport.com/
    atlanta-committee-for-progress-to-help-fight-crime-in-the-city/sections/
    reports/maria_saporta/.

30. Joe Parker, "The Rise and Fall of the Buckhead Cityhood Movement: An
    Updated Timeline," *Buckhead*, March 10, 2023, https://www.buckhead.
    com/the-rise-and-fall-of-the-buckhead-cityhood-movement-a-timeline/.

31. J. D. Capelouto and Jennifer Peebles, "City of Buckhead: Data Shows What
    Proposed Buckhead City Would Look Like," *Atlanta Journal-Constitution*,
    April 25, 2021, https://www.ajc.com/news/atlanta-news/what-would-
    buckhead-city-look-like-we-crunched-the-numbers/WRIYJBY2PBCE-
    JFKWTFK2YDWXYA/.

32. Herskind, "Cop City and the Prison Industrial Complex in Atlanta."

33. Herskind, "Cop City and the Prison Industrial Complex in Atlanta."

34. Sam Worley and Myrydd Wells, "Next Stop, Cop City? What's Hap-
    pening with the Controversial Plan for a New Police and Fire Training
    Center in DeKalb," *Atlanta Magazine*, September 8, 2021, https://www.
    atlantamagazine.com/news-culture-articles/next-stop-cop-city-whats-
    happening-with-the-controversial-plan-for-a-new-police-and-fire-training-
    center-in-dekalb/.

35. Herskind, "Cop City and the Prison Industrial Complex in Atlanta."

36. Jon Shirek, "Atlanta Residents Push for Tougher Street Racing Penalties,"
    11Alive, September 10, 2020, https://www.11alive.com/article/news/
    local/atlanta-residents-push-for-tougher-street-racing-penalties/85-
    ac6628e5-5a98-4aa7-9af5-19d3e1f60bd7.

37. Atlanta City Council, "Atlanta City Council Members J. P. Matzigkeit,
    Howard Shook and Matt Westmoreland Donate $125,000 to Buckhead
    Security Plan," press release, December 28, 2020, https://citycouncil.
    atlantaga.gov/Home/Components/News/News/2374/.

38. Madeline Thigpen, "Understanding Atlanta's Great Jail Debate," *Capital B
    Atlanta*, September 14, 2022, https://atlanta.capitalbnews.org/acdc-fulton-
    jail-explainer/.

39. Wilborn P. Nobles, "Atlanta's Mayoral Candidates Resume Focus on Fighting Crime at Latest Debate," *Atlanta Journal-Constitution*, October 14, 2021, https://www.ajc.com/news/atlanta-news/atlantas-mayoral-candi-dates-resume-focus-on-fighting-crime-at-latest-debate/2LTW5EO4CZH-VHO5VTPBPVY4P5E/.

40. Wilborn P. Nobles, "Atlanta Mayor Touts Plans to Open New Police Train-ing Center," *Atlanta Journal-Constitution*, April 1, 2021, https://www.ajc.com/news/atlanta-news/atlanta-mayor-touts-plans-to-open-new-police-training-center/SD57ADXAEVEAXKCEQWG353JUJI/.

41. John Ruch, "How Atlanta Might—and Might Not—Share Its Controver-sial Public Safety Training Center," *Saporta Report*, July 12, 2021, https://saportareport.com/how-atlanta-might-and-might-not-share-its-controver-sial-public-safety-training-center/columnists/johnruch/.

42. Nobles, "Atlanta Mayor Touts Plans to Open New Police Training Center."

43. Anjali Huynh, "Atlanta Mayor Bottoms Says Forested Land Only Option for Public Safety Training Center," *Atlanta Journal-Constitution*, September 9, 2021, https://www.ajc.com/news/atlanta-mayor-bot-toms-says-forested-land-only-option-for-public-safety-training-center/LMYFNLZQRRE4ZGDFQDTHIIPDYA/.

44. Alanta Committee for Progress, "Atlanta Committee for Progress to Support Mayor Bottoms' Plan to Address Violent Crime," press release, April 1, 2021, https://www.atlprogress.org/_pdf/ACP_Public_Safety_Release_04-01-21.pdf; Huynh, "Atlanta Mayor Bottoms Says Forested Land Only Option for Public Safety Training Center."

45. Ruch, "How Atlanta Might—and Might Not—Share Its Controversial Public Safety Training Center."

46. Charles Bethea, "The New Fight over an Old Forest in Atlanta," *New Yorker*, August 3, 2022, https://www.newyorker.com/news/letter-from-the-south/the-new-fight-over-an-old-forest-in-atlanta.

47. Editorial Board, "Crime Wave Should Spur Action on Center," *Atlanta Journal-Constitution*, July 28, 2021, https://www.ajc.com/opinion/opinion-crime-wave-should-spur-action-on-center/E2G7BMPL2BEZH-POW4AOJBXUG64/.

48. Herskind and Roberts, "The Failure of Police Reform."

49. Herskind, "Cop City and the Prison Industrial Complex in Atlanta."

50. "Your Voice Is Needed SUNDAY, 9/6 @ 4pm," Atlanta Police Foundation, email, September 3, 2021, https://drive.google.com/file/d/1sGoCn8P7hk-9CoUFnLH2MFfh0gAJwje1C/view.

51. Aja Arnold, "Why Atlantans Are Pushing to Stop 'Cop City,'" The Appeal, December 8, 2021, https://theappeal.org/atlanta-cop-city-police-train-ing-facility/.

52. Wilborn P. Nobles, "Atlanta Police Foundation Unveils Preliminary Renderings of New Training Center," *Atlanta Journal-Constitution*, April 12, 2021, https://www.ajc.com/news/atlanta-news/atlanta-police-foundation-unveils-renderings-of-new-public-safety-academy/G2EUT-PUTH5ARDK5M54MWACJMIU/.

53. Kristal Dixon, "Violent Crime in Atlanta Dropped During 2023," *Axios*, January 5, 2024, https://www.axios.com/local/atlanta/2024/01/05/atlanta-crime-stats-2023-homicide-car-theft.

54. Leo Goldsmith, "Town and Country," *Artforum*, September 15, 2022, https://www.artforum.com/film/the-american-auguries-of-riotsville-usa-89247.

55. Jennifer Bamberg, "Controversial West Side Cop Academy Will Have Mock Neighborhood for Training. Here's What It Will Look Like," *Block Club Chicago*, August 10, 2022, https://blockclubchicago.org/2022/08/10/controversial-west-side-cop-academy-will-have-mock-neighborhood-for-training-heres-what-it-will-look-like/.

56. Kiran Misra, "#NoCopAcademy and the Movement to Defund the Police," *Belt Magazine*, July 31, 2020, https://beltmag.com/no-cop-academy-movement-defund-police-chicago/.

57. Renee Johnston, "Cop Cities, USA," *Is Your Life Better* (Substack), https://isyourlifebetter.net/cop-cities-usa/.

58. Stuart Schrader, "Defund the Global Policeman," *N+1*, Fall 2020, https://www.nplusonemag.com/issue-38/politics/defund-the-global-policeman/.

59. Oded Balilty, "Israelis Train in Ghost Town Dubbed 'Mini Gaza,'" Associated Press, June 22, 2022, https://apimagesblog.com/blog/2022/6/19/israelis-train-in-ghost-town-dubbed-mini-gaza.

60. Matthew Petti, "U.S. Cops Don't Need Israeli Counterterrorism Training," *Reason*, https://reason.com/2022/06/20/do-small-town-cops-need-training-in-israeli-counterterror-techniques/.

61. Rose Scott, "PAD Responds to Overcrowding at Fulton County's Jail," WABE, November 21, 2022, https://www.wabe.org/podcasts/closer-look/pad-responds-to-overcrowding-at-fulton-countys-jail-communication-app-for-children-now-available-in-south-africa-the-healthcare-georgia-foundation-receives-9-million-donation/; Shaddi Abusaid, "Atlanta Officials Unveil New Buckhead Police Precinct," *Atlanta Journal-Constitution*, January 14, 2022, https://www.ajc.com/news/atlanta-officials-unveil-new-buckhead-police-precinct/OXKWEEFXGRH4ZE-JMFHXUWRLSDA/.

62. Bob Pepalis, "New Fulton County Jail Could Cost $2 Billion, According to Study," Georgia Public Broadcasting, December 8, 2023, https://www.

gpb.org/news/2023/12/08/new-fulton-county-jail-could-cost-2-billion-according-study.

63. Herskind, "The Fight to Stop Cop City Has Decades-Old Roots."

64. Greg Bluestein, "Atlanta Loses Bid for Democratic National Convention to Chicago," *Atlanta Journal-Constitution*, November 9, 2017, https://www.ajc.com/politics/atlanta-loses-bid-for-democratic-national-convention-to-chicago/GLMOV35VZNFJVNDIMDDHT4YZPA/.

65. Hannah Appel, "Public Thinker: Destin Jenkins on Breaking Bonds," *Public Books*, December 13, 2021, https://www.publicbooks.org/public-thinker-destin-jenkins-on-breaking-bonds/.

66. Bethea, "The New Fight over an Old Forest in Atlanta."

67. Drew Kann, "As Atlanta Grows, Its Trademark Tree Canopy Suffers," *Atlanta Journal-Constitution*, January 20, 2023, https://www.ajc.com/news/as-atlanta-grows-its-trademark-tree-canopy-suffers/NM7Y6L3X-UBDZTJYWPXHNIV5WC4/.

68. Micah Herskind and Hannah Riley, "Atlanta's 'Cop City' Is Putting Policing Before the Climate," *Teen Vogue*, January 30, 2023, https://www.teen-vogue.com/story/stop-cop-city-tortugita-oped; John Ruch, "South River Forest: A Big Green Dream Starts Coming True," *Saporta Report*, June 8, 2021, https://saportareport.com/south-river-forest-a-big-green-dream-starts-coming-true/columnists/johnruch/; David Pendered, "National Spotlight Shines on South River as Example of Environmental Injustice," *Saporta Report*, April 14, 2021, https://saportareport.com/national-spot-light-shines-on-south-river-as-example-of-environmental-injustice/sections/reports/david/.

69. Ryan Gravel, "FAQ > 'What Process Would We Expect?,'" August 21, 2021, https://ryangravel.com/2021/08/21/faq-what-process-would-we-expect/.

70. Tyler Estep, "DeKalb Commission Approves Controversial Blackhall Land Swap," *Atlanta Journal-Constitution*, October 13, 2020, https://www.ajc.com/news/atlanta-news/dekalb-commission-approves-controver-sial-blackhall-land-swap/D6TXV35KDVFOZDQ6HGD3HEPGRQ/.

71. David Pendered, "Blackhall Studios Sale Did Not Include 40 Acres Once in DeKalb County's Intrenchment Creek Park," *Saporta Report*, June 6, 2021, https://saportareport.com/blackhall-studios-sale-did-not-include-40-acres-once-in-dekalb-countys-intrenchment-creek-park/sections/reports/david/.

72. Atlanta Community Press Collective, "Stop the Swap Lawsuit Plaintiffs File Emergency Motion in Response to Destruction at Weelaunee People's Park," December 23, 2022, https://atlpresscollective.com/2022/12/23/stop-the-swap-lawsuit-plaintiffs-file-emergency-motion-in-response-to-destruction-at-weelaunee-peoples-park/.

73. Maria Saporta, "Ryan Millsap Sells Blackhall Studios, Plans New Ventures," *Saporta Report*, April 28, 2021, https://saportareport.com/ryan-millsap-sells-blackhall-studios-plans-new-ventures/sections/reports/maria_saporta/.

74. Dan Immergluck, "Atlanta's BeltLine Shows How Urban Parks Can Drive 'Green Gentrification' If Cities Don't Think About Affordable Housing at the Start," *The Conversation*, January 25, 2023, https://theconversation.com/atlantas-beltline-shows-how-urban-parks-can-drive-green-gentrification-if-cities-dont-think-about-affordable-housing-at-the-start-193204.

Chapter 2: Boss Terror: How the Capital of the South Funded Cop City

1. Passive investment strategy seeks to maximize returns by minimizing buying and selling.

2. Bocar A. Ba, Roman Rivera, and Alexander Whitefield, "Market Response to Racial Uprisings," National Bureau of Economic Research, August 2023, https://www.nber.org/system/files/working_papers/w31606/w31606.pdf

3. Color of Change, *Police Foundations: A Corporate-Sponsored Threat to Democracy*, October 2021.

4. Alex Ross, "How American Racism Influenced Hitler," *New Yorker*, April 23, 2018.

5. Edmund Drago, "Black Legislators During Reconstruction," New Georgia Encyclopedia, last modified July 25, 2023, https://www.georgiaencyclopedia.org/articles/history-archaeology/black-legislators-during-reconstruction/.

6. Drago, "Black Legislators During Reconstruction."

7. Douglas Blackmon, *Slavery by Another Name: The Re-enslavement of Black Americans from the Civil War to World War II* (New York: Doubleday, 2008).

8. Gilbert Lewis, "A Negro Tuul Organizer in the South of the USA," *Negro Worker* 3, no. 7 (May 1930); Matthew Hild, "Organizing Across the Color Line: The Knights of Labor and Black Recruitment Efforts in Small-Town Georgia," *Georgia Historical Quarterly* 81, no. 2 (1997): 287–310.

9. Stewart Tolnay and E. Beck, "Lynching," New Georgia Encyclopedia, last modified August 12, 2020, https://www.georgiaencyclopedia.org/articles/history-archaeology/lynching/.

10. Gina Echevarria, "How Coca-Cola Invented Fanta During World War II," *Business Insider*, March 14, 2021; Juan Forero, "Union Says Coca-Cola in Colombia Uses Thugs," *New York Times*, July 26, 2001.

11. Coca-Cola Company, "Coke Foundation Pledges $2 Million to Atlanta Police Foundation," October 9, 2018, https://www.coca-colacompany.com/news/coke-foundation-pledges-2-m-to-atlantapolice.

12. Ayla Kahn, "Sterk Leaves Atlanta Police Foundation Board of Trustees, University Denies Connections Following Cop City Protests," *Emory Wheel,* February 26, 2023. Others schools, including Georgia State University and Morehouse, hold seats on the board of the Atlanta Committee for Progress, as discussed in Micah Herskind's chapter in this volume.

13. SunTrust Foundation, "SunTrust Foundations Award $3 Million to Atlanta Police Foundation," PR Newswire, September 17, 2019.

14. Barry T. Hirsch, David A. McPherson, and Wayne G. Vroman, "Estimates of Union Density by State, 1964–2000," *Monthly Labor Review,* July 2001.

15. Hannah Bowlus, "Norfolk Southern Donated $100,000 to Cop City," *In These Times,* February 28, 2023, https://inthesetimes.com/article/norfolk-southern-cop-city-east-palestine-railroads.

16. Bowlus, "Norfolk Southern Donated $100,000 to Cop City."

17. John Ruch, "Atlanta's Overlooked Labor Union History May Show the Future of Changing Times," *Saporta Report,* August 15, 2022, https://saportareport.com/atlantas-overlooked-labor-union-history-may-show-the-future-of-changing-times/columnists/johnruch/.

18. "Baggage Handler Hourly Salaries, in Atlanta, GA at Delta Air Lines," Indeed, https://www.indeed.com/cmp/Delta-Air-Lines/salaries/Baggage-Handler/Atlanta-GA; "Living Wage Calculation for Atlanta-Sandy Springs-Alpharetta, GA," Living Wage Calculator, https://livingwage.mit.edu/metros/12060.

19. Color of Change, *Police Foundations.*

20. "Waffle House Inc Profile: Summary," Open Secrets, https://www.opensecrets.org/orgs/waffle-house-inc/summary?id=D000029728.

21. US Department of Labor, "US Department of Labor Recovers $47K in Back Wages, Damages for Employees of Utah Chick-fil-A Franchisee, Fines Employer $187K," press release, September 28, 2023, https://www.dol.gov/newsroom/releases/whd/whd20230928; Steve Mollman, "A Chick-fil-A That Paid Workers with Sandwiches Instead of Actual Money Was Just Fined by the Department of Labor," *Fortune,* December 22, 2022, https://fortune.com/2022/12/22/chick-fil-a-paid-workers-sandwiches-not-wages-fined-department-of-labor/.

22. K Agbebiyi, Azani Creeks, and Amanda Mendoza, *P.E. Profits from Destroying the Atlanta Forest,* Private Equity Stakeholder Project, March 2023.

23. Ihna Mangundayao et al., "More Than $3 Billion in Stolen Wages Recovered for Workers Between 2017 and 2020," Economic Policy Institute, December 22, 2021.

24. Jamie Bynum, "The Uprising of '34," West Georgia Textile Heritage Trail, February 25, 2022.

25. Bynum. "The Uprising of '34."

26. James Swift, "Bill Would Exclude Some Nonprofit Data from Open Records Laws," *Dalton Daily Citizen*, February 21, 2024, https://www.dailycitizen.news/news/local_news/bill-would-exclude-some-non-profit-data-from-open-records-laws/article_0f9bf8ca-cf4a-11ee-a6c8-43d75b0916d7.html.

Chapter 3: A Brief History of the Atlanta Prison Farm

1. "Life on the Farm: 'Many of Our Drunks Leave Here After Breakfast and Are Back by Supper . . . ,'" *Atlanta Journal-Constitution*, May 21, 1976.
2. "Arkansas Prison Said Graveyard of Murdered Men," *Desert Sun*, January 30, 1968.
3. "Coroner's Jury Will Probe Death of Prisoner; Brown Urges Full Investigation," *Atlanta Daily World*, April 14, 1953.
4. "Prisoner Drops Dead," *Atlanta Daily World*, May 28, 1957.
5. "Prison Death Brings Lawsuit Against City," *Atlanta Journal-Constitution*, July 27, 1977.
6. "Recorder Suggests City Prison Farm," *Atlanta Constitution*, January 5, 1915.
7. "Provision Is Made for New Schools," *Atlanta Constitution*, June 1, 1918.
8. "State Will Probe Flogging Charges at City Stockade," *Atlanta Constitution*, January 10, 1920.
9. "Whipping Women at City Stockade Ordered Stopped," *Atlanta Constitution*, January 13, 1920.
10. "Flogging Ended at City Prison," *Atlanta Constitution*, January 25, 1920.
11. "Prison Committee to Meet Today," *Atlanta Constitution*, November 11, 1922.
12. "304 Prisoners Held in Atlanta Stockade," *Atlanta Constitution*, March 14, 1925.
13. "African-American Experience," Atlanta: A National Register of Historic Places Travel Itinerary, National Park Service Atlanta, 2021, https://www.nps.gov/nr/travel/atlanta/africanamerican.html.
14. Conor Lee, "Doll's Head Trail at Constitution Lakes," History Atlanta, July 9, 2014, http://historyatlanta.com/dolls-head-trail-constitution-lakes/.
15. "Arnall to See Prison Opening," *Atlanta Constitution*, May 17, 1944.
16. "Life on the Farm: 'Many of Our Drunks Leave Here After Breakfast.'"
17. B. Tarleton, "New Atlanta Prison 'Good Investment,'" *Atlanta Journal-Constitution*, November 4, 1946.
18. T. Cooper, "'Slave Labor' Gone at the Prison Farm, but Inmates Still Tend Cattle, Hogs," *Atlanta Constitution*, December 22, 1982.
19. "Conflicting Pictures Are Drawn of Prison Farm Conditions Here," *Atlanta Constitution*, June 22, 1938.
20. "Atlanta Police Department," *Atlanta Constitution*, May 2, 1936.

21. "Prison Head Urgently Needed for City System. New Wing Is Finished on Atlanta Penal Farm Building," *Atlanta Constitution*, January 1, 1938.

22. "Conflicting Pictures Are Drawn of Prison Farm Conditions Here."

23. "DeKalb Jury Findings Merit Careful Attention," *Atlanta Constitution*, November 26, 1958.

24. "Steps in Right Direction Taken at Prison Farm," *Atlanta Constitution*, December 24, 1958; "Jury Raps Prison Overcrowding," *Atlanta Constitution*, October 29, 1960.

25. Dick Herbert, "City Prison's a Much Better Place These Days," *Atlanta Constitution*, December 9, 1965.

26. G. Stephens, "Mayor's Office and Stockade Boss Disagree," *Atlanta Constitution*, October 16, 1970.

27. "Alderman Dodson's Record of Progress and Dedication," *Atlanta Voice*, September 1, 1973.

28. William J. Todd, Fulton DeKalb Hospital Authority, Inter-office Communication, May 28, 1976, Mary N. Long Papers, Series II, Grady Memorial Hospital, 1969–1987, box 3, folder 8, entitled "Grady Memorial Hospital: City of Atlanta Prison and Farm, 1971–1979," undated, Special Collections and Archives, Georgia State University.

29. H. Woodhead, "Can Respect Keep Men Out of Jail," *Atlanta Constitution*, July 23, 1972.

30. "Keep the Heat on Prisons," *Atlanta Constitution*, November 28, 1982; "Two Atlanta Escapees Back in Jail," *Atlanta Constitution*, November 28, 1982.

31. Katheryn Hayes, "City Agrees to $4,500 Settlement with Former Prison Farm Inmates," *Atlanta Constitution*, May 31, 1985.

32. "Firm Wins City Contract Three Months After Investigation," Atlanta Constitution, May 3, 1987.

33. Tracy Hresko, "In the Cellars of the Hollow Men: Use of Solitary Confinement in U.S. Prisons and Its Implications Under International Laws Against Torture," *Pace International Law Review* 18, no. 1 (2006).

34. Atlanta Community Press Collective, "A Brief History of the Atlanta Prison Farm," August 14, 2021, https://atlpresscollective. com/2021/08/14/history-of-the-atlanta-city-prison-farm/.

Chapter 4: Becoming External Enemies: From Occupy Atlanta to Stop Cop City

1. Ernie Suggs, "Atlanta Way Challenged After Violent Night of Protests," *Atlanta Journal-Constitution*, May 30, 2020.

2. Kayla Edgett and Sarah Abdelaziz, "The Atlanta Way: Repression, Mediation, and Division of Black Resistance from 1906 to the 2020 George Floyd

Uprising," *Atlanta Studies*, October 4, 2021; Charles Rutheiser, *Imagineering Atlanta: The Politics of Place in the City of Dreams* (London: Verso, 1996).

3. W. E. B. Du Bois, *Black Reconstruction in America: An Essay Toward a History of the Part Which Black Folk Played in the Attempt to Reconstruct Democracy in America, 1860–1880*, with an introduction by David Levering Lewis (New York: Free Press, 1992).

4. Wei Lu and Alexandre Tanzi, "In America's Most Unequal City, Top Households Rake in $663,000," *Bloomberg*, November 2, 2019; Jurgita Lapienytė, "This Is the Most Heavily Surveilled City in the US," *CyberNews*, February 22, 2021.

5. Edgett and Abdelaziz, "The Atlanta Way"; Micah Herskind, "Cop City: A Timeline of Policing in Atlanta," *Scalawag Magazine*, May 2023.

6. See Eva Dickerson's chapter in this book.

7. See Winston Grady-Willis, *Challenging U.S. Apartheid: Atlanta and Black Struggles for Human Rights, 1960–1977* (Durham, NC: Duke University Press, 2006); Akira Drake Rodriguez, *Diverging Space for Deviants* (Athens: University of Georgia Press, 2021); Kayla Edgett, "Competing Spatial Imaginaries and Counterinsurgency in the 'Black Mecca': A Case Study of the Ron Carter Patrol" (master's thesis, Georgia State University, 2022); Maurice J. Hobson, *The Legend of the Black Mecca: Politics and Class in the Making of Modern Atlanta* (Chapel Hill: University of North Carolina Press, 2017.

8. Thank you, Amilcar Cabral. Thank you, Lydia Pelot-Hobbs.

9. There are many ways in which the movement can be "traced back." I offer one way, from my limited perspective, no doubt with shortcomings and failures. Many lineages should be written, and all should be taken as partial.

10. Thank you, Mariame Kaba.

11. Thank you, Ruth Wilson Gilmore.

12. Malcolm X Grassroots Movement, "Operation Ghetto Storm," Every 36 Hours Campaign, April 2013. Between 2010 and 2020, over ninety Black people were killed by police in metro Atlanta. Say their names: Joetavius Stafford, Ariston Waiters, Alexia Christian, Anthony Hill, Deaundre Phillips, Shukri Said, Oscar Cain, and so many more, may they rest in power. See "Over the Line," *Atlanta Journal-Constitution*, originally published December 20, 2015, https://investigations.ajc.com/overtheline/.

13. For more thorough analyses of the early years of the movement for Black lives in Atlanta, see Sarah Abdelaziz, "Ratcheting a Way Out of the Respectable: Genealogical Interventions into Atlanta's Respectability Politics" (master's thesis, Georgia State University, 2017); and Taryn Jordan, "The Politics of Impossibility: CeCe McDonald and Trayvon Martin— the Bursting of Black Rage" (master's thesis, Georgia State University, 2014).

14. Matt Kempner, "Andrew Young: Atlanta Police Face 'Unlovable Little Brats Some Times,'" *Atlanta Journal-Constitution*, August 12, 2016.

15. Hobson, *The Legend of the Black Mecca.*

16. For more on this see, Micah Herskind, "Cop City and the Prison Industrial Complex in Atlanta," *Mainline*, February 7, 2022, https://www.mainlinezine.com/cop-city-and-the-prison-industrial-complex-in-atlanta/.

17. For a more in-depth discussion of repression against the movement, see Kamau Franklin's chapter in this book.

18. Sean Summers, "Hundreds Set to Launch Hunger Strike Inside Stewart Detention Center," *Unicorn Riot*, September 6, 2023.

19. Angela Y. Davis, *Abolition Democracy: Beyond Empire, Prisons, and Torture* (New York: Seven Stories Press, 2005).

20. Salar Mohandesi, "Party as Articulator," *Viewpoint Magazine*, September 4, 2020.

21. Ruth Wilson Gilmore, *Abolition Geography: Essays Towards Liberation* (Verso Books, 2022), 491.

Chapter 5: How the Black Misleadership Class Provides Cover to Cop City

1.   Julie Varughese, "The Late Glen Ford's 'The Black Agenda' Lays Out Blueprint for Honest Journalism," *Toward Freedom*, July 27, 2022, https://towardfreedom.org/reviews/book-review-the-late-glen-fords-the-black-agenda-lays-out-blueprint-for-honest-journalism/.

2.   Dorrie Toney, "ACLU of Georgia Leaves Public Safety Training Center Task Force over Concerns About Transparency," ACLU of Georgia, April 20, 2023, https://www.acluga.org/en/press-releases/press-release-aclu-georgia-leaves-public-safety-training-center-task-force-over.

3.   Kayla Edgett and Sarah Abdelaziz, "The Atlanta Way: Repression, Mediation, and Division of Black Resistance from 1906 to the 2020 George Floyd Uprising," *Atlanta Studies*, October 4, 2021, https://atlantastudies.org/2021/10/04/the-atlanta-way-repression-mediation-and-division-of-black-resistance-from-1906-to-the-2020-george-floyd-uprising/.

4.   Gregory Krieg and Paul LeBlanc, "Atlanta Mayor Keisha Lance Bottoms Steps into National Spotlight with Passionate Plea to Protesters," CNN, June 1, 2020, https://www.cnn.com/2020/05/29/politics/atlanta-protests-keisha-lance-bottoms/index.html.

5.   Dan Klepal, "Turner Field Community Benefits Coalition Presents Petition," *Atlanta Journal-Constitution*, April 18, 2016, https://www.ajc.com/news/local-govt--politics/turner-field-community-benefits-coalition-presents-petition/iR09iOWo2gsUbGM5D1akSP/; Ariana Brazier, "The

Taking of Peachtree-Pine and the Dawning of Cop City," *Scalawag*, May 3, 2023, https://scalawagmagazine.org/2023/05/peachtree-pine-cop-city.

6. Tayari Jones, "A Mayor Named Keisha," *Glamour*, October 13, 2020, https://www.glamour.com/story/keisha-lance-bottoms-women-of-the-year-2020.

7. Fox 5 Atlanta Digital Team, "Ex-Atlanta Mayor Keisha Lance Bottoms Appointed to Biden's Export Council," Fox 5 Atlanta, July 17, 2023, https://www.fox5atlanta.com/news/keisha-lance-bottoms-former-atlanta-mayor-biden-administration-export-council.

8. Kasim Reed (@KasimReed), "The Atlanta Way is alive and well," X, December 20, 2017, https://twitter.com/KasimReed/status/943892461738479616?s=20.

9. Patricia Murphy, "'Atlanta Way' Long Gone as City Leaders Face Death Threats over Training Center," *Atlanta Journal-Constitution*, June 10, 2023, https://www.ajc.com/politics/opinion-atlanta-way-long-gone-as-city-leaders-face-death-threats-over-training-center/7Q57D-5ND4ZH25BSJ2WOLPYW2D4/.

10. Ernie Suggs and Rosalind Bentley, "Violent Protest Puts Spotlight on 'Atlanta Way' of Peaceful Marches," *Atlanta Journal-Constitution*, May 30, 2020, https://www.ajc.com/news/atlanta-way-challenged-after-violent-night-protests/HWsEwkX0ZN6xD4kesoElSO/.

11. 11Alive Staff, "Raphael Warnock Eulogy for Rayshard Brooks," 11Alive, June 23, 2020, https://www.11alive.com/article/news/local/raphael-warnock-eulogy-for-rayshard-brooks/85-dd5d474c-faf3-4e4f-ae06-99d076a1d81a.

12. Prem Thakker, "Atlanta Mayor Dismisses Cop City Referendum as 'Not an Election,'" *The Intercept*, September 27, 2023, https://theintercept.com/2023/09/27/cop-city-referendum-atlanta-andre-dickens/.

13. Emma Hurt, "Stacey Abrams Wants to Fund the Police," *Axios*, June 23, 2022, https://www.axios.com/local/atlanta/2022/06/23/exclusive-stacey-abrams-wants-fund-the-police.

14. Riley Bunch, "Abrams Supports Putting Atlanta's Training Center to a Vote," *Atlanta Journal-Constitution*, September 17, 2023, https://www.ajc.com/news/atlanta-news/abrams-supports-putting-atlantas-training-center-to-a-vote/JOZWWL2S65FTPPD7K7GY7AP47E/.

15. Atlanta Community Press Collective (@ACPC_Live), "You're taking care of all the kids in the city . . ." X, June 20, 2023, https://twitter.com/ACPC_Live/status/1671265919568584704?s=20.

16. Natasha Lennard, "Atlanta Cop City Protesters Charged with Domestic Terror for Having Mud on Their Shoes," *The Intercept*, March 8, 2023, https://theintercept.com/2023/03/08/atlanta-cop-city-protesters/.

17. Bill Torpy, "The Privileged, Transient Warriors Protesting Police Training Center," *Atlanta Journal-Constitution*, March 8, 2023, https://www.ajc.

com/opinion/columnists/opinion-cop-citys-privileged-transient-war-riors/KZ5UDGLLLZGXTPXW6KAMJH5SPI/.

18.   Timothy Pratt, "Atlanta's Black Community Raises Voice Against 'Cop City' Police Base," *The Guardian*, March 12, 2023, https://www.theguardian.com/us-news/2023/mar/12/atlanta-cop-city-black-community-protest.

19.   Andre Dickens (@andreforatlanta), "We focused on youth, night-life . . ." X, July 27, 2023, https://twitter.com/andreforatlanta/status/1684585610466545665?s=20.

20.   Unity and Struggle, *Big Brick Energy: A Multi-city Study of the 2020 George Floyd Uprising*, July 2022, http://www.unityandstruggle.org/2022/07/big-brick-energy-a-multi-city-study-of-the-2020-george-floyd-uprising/.

Chapter 9: Base Building to Stop Cop City: Successes, Failures, Reflections, and Lessons for Future Organizers

1.   A 1-1 is a tool used by organizers for effective base building that involves sitting down for an hour long meeting with a member. It gives the organizer an opportunity to get to know members, connect them to a group, and contribute to their leadership development by asking them to take on some sort of task (e.g. making phone calls, giving a speech at a rally, bringing food to the next meeting, or canvassing their neighbors.)

2.   Provided to author by Lily Ponitz.

3.   Data based on information collected in reflective conversations with can-vassers after each outreach session.

Chapter 10: Is This Enough Black Folks for You, Andre Dickens?

1.   Gabrielle Chung, "6 Atlanta Officers Charged After Body Cam Footage Shows Them Using Tasers on Black College Students," *People*, June 2, 2020, https://people.com/crime/atlanta-officers-charged-after-body-cam-foot-age-shows-them-using-taser-on-black-students/.

2.   Malachy Browne et al., "The Killing of Rayshard Brooks: How a 41-Min-ute Police Encounter Suddenly Turned Fatal," *New York Times*, June 22, 2020, https://www.nytimes.com/video/us/100000007198581/rayshard-brooks-killing-garrett-rolfe.html.

3.   Chauncey Alcorn, "Key Dates and Moments in Atlanta's 'Cop City' Con-troversy," *Capital B Atlanta*, June 5, 2023, https://atlanta.capitalbnews.org/cop-city-timeline/.

4.   Bo Emerson, "Pro-Palestinian Protesters Denounce Israel as Violence in Gaza Grows," *Atlanta Journal-Constitution*, May 15, 2021, https://www.ajc.com/news/pro-palestinian-protesters-denounce-israel-as-violence-in-ga-za-grows/V772FS5VONCAPHLBELUAABHOPY/.

5. Tyler Estep, "Longtime Atlanta City Council Members Ousted in Runoffs," *Atlanta Journal-Constitution*, December 2, 2021, https://www.ajc.com/neighborhoods/dekalb/longtime-atlanta-city-council-members-ousted-in-runoffs/Z64S2FLGQRF37AOU5ODKPTWPXY/.

6. Chauncey Alcorn, "Environmental Impact Targeted in New Push Against 'Cop City,'" Center for Public Integrity, November 15, 2023, https://publicintegrity.org/environment/pollution/environmental-justice-denied/environmental-impact-targeted-in-new-push-against-cop-city/.

7. Sinduja Rangarajan, Hannah Levintova, and Laura Thompson, "The Blue Budget: What Cities Spend on Police," *Mother Jones*, September 2020.

8. Doug Richards, "Atlanta Census Data: Black Population No Longer Majority," 11Alive, August 26, 2021, https://www.11alive.com/article/news/local/census-no-more-black-majority-in-atlanta/85-645bed51-b9bd-4263-bbd3-40c1a97ded61.

9. City of Atlanta, "FAQs on Nationwide Calls for Police Reform," One Atlanta, 2020, https://justicereform.atlantaga.gov/faq#training-updates-2.

10. Linda Qiu, "Justice Dept. to Investigate Fulton County Jail in Georgia," *New York Times*, July 13, 2023, https://www.nytimes.com/2023/07/13/us/politics/georgia-jail-death-investigation.html.

11. Benjamin Stumpf, "'Outside Agitators' from the Civil Rights Movement to Stop Cop City," *Abusable Past*, April 5, 2023, https://abusablepast.org/outside-agitators-from-the-civil-rights-movement-to-stop-cop-city/.

12. Timothy Pratt, "Atlanta's Black Community Raises Voice Against 'Cop City' Police Base," *The Guardian*, March 12, 2023, https://www.theguardian.com/us-news/2023/mar/12/atlanta-cop-city-black-community-protest.

13. "'Because We Need It': Atlanta Mayor Moves Forward with Police Training Center Following Task Force Meeting," 11Alive, April 19, 2023, https://www.11alive.com/article/news/politics/andre-dickens-press-conference-public-safety-training-center-cop-city-task-force/85-81fdbfe0-0e81-46c2-8d84-7237eea06a92.

14. Nicholas Wooten, "Buckhead City Atlanta Cop City Poll," 11Alive, March 17, 2023, https://www.11alive.com/article/news/politics/emory-poll-atlanta-residents-buckhead-city-cop-city-public-safety-training-center/85-4edd2e82-39f9-49f6-9b1a-c5c20489197d.

15. Timothy Franzen, "Stop Cop City Ballot Initiative Has over 116,000 Signatures," American Friends Service Committee, September 14, 2023, https://afsc.org/news/stop-cop-city-ballot-initiative-has-over-116000-signatures.

Chapter 11: Protecting the South River Forest

1. Intrenchment Creek Park is known to the movement as Weelaunee People's Park.
2. Hence the Cop City slogan "No Cop City, No Hollywood Dystopia."
3. Dr. Echols later clarified, "I had not attended any of the other hearings for demonstrators charged with various lesser crimes. This was the first RICO hearing related to an arrest since the governor decided to pursue racketeering charges."
4. Riley Bunch, "Judge Denies Attempt to Halt Atlanta Police Training Center Construction," *Atlanta Journal-Constitution*, January 18, 2024, https://www.ajc.com/news/atlanta-news/judge-denies-attempt-to-halt-training-center-construction/U2YGHWNYSBERXKN5G2U2EPGFZ4/.

Chapter 13: Students vs. Cop City

1. Anna Simonton, "Inside GILEE, the US-Israel Law Enforcement Training Program Seeking to Redefine Terrorism," *Mondoweiss*, January 5, 2016, https://mondoweiss.net/2016/01/enforcement-training-terrorism/.

Chapter 15: The Roots of Resistance: Building Narrative Power

1. GORAFORRAU (@InoperableSink), "Ajc publisher Andrew Morse offers media services . . . ," X, January 8, 2024, https://twitter.com/InoperableSink/status/1744453040457797804/photo/1.
2. "Ethics Code," *Atlanta Journal-Constitution*, https://www.ajc.com/ethics-code/; "Who We Are," *Atlanta Journal-Constitution*, https://www.ajc.com/about-us/who-we-are/DT6HW7HAYVFG7N2N6TIIHHTTVE/.
3. Kerry Dolan, "Billion Dollar Dynasties: These Are the Richest Families in America," *Forbes*, December 17, 2020, https://www.forbes.com/sites/kerryadolan/2020/12/17/billion-dollar-dynasties-these-are-the-richest-families-in-america/?sh=a1cd043772c7; "A Commitment to New Media," Cox Enterprises, https://www.coxenterprises.com/businesses/cox-new-growth/digital-media; Cox Media Group, https://www.cmg.com/.
4. "James M. Cox," Britannica, https://www.britannica.com/biography/James-M-Cox.
5. Clifford Kuhn and Gregory Mixon, "Atlanta Race Massacre of 1906," *New Georgia Encyclopedia*, November 14, 2022, https://www.georgiaencyclopedia.org/articles/history-archaeology/atlanta-race-massacre-of-1906/.
6. Charles Bethea, "Can 'Cop City' Be Stopped at the Ballot Box?," *New Yorker*, August 12, 2023, https://www.newyorker.com/news/letter-from-the-south/can-cop-city-be-stopped-at-the-ballot-box.

7. Allyson Chiu, 'Every Atlanta Police Officer Gets $500 Bonus from Police Foundation for 'Low Morale' as Sick-Outs Continue,' *Washington Post*, June 19, 2020, https://www.washingtonpost.com/nation/2020/06/19/atlanta-police-bonus-protests/; Kristal Dixon, "Low Morale Hinders Atlanta Police Recruitment," *Axios Atlanta*, October 4, 2021. https://www.axios.com/local/atlanta/2021/10/04/atlanta-kemp-law-enforcement-job-bonuses

8. Editorial Board, "Crime Wave Should Spur Action on Center," *Atlanta Journal-Constitution*, August 21, 2021, https://www.ajc.com/opinion/opinion-crime-wave-should-spur-action-on-center/E2G7BMPL2BEZHPOW4AOJBXUG64/.

9. Stephanie Desmon, "Gun Deaths Spiked During the Pandemic," Johns Hopkins Bloomberg School of Public Health, November 17, 2022, https://publichealth.jhu.edu/2022/gun-deaths-spiked-during-the-pandemic.

10. Robert C. Loudermilk Jr., "Opinion: Atlanta City Council Needs to Step Up, Prioritize Public Safety?," *Atlanta Journal-Constitution*, August 21, 2021, https://www.ajc.com/opinion/opinion-does-atlanta-city-council-really-care-about-public-safety/MBMGNS2I2BBLBHJ7HHFPTVCQ5I/.

11. Dave Wilkinson, "City's Crime Rise Can Be Reversed Once More," *Atlanta Journal-Constitution*, January 15, 2021, https://www.ajc.com/opinion/citys-crime-rise-can-be-reversed-once-more/NXZT4APRCRHD5N-TEPFFZZR3YYE/; Dave Wilkinson, "The Sometimes-Messy but Inexorable March to Public Safety," *Atlanta Journal-Constitution*, May 8, 2021, https://www.ajc.com/opinion/opinion-the-sometimes-messy-but-inexorable-march-to-public-safety/BYFEJFLAVFA6PFWP2E6554QGKA/.

12. Timothy Pratt, "'Cop City' Backers and Opponents Battle for Public Opinion over $90m Project," *The Guardian*, April 2, 2023, https://www.theguardian.com/us-news/2023/apr/02/atlanta-cop-city-public-opinion-poll.

13. The Daily Show, "Roy Wood Jr. Explores Police Militarization & Atlanta's 'Cop City.'" YouTube, January 26, 2023, https://www.youtube.com/watch?v=ibLb-LGP9W8&ab_channel=TheDailyShow.

14. Micah Herskind and Hannah Riley, "Atlanta's 'Cop City' Is Putting Policing Before the Climate," *Teen Vogue*, January 30, 2023, https://www.teenvogue.com/story/stop-cop-city-tortugita-oped.; Natasha Lennard, "Police Shot Atlanta Cop City Protester 57 Times, Autopsy Finds," *The Intercept*, April 20, 2023, https://theintercept.com/2023/04/20/atlanta-cop-city-protester-autopsy/.

15. Timothy Pratt, "Atlanta's Black Community Raises Voice Against 'Cop City' Police Base," *The Guardian*, March 12, 2023, https://www.theguardian.com/us-news/2023/mar/12/atlanta-cop-city-black-community-protest.

16. Madeline Thigpen, "Let the People Decide: Organizers Want a Referendum on Cop City," *Capital B Atlanta*, June 8, 2023, https://atlanta.capitalbnews.org/cop-city-referendum/.

17. The People's RICO, https://thepeoplesrico.org.

18. Atlanta Community Press Collective, "Backroom Deals and Elasticity Clause Increase Public Cost of Cop City," May 24, 2023, https://atlpresscollective.com/2023/05/24/backroom-deals-and-elasticity-clause-increase-public-cost-of-cop-city/.

19. "An Annotated Version of the Indictment Filed Against #StopCopCity Organizers," Interrupting Criminalization, 2023, https://www.interruptingcriminalization.com/resources-all/annotated-indictment.

Chapter 16: Let the People Decide

1. Riley Bunch and Brian Eason, "City Council Passes Funding Legislation for Training Center," *Atlanta Journal-Constitution*, June 6, 2023, https://www.ajc.com/news/atlanta-news/city-council-passes-funding-legislation-for-training-center/H4Z4QYFECRDJBOLQ3YMW43GTCA/.

2. Alex Binder, "'We Do Not Need a School for Assassins': Hours of Public Comment Unanimously Against 'Cop City,'" *Unicorn Riot*, May 16, 2023, https://unicornriot.ninja/2023/we-do-not-need-a-school-for-assassins-hours-of-public-comment-unanimously-against-cop-city/.

3. ACPC Staff, "Stop Cop City Activists Launch Referendum Campaign to Cancel Lease," Atlanta Community Press Collective, June 8, 2023, https://atlpresscollective.com/2023/06/08/stop-cop-city-activists-launch-referendum-campaign-to-cancel-lease/.

4. ACPC Staff, "Stop Cop City Activists Launch Referendum Campaign to Cancel Lease."

5. ACPC Staff, "Stop Cop City Activists Launch Referendum Campaign to Cancel Lease."

6. Russ Bynum, "Vote to Block Georgia Spaceport Upheld by State's High Court," AP News, February 7, 2023, https://apnews.com/article/politics-georgia-state-government-constitutions-referendums-880fc-c37bf74f5970fda6e0dfa123444.

7. Dyana Bagby, "DeKalb Residents Sue Atlanta over 'Cop City' Referendum," *Rough Draft Atlanta*, July 9, 2023, https://roughdraftatlanta.com/2023/07/09/report-dekalb-residents-sue-atlanta-over-cop-city-referendum/.

8. Dyana Bagby, "Judge Rules Residents Living Outside Atlanta Can Collect Signatures for 'Cop City' Referendum Petition," *Rough Draft Atlanta*, July 27, 2023, https://roughdraftatlanta.com/2023/07/27/

judge-rules-residents-living-outside-atlanta-can-collect-signa-tures-for-cop-city-referendum-petition/.

9. Matt Scott, "Body Camera Footage of the Killing of Johnny Hollman Finally Sees the Light of Day," Atlanta Community Press Collective, November 22, 2023, https://atlpresscollective.com/2023/11/22/body-camera-footage-of-the-killing-of-johnny-hollman-finally-sees-the-light-of-day/.

10. R. J. Rico, "'Stop Cop City' Petition Campaign in Limbo After Signa-tures Presented to Atlanta Officials," AP News, September 11, 2023, https://apnews.com/article/atlanta-cop-city-referendum-signa-tures-4b617a220807b6701c9f46745e4762c4.

11. Atlanta Community Press Collective (@atlanta_press), "Today on the Adams Crossing Neighborhood FB Page . . . ," X, July 7, 2023, https://twit-ter.com/atlanta_press/status/1677426999961214977.

12. Rico, "'Stop Cop City' Petition Campaign in Limbo After Signatures Pre-sented to Atlanta Officials."

13. Riley Bunch, "Training Center Petitions Posted on Atlanta City Website After Initial Glitch," Atlanta Journal-Constitution, September 29, 2023, https://www.ajc.com/news/atlanta-news/training-center-petitions-post-ed-on-atlanta-city-website/CRMWRVSQKJFJLEXIOSZKLFP2LY/.

14. Chauncey Alcorn, "Black Atlantans Divided on 'Cop City' Support Ballot Measure for Public Vote," Capital B Atlanta, September 25, 2023, https://atlanta.capitalbnews.org/cop-city-voting-rights/.

15. Riley Bunch, "Atlanta City Council Passes Referendum Legislation After Pushback," Atlanta Journal-Constitution, February 6, 2024, https://www.ajc.com/news/atlanta-news/atlanta-city-council-passes-referendum-legis-lation-after-pushback/BSQM6CP6BFH67A5U3VN45Q5UKY/.

16. Renee Johnston, "Cop Cities, USA.," Is Your Life Better, 2024, https://isyourlifebetter.net/cop-cities-usa/.

Chapter 17: Children Have Always Been at the Center

1. Turtles have become a symbol in the movement, as "Tortuguita" translates to "Little Turtle."

Chapter 18: Dear Andre Dickens, Save Weelaunee

1. Sasha Von Hannah, The Kids of Weelaunee, Weelaunee Coalition Press, May 2023, https://www.themissvon.com/library/kids-of-weelaunee.

Chapter 19: Little Turtle's War

1.   David. Peisner, "The Forest for the Trees," *Bitter Southerner*, December 13, 2022, https://bittersoutherner.com/feature/2022/the-forest-for-the-trees-atlanta-prison-farm.

Chapter 21: In Their Own Words

1.   Timothy Pratt, "'It's Alarming': Diary of Killed Cop City Activist to Play Role in Georgia Lawsuit," *The Guardian*, November 27, 2023, https://www.theguardian.com/us-news/2023/nov/27/cop-city-tortuguita-georgia-manuel-paez-teran.

Chapter 22: How Georgia Indicted a Movement

1.   Matt Scott, "Construction Work Stopped Briefly as Cop City Protesters Enter Site," Atlanta Community Press Collective, September 7, 2023, https://atlpresscollective.com/2023/09/07/construction-work-stopped-briefly-as-cop-city-protesters-enter-site/.
2.   Tiffany Roberts, "The Collapse of Criminal Legal Reform in the Black Mecca," *Essence*, October 4, 2021, https://www.essence.com/news/atlanta-cop-city/.
3.   Natasha Lennard, "Atlanta Cop City Protesters Charged with Domestic Terror for Having Mud on Their Shoes," *The Intercept*, March 8, 2023, https://theintercept.com/2023/03/08/atlanta-cop-city-protesters/.
4.   GA Code Ann., §16-11-220 (2023).
5.   James Salzer, "Kemp Signs $75 Million in Tax Breaks for People Who Donate to Police," *Atlanta Journal-Constitution*, May 29, 2022, https://www.ajc.com/politics/kemp-signs-75-million-in-tax-breaks-for-people-who-donate-to-police/O6ZI7XVDUNGMNN3XGS6Q5WOE6I/.
6.   The People's RICO, https://thepeoplesrico.org/.
7.   Teddy Grant, "Another Inmate Dies at Fulton County Jail, 10th Inmate Death This Year," ABC News, September 6, 2023, https://abcnews.go.com/US/inmate-dies-fulton-county-jail-atlanta-10th-death-this-year/story?id=102974414.
8.   John A. Regan, "RICO 101," Prosecuting Attorneys' Council of Georgia, https://drive.google.com/file/d/1aSON-G8srQR2psMclYAB0QbjFfe-pAdq4/view?usp=sharing.
9.   Nitish Pahwa, "RICOp City," *Slate*, September 13, 2023, https://slate.com/news-and-politics/2023/09/cop-city-defend-the-atlanta-forest-rico-charges-criminal-conspiracy.html.
10. GA Code § 16-14-2 (2022).

11. Natasha Lennard and Akela Lacy, "Activists Face Felonies for Flyers on 'Cop City' Protester Killing," *The Intercept*, May 2, 2023, https://theintercept.com/2023/05/02/cop-city-activists-arrest-flyers/.

12. Jeff Amy, "Georgia Bill Is Latest GOP Effort Targeting Prosecutors," AP News, March 28, 2023, https://apnews.com/article/georgia-prosecutor-district-attorney-remove-discipline-dd06c56d0d0672e38ef11f4c63dda468.

13. Stanley Dunlap, "Georgia Courts Still Struggle with Pandemic-Era Backlogs, State Supreme Court Chief Justice Says," *Georgia Recorder*, March 8, 2023, https://georgiarecorder.com/brief/georgia-courts-still-struggle-with-pandemic-era-backlogs-state-supreme-court-chief-justice-says/.

14. George Chidi, "Young Thug Trial: Court Slowdowns, Prosecution Delays," *Rolling Stone*, March 4, 2023, https://www.rollingstone.com/music/music-features/young-thug-trial-ysl-court-delay-1234687224/.

15. Anna Simonton, "Prosecutor Lauded for Investigating Trump Also Wants to Send Educators to Prison," *The Appeal*, July 6, 2022, https://theappeal.org/atlanta-cheating-prosecutions-fani-willis-rico/.

16. Christina Lee, "What (or Who) Is Behind the Rise of RICO?" *Atlanta Magazine*, June 14, 2023, https://www.atlantamagazine.com/news-culture-articles/what-or-who-is-behind-the-rise-of-rico/.

17. "Criminal Bond Motions Calendar," Superior Court of Fulton County, 2023, https://drive.google.com/file/d/1CAMGehvOIyq3gUvQo-FO5aYoZfD7c9FOW/view.

18. Jim Burress, "YSL Trial Enters Second Year with No End in Sight in Fulton County Court," WABE, February 14, 2024, https://www.wabe.org/ysl-trial-enters-second-year-with-no-end-in-sight-in-fulton-county-court/.

19. 11Alive Staff, "Lawyer for YSL RICO Defendant Asks to Withdraw, Citing 'Egregiously Low' Pay and Length of Trial," 11Alive, April 13, 2023, https://www.11alive.com/article/news/crime/ysl-trial/ysl-rico-trial-public-defender-requests-withdraw-low-pay-long-commitment/85-d259045e-9ca8-49c7-a2d3-1ba98aef49ed.

20. Kristal Dixon, "Atlanta Police Use Billboards to Solve 'Cop City' Arsons," *Axios*, January 17, 2024, https://www.axios.com/local/atlanta/2024/01/17/cop-city-arson-atlanta-police-billboards.

21. Timothy Pratt, "Georgia Police and FBI Conduct Swat-Style Raids on 'Cop City' Activists' Homes," *The Guardian*, February 10, 2024, https://www.theguardian.com/us-news/2024/feb/10/georgia-police-fbi-raids-cop-city-activists-atlanta.

Chapter 23: Thirty-One Days in DeKalb County Hell

1. Brandon Drenon, "Lashawn Thompson: US Inmate Died in Insect-Infested 'Death Chamber,'" BBC, April 20, 2023, https://www.bbc.com/news/world-us-canada-65338593.
2. Sarah Kallis, "10 Inmates Have Died in the Overcrowded Fulton County Jail in Atlanta," NPR, November 12, 2023, https://www.npr.org/2023/11/12/1212534845/10-inmates-have-died-in-the-overcrowded-fulton-county-jail-in-atlanta.
3. Nolan Huber-Rhoades, "Despite Promises, Atlanta's Detention Center Lease Is Not Saving Lives," Atlanta Community Press Collective, July 17, 2023, https://atlpresscollective.com/2023/07/17/despite-promises-atlantas-detention-center-lease-is-not-saving-lives/.
4. Mark Spencer, "Beware the Healthier Cage," *Inquest*, August 21, 2023.
5. Robins S. Engel, Nicholas Corsaro, and M. Murat Ozer, "The Impact of Police on Criminal Justice Reform," *Criminology and Public Policy* 16, no. 2 (2017): 375–402.

Chapter 24: Defending the Movement: Lessons in Anti-repression

1. George Chidi, "Georgia Senate Passes Bill Curtailing Charitable Bail Funds for Protest Groups," *The Guardian*, February 2, 2024, https://www.theguardian.com/us-news/2024/feb/01/georgia-senate-restricts-cash-bail-protestors-jail-overcrowding.

Chapter 26: From No Cop Academy to Stop Cop City

1. No Cop Academy, https://nocopacademy.com/.
2. No Cop Academy, "No Cop Academy: The Report," 2018, https://nocopacademy.com/report/.
3. Jonah Newman, "To Build Cop Academy, Chicago Picks AECOM, Firm with Checkered Past," *Chicago Reporter*, January 24, 2019, https://www.chicagoreporter.com/to-build-cop-academy-chicago-picks-aecom-firm-with-checkered-past/.
4. American Friends Service Committee, "The Companies and Foundations Behind Cop City," September 2023, https://afsc.org/companies-and-foundations-behind-cop-city.
5. Fran Spielman, "Emanuel Plays Hardball with Opponents of $95M Police Academy," *Chicago Sun-Times*, May 23, 2018, https://chicago.suntimes.com/2018/5/23/18431816/emanuel-plays-hardball-with-opponents-of-95m-police-academy.

Chapter 27: Cop Cities in a Militarized World

1. Jessica Corbett, "Rights Advocates Demand Probe into Murder of Environmental Defenders in Honduras," *Common Dreams*, January 11, 2023, https://www.commondreams.org/news/honduras-environmental-defenders.

2. Vinicius Madureira, "Seven Peasant Activist Killed in Two Months in Honduras," Organized Crime and Corruption Reporting Project, February 15, 2023, https://www.occrp.org/en/daily/17325-seven-peasant-activist-killed-in-two-months-in-honduras.

3. Nina Lakhani, "Salvadoran Environmental Defenders Detained for Decades-Old Crimes," *The Guardian*, January 14, 2023, https://www.theguardian.com/world/2023/jan/14/el-salvador-environmental-defenders-arrested-mining-ban.

4. Ali Hines, "Decade of Defiance," Global Witness, May 10, 2023, https://www.globalwitness.org/en/campaigns/environmental-activists/decade-defiance/#a-global-analysis-2021; Julett Pineda, "Defending the Environment Can Be a Death Sentence," *Deutsche Welle*, December 1, 2022, https://www.dw.com/en/defending-the-environment-can-be-a-death-sentence/a-63837132.

5. Reuters in San Salvador, "El Salvador Moves Suspected Gang Members to 40,000-Capacity 'Megaprison,'" *The Guardian*, February 25, 2023, https://www.theguardian.com/world/2023/feb/25/el-salvador-moves-2000-suspected-gang-members-to-new-megaprison.

6. Dany D. Mejía, "State of Emergency in El Salvador Brings Arbitrary Detentions and Violence," *America Magazine*, December 22, 2022, https://www.americamagazine.org/politics-society/2022/12/22/detentions-human-rights-abuses-state-emergency-el-salvador-244412.

7. Marcos Alemán, "El Congreso de El Salvador prorroga por 26 veces el régimen de excepción para combatir las pandillas," Associated Press, May 9, 2024, https://apnews.com/world-news/general-news-93717aaa0c3d-792de8239c7d197577c5.

8. Nelson Renteria, "El Salvador Backs Mass Trials for Thousands Held in Crime Crackdown," *Reuters*, July 26, 2023, https://www.reuters.com/world/americas/el-salvador-approves-group-trials-amid-crime-crackdown-2023-07-26/.

9. Leisy J. Abrego and Steven Osuna, "The State of Exception: Gangs as a Neoliberal Scapegoat in El Salvador," *Brown Journal of World Affairs* 29, no. 1 (Fall/Winter 2022): 59–73.

10. Committee in Solidarity with the People of El Salvador, "Terrorism Charges for Water Protests Dropped Against 'Suchitoto 13,'" North American Congress on Latin America, March 13, 2008, https://nacla.org/news/

terrorism-charges-water-protests-dropped-against-%E2%80%98suchito-to-13%E2%80%99.

11. "Most Notorious SOA Graduates," School of the Americas Watch, March 6, 2019, https://soaw.org/notorious-soa-graduates.

12. "Fiscal Year 2019 Report," Western Hemisphere Institute for Security Cooperation, https://defenseassistance.org/primarydocs/200129_whinsec_rept.pdf.

13. "ILEA San Salvador," US Department of State, https://2009-2017.state.gov/j/inl/c/crime/ilea/c11286.htm.

14. City of Atlanta, "Atlanta Police Officers Travel to San Salvador to Train International Law Enforcement Officers," July 6, 2016, https://www.atlantaga.gov/Home/Components/News/News/4589/.

15. United States Government Accountability Office, "Mérida Initiative: The United States Has Provided Counternarcotics and Anticrime Support but Needs Better Performance Measures," July 2010, https://www.gao.gov/assets/gao-10-837.pdf.

16. "The Central America Regional Security Initiative: A Shared Partnership," US Department of State, 2010, https://2009-2017.state.gov/r/pa/scp/fs/2010/145747.htm.

17. Geoff Thale and Kevin Amaya, "Amid Rising Violence, El Salvador Fails to Address Reports of Extrajudicial Killings," Washington Office on Latin America, November 3, 2017, https://www.wola.org/analysis/amid-rising-violence-el-salvador-fails-address-reports-extrajudicial-killings/; Agnes Callamard, "El Salvador End of Mission Statement," United Nations Office of the High Commissioner of Human Rights, February 5, 2018, https://www.ohchr.org/en/statements/2018/02/el-salvador-end-mission-statement.

18. Adam Isacson and Sarah Kinosian, "Which Central American Military and Police Units Get the Most U.S. Aid?" Washington Office on Latin America, https://www.wola.org/analysis/which-central-american-military-and-police-units-get-the-most-u-s-aid/.

19. Nick P. Walsh, Barbara Arvanitidis, and Bryan Avelar, "US-Funded Police Linked to Illegal Executions in El Salvador," CNN, May 29, 2018, https://www.cnn.com/interactive/2018/05/world/el-salvador-police-intl/.

20. Isacson and Kinosian, "Which Central American Military and Police Units Get the Most U.S. Aid?"

21. Carlos Maradiaga, "Honduras: Policías 'Tigres' dejaron enlibertad al capo Wilter Blanco Ruiz," El Heraldo, October 16, 2016, https://www.elheraldo.hn/honduras/honduras-policias-tigres-dejaron-enlibertad-al-capo-wilter-blanco-ruiz-PVEH1009116#image-1.

22. Ilise Benshushan Cohen and Azadeh Shahshahani, "U.S. Police Are Being Trained by Israel—and Communities of Color Are Paying the Price," *The Progressive*, October 7, 2019, https://progressive.org/latest/us-police-trained-by-israel-communities-of-color-paying-price-shahshahani-cohen-191007/.

23. Michael D. McDonald, Sally Bakewell, and Nancy Cook, "El Salvador Jails 64,000 Gangsters in Crime Crackdown," *Bloomberg*, February 28, 2023, https://www.bloomberg.com/news/articles/2023-02-28/el-salvador-has-jailed-64-000-gangsters-defense-minister-says.

24. Tucker Carlson Tonight, "How Has El Salvador Transitioned from Being the Murder Capital of the World?" Fox News, September 21, 2022, https://www.foxnews.com/video/6312679081112.

25. Trevor Williams, "El Salvador Sells Its National 'Rebranding' in Atlanta with Ambassador Visit," Global Atlanta, March 10, 2023, https://www.globalatlanta.com/el-salvador-sells-its-national-rebranding-in-atlanta-with-ambassador-visit/.

26. Milena Mayorga (@MilenaMayorga), "Hoy visitamos al Alcalde de Atlanta," X, March 6, 2023, https://twitter.com/MilenaMayorga/status/1632864504890392576

27. Luigi Morris, "SOUTHCOM Chief Aims to Increase Imperialist Plunder of Latin America's Resources," *Left Voice*, January 6, 2023, https://www.leftvoice.org/southcom-chief-aims-to-increase-imperialist-plunder-of-latin-americas-resources/.

28. Owen Schalk, "El Salvador's Historic Metal Mining Ban Is in Danger," *Jacobin*, February 5, 2023, https://jacobin.com/2023/02/el-salvador-mining-ban-threat-water-pollution-nayib-bukele.

29. US Congressman Jesús G. "Chuy" García, "Representatives García, Bush, Omar, Schakowsky & Bowman Introduce Resolution to Affirm Rights of Honduras' Garífuna People," press release, December 14, 2022, https://chuygarcia.house.gov/media/press-releases/representatives-garcia-bush-omar-schakowsky-bowman-introduce-resolution-to-affirm-rights-of-honduras-garifuna-people.

30. Nina Lakhani, "UN Rapporteur 'Appalled' by Convictions for Honduran Environmentalists Who Opposed Open-Pit Mine," *The Guardian*, February 9, 2022, https://www.theguardian.com/world/2022/feb/09/honduras-environmentalists-guilty-crimes-mining-company.

31. Mike Ludwig, "Champions of El Salvador's Historic Mining Ban Face Legal Persecution," *Truthout*, January 11, 2024, https://truthout.org/articles/champions-of-el-salvadors-historic-mining-ban-face-legal-persecution/.

Chapter 28: Atlanta's Attack on Protesters Should Be a Warning to Us All

1. Sam Levin, "'It Never Stops': Killings by US Police Reach Record High in 2022," *The Guardian*, January 6, 2023, https://www.theguardian.com/us-news/2023/jan/06/us-police-killings-record-number-2022.

2. Patrick Greenfield, "More Than 1,700 Environmental Activists Murdered in the Past Decade," *The Guardian*, September 28, 2022, https://www.theguardian.com/environment/2022/sep/29/global-witness-report-1700-activists-murdered-past-decade-aoe.

3. Ryan Fatica and Chris Schiano, "'Community' Committee Cheers Police Violence as Authorities Repress Resistance to 'Cop City,'" *Unicorn Riot*, February 24, 2023, https://unicornriot.ninja/2023/community-committee-cheers-police-violence-as-authorities-repress-resistance-to-cop-city/.

4. Jasmine Browley, "Atlanta Has the Highest Income Inequality in the Nation," *Essence*, January 18, 2023, https://www.essence.com/news/money-career/atlanta-highest-income-inequality/.

Chapter 29: Please Keep Playing: A Letter to My Son, Remix

1. Brad Schrade, Jeff Ernsthausen, and Jennifer Peebles, "Over the Line: Police Shootings in Georgia," *Atlanta Journal-Constitution*, n.d., accessed March 9, 2024, https://investigations.ajc.com/overtheline/shot-at-home/.

Conclusion

1. Renee Johnston, "Cop Cities, USA," Is Your Life Better, 2024, https://isyourlifebetter.net/cop-cities-usa/.

2. Judah Schept, "The Carceral Conjuncture in Central Appalachia," *LPE Project*, March 20, 2023, https://lpeproject.org/blog/the-carceral-conjuncture-in-central-appalachia/.

3. Katie Myers, "Inside the Last-Ditch Effort to Stop the Mountain Valley Pipeline," *Grist*, January 16, 2024, https://grist.org/protest/inside-the-last-ditch-effort-to-stop-the-mountain-valley-pipeline/.

4. Kelly House, "Michigan Rejects Camp Grayling Expansion, Instead Offering Annual Use Permits," *Bridge Michigan*, April 28, 2023, https://www.bridgemi.com/michigan-environment-watch/michigan-rejects-camp-grayling-expansion-instead-offering-annual-use.

5. Stuart Schrader, "Defund the Global Policeman," *N+1*, Fall 2020, https://www.nplusonemag.com/issue-38/politics/defund-the-global-policeman/.

6. Piper French, "A Weapon by the State to Silence Our Voices," *Bolts Magazine*, April 3, 2023, https://boltsmag.org/critical-infrastructure-laws/.

7. John Legend and Jocelyn Simonson, "Bail Funds Are Essential to Democracy. A Georgia Bill Threatens to Stifle Them," *Time*, February 27, 2024, https://time.com/collection/time100-voices/6835328/bail-funds-georgia-john-legend-essay/.

8. Jon Gambrell, "Crews Extinguish Fire on Tanker Hit by Houthi Missile off Yemen After US Targets Rebels in Airstrike," AP News, January 27, 2024, https://apnews.com/article/yemen-houthi-red-sea-israel-hamas-war-attacks-f36fc8911e069a5b4dbc4d9e67f31e50.

9. Jennifer Lifsey and Don Shipman, "Atlanta Police, FBI, ATF Looking into Fires at Construction Site," *Atlanta News First*, January 26, 2024, https://www.atlantanewsfirst.com/2024/01/26/police-look-into-cause-fire-construction-site-southeast-atlanta/.

10. Atlanta Community Press Collective (@atlanta_press), "BREAKING: Two activists are using reinforced pipes . . ." X, January 29, 2024, https://twitter.com/atlanta_press/status/1751929183343677576.

11. Appalachians Against Pipelines, "Happening now!! Madeline Fitch, Appalachian mother, locked herself to a MVP drill," X, January 29, 2024, https://twitter.com/stopthemvp/status/1751935541937852762.

12. "Transport Company Cuts Ties with Israeli Weapons Manufacturer Elbit," *Middle East Monitor*, February 2, 2024. https://www.middleeastmonitor.com/20240202-transport-company-cuts-ties-with-israel-weapons-manufacturer-elbit/.

About the Editors

Kamau Franklin is the founder of Community Movement Builders, a Black, member-based collective of community residents and organizers. Kamau has been a dedicated community organizer for over thirty years and is a former practicing attorney, beginning in New York City and now based in Atlanta.

Micah Herskind is an organizer, writer, and law student. He is active in abolitionist movements against police and jail expansion, and has written for outlets including *New York Magazine*, *Scalawag*, MSNBC, *Teen Vogue*, and *Race & Class*.

Mariah Parker is an emcee and labor organizer born and raised in the South. Their cultural work and organizing have been featured in *The New York Times*, *Rolling Stone*, *Teen Vogue*, *SPIN*, Al Jazeera, *Scalawag*, and *Hammer & Hope*.

About Haymarket Books

Haymarket Books is a radical, independent, nonprofit book publisher based in Chicago. Our mission is to publish books that contribute to struggles for social and economic justice. We strive to make our books a vibrant and organic part of social movements and the education and development of a critical, engaged, and internationalist left.

We take inspiration and courage from our namesakes, the Haymarket Martyrs, who gave their lives fighting for a better world. Their 1886 struggle for the eight-hour day—which gave us May Day, the international workers' holiday—reminds workers around the world that ordinary people can organize and struggle for their own liberation. These struggles—against oppression, exploitation, environmental devastation, and war—continue today across the globe.

Since our founding in 2001, Haymarket has published more than nine hundred titles. Radically independent, we seek to drive a wedge into the risk-averse world of corporate book publishing. Our authors include Angela Y. Davis, Arundhati Roy, Keeanga-Yamahtta Taylor, Eve L. Ewing, aja monet, Mariame Kaba, Naomi Klein, Rebecca Solnit, Mohammed El-Kurd, José Olivarez, Noam Chomsky, Winona LaDuke, Robyn Maynard, Leanne Betasamosake Simpson, Howard Zinn, Mike Davis, Marc Lamont Hill, Dave Zirin, Astra Taylor, and Amy Goodman, among many other leading writers of our time. We are also the trade publishers of the acclaimed Historical Materialism Book Series.

Haymarket also manages a vibrant community organizing and event space in Chicago, Haymarket House, the popular Haymarket Books Live event series and podcast, and the annual Socialism Conference.